WARREN BALLPARK

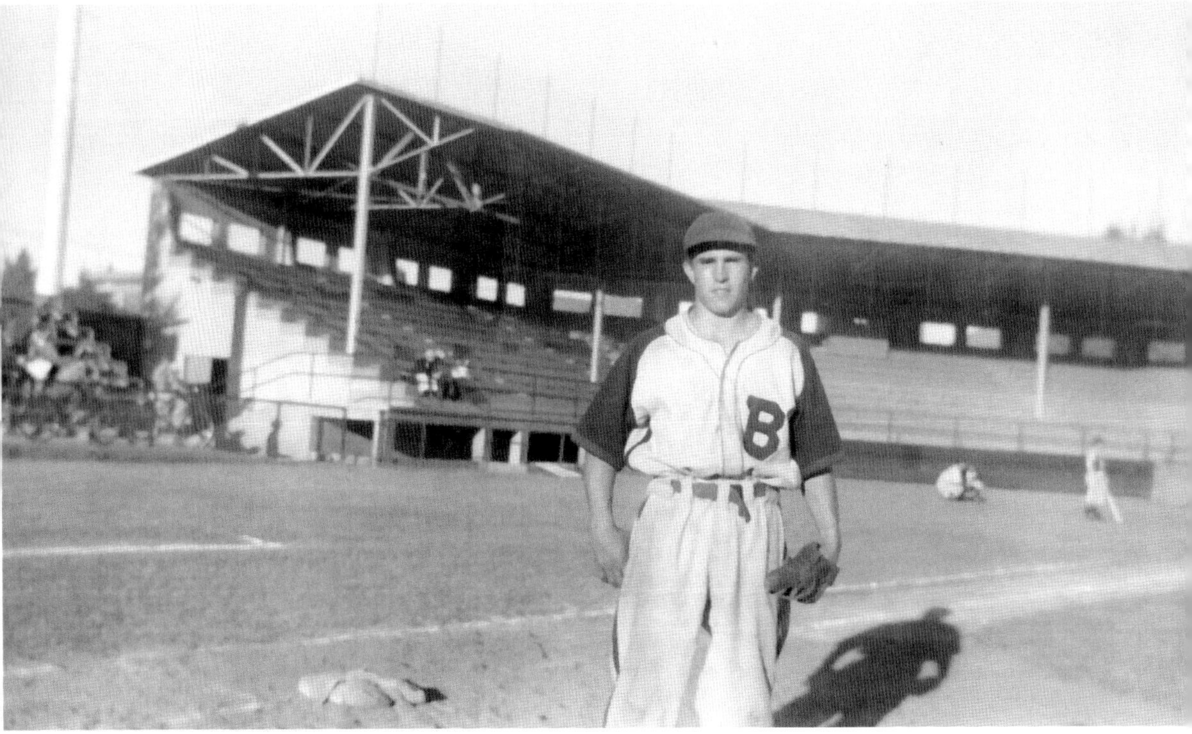

Like the unknown soldier entombed in Arlington National Cemetery, this unidentified member of the 1939 Bisbee Bees minor league team is representative of the thousands of young men and boys who played baseball at Warren Ballpark over the past 103 years. If he were to return there today, he would see no difference in the appearance of the grandstands. He would, however, likely comment favorably on the addition of field lights. (Courtesy Bobby Holland collection.)

ON THE FRONT COVER: Promotions and special events have been a part of baseball for as long as fans have paid to see games. The 1950 Bisbee-Douglas Copper Kings wore Bermuda shorts and Hollywood Stars uniform shirts donated by a sponsor for a game that summer. (Courtesy Dick Smith.)

COVER BACKGROUND: The last barnstorming exhibition game played by major league teams at Warren Ballpark took place on March 15, 1947, when the Cleveland Indians and the New York Giants took the field in Bisbee. The Giants, led by field manager Mel Ott, routed the Indians, who were managed by Lou Boudreau, 17-7. (Courtesy Tim Kusmertz.)

ON THE BACK COVER: Semiprofessional teams played baseball on a dirt field at Warren Ballpark during its first two decades of operation.

WARREN BALLPARK

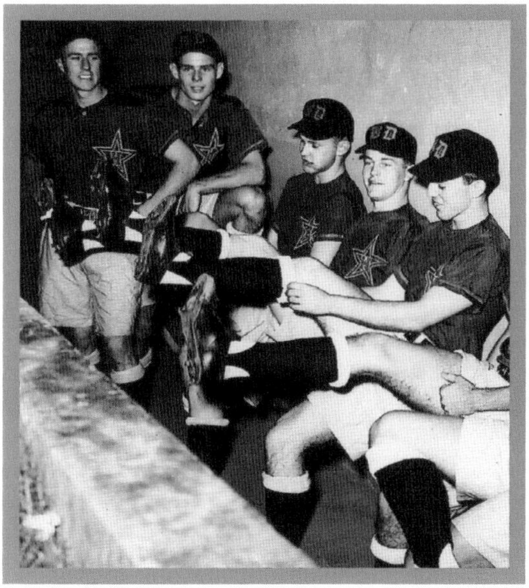

Mike Anderson

ARCADIA
PUBLISHING

ISBN 978-0-7385-9643-3

Published by Arcadia Publishing
Charleston, South Carolina

Printed in the United States of America

Library of Congress Control Number: 2012945314

For all general information, please contact Arcadia Publishing:
Telephone 843-853-2070
Fax 843-853-0044
E-mail sales@arcadiapublishing.com
For customer service and orders:
Toll-Free 1-888-313-2665

Visit us on the Internet at www.arcadiapublishing.com

To my wife and lifelong companion, Judy.

CONTENTS

ACKNOWLEDGMENTS

This book would not have been completed without the help of many good people along the way. Foremost among them are the former players, coaches, and managers who allowed me to interview them and share their stories. Charlie Metro, Frank Lucchesi, Pete and Danny Vucurevich, Jim Propst, Sam Kitterman, Dick Smith, Russ Kusmertz, Dick Atkinson, Ted Sorich, Doug Knipp, Fred Giacoletti, and Hadley Hicks took the time to patiently answer questions and to help in any way they were asked.

Ann Henry, the wife of Bob Henry and a very fine athlete in her own right, shared photographs, scrapbooks, and memories. Snoody Borowiec, a star softball player, shared an extensive collection of photographs taken at Warren Ballpark by her late husband, Bob, as well as her own fascinating collection of memorabilia.

Ann Longmore, the niece of Syd Cohen, a legendary baseball figure in the southwest who played and managed in Bisbee, provided countless photographs, letters, and stories about her uncle.

Elena Metro, the daughter of Charlie Metro, shared stories about her father and her reminiscences of growing up in professional baseball. Luche Giacomino provided ideas and the names of local persons who might be helpful in preparing this book. Bisbee High School baseball coach Mike Frosco shared his experiences as a player and coach.

My very special thanks go to Carrie Gustavson, the director of the Bisbee Mining and Historical Museum, as well as to curator Annie Larkin and secretary Ana Garcia. Their generosity and assistance were absolutely crucial to the successful completion of this project. Unless specific credit is given otherwise, all photographs used in this book are from the archives of the Bisbee Mining and Historical Museum.

Tom Mosier and Frank Barco, the owners of the now-defunct Bisbee Copper Kings baseball club, were of great help. Frank continues to bring quality baseball to our community in the form of the Bisbee Ironmen baseball club. Thanks are also due to Butch Hammett and Bill Moore, former field managers for the modern Copper Kings.

My thanks to Phil Vega, the publisher of the *Sierra Vista Herald–Bisbee Daily Review*, for allowing me use of several photographs, and to photographer Mark Levy for finding them. And to all others who provided material, ideas, and inspiration for this project, I am deeply grateful.

INTRODUCTION

Bisbee's Warren Ballpark is America's oldest multisport facility. Located in the Mule Mountains of southeast Arizona, almost one mile above sea level, it continues to provide a venue for wholesome and healthy athletic entertainment and other community events. From its earliest days as a baseball field, Warren Ballpark, now 103 years old, hosted high school teams, town teams, semiprofessional teams, outlaw teams, minor league teams, and barnstorming major league teams.

On November 7, 1913, the New York Giants and Chicago White Sox stopped to play an exhibition game during their trip by train and steamship around the world. That day, six future Hall of Famers and legendary Olympic athlete Jim Thorpe took the field to play for a Bisbee crowd. Other major league teams stopped here as well, including the Chicago Cubs, who were frequent visitors, the Cleveland Indians, the Pittsburgh Pirates, and the Philadelphia Athletics. On April 2, 1940, two of baseball's most revered figures, Connie Mack and Honus Wagner, appeared on the field at Warren Ballpark.

From 1926 through the 1927 season, the ballpark was the home field for the Bisbee Miners, a team in the outlaw "Copper League." During those years, several members of the Chicago White Sox team who were banned from baseball for fixing the 1919 World Series played on visiting teams, including Buck Weaver, Chick Gandil, and Lefty Williams. Former New York Giants Hal Chase and Jimmie O'Connell, also banned from organized baseball for throwing games, played on visiting teams as well.

As the only large outdoor community center in the Warren mining district, Warren Ballpark was in constant use. English immigrants used it to play soccer, rugby, and cricket; owners of traveling rodeos and Wild West shows rented it for their events; circuses and professional wrestling matches were staged there; and local theaters used it to show blockbuster feature films.

In 1937, the original wooden stands, built in 1909, were demolished, and the grandstands used today were constructed. The first game played to dedicate the new ballpark was between the Chicago Cubs and the Chicago White Sox on April 6, 1937. The game was broadcast live to listeners in Chicago with the assistance of Bisbee's KSUN radio station.

In its 19 years as a minor league baseball venue, the ballpark was the starting point or way station for four major league managers, Tom Seaton (an ace major league hurler turned outlaw manager), and many talented major league players. In addition, from 1928 through 1955—except during the height of the Great Depression and during World War II—many fine players who spent substantial time in the minor leagues started their careers or spent several seasons on the rosters of the Bisbee Bees, Javelinas, Miners, or Bisbee-Douglas Copper Kings, of the Arizona State and Arizona-Texas Leagues.

For half a century after minor league baseball left Warren Ballpark, the field was used primarily for high school athletics. That time was well spent, as the five state baseball championships and four state football championships earned by the Pumas from then until today can readily attest. Even when the adult game had disappeared, Bisbee remained a great town for sports.

The return of the Copper Kings as a minor league baseball team in 2003 brought initial excitement and subsequent disappointment after the team quickly folded. The onset of summer league semiprofessional ball in 2006 has been a source of entertainment and pride for our community every year since. The Copper Kings and now the Ironmen brought the tradition of adult baseball back to Bisbee.

Warren Ballpark is also the home field for the Bisbee Pumas football team, which has played its home games there since 1909. The Puma varsity gridders have never failed to thrill local fans and have always been a keen source of hometown pride. To date, Bisbee has won four "unofficial" state football championships. The Bisbee-Douglas high school football rivalry, one of the longest-running and most frequently played in the nation, remains a must-attend annual event for fans of both communities.

The influence of immigrants in Bisbee is reflected in the competitive sports that were played at Warren Ballpark in its first two decades. Entertainment and athletic events taking place there have continued to reflect the local economy and culture over the years.

But Warren Ballpark has also had its more serious moments. From 1913 to 1916, American troops were bivouacked across the street from the ballpark to protect the Warren mining district from violence spilling across the nearby border with Mexico. In July 1917, the ballpark served as a detention facility for 1,500 striking miners rounded up by vigilantes during the event known as the Bisbee Deportation. The deportation, a key moment in the history of the American labor movement, remains a point of contention and controversy in Bisbee today.

Still owned by the Bisbee Unified School District, Warren Ballpark remains in year-round use for sporting events, other school-related events, and community activities such as the Bisbee Blues Festival.

Yankee Stadium, the Polo Grounds, Ebbetts Field, Shibe Park, and Tiger Stadium are gone. They exist today only in memory, photographs, and museum artifacts. Warren Ballpark, nestled in a sedate neighborhood of a small Arizona copper-mining town, is a direct connection to those ballparks and to all of the long-vanished fields that were once a vital part of community life in hundreds of towns and cities across America.

It is a living history museum, a ballpark still in use that gives us an insightful look into the world of sports and small-town community culture of decades gone by. If there really are ghosts of baseball players past who return each night to play out their glory days on a field of dreams, this is the place they return to: the real "field of dreams."

1

No Place for a Ballpark

A search for signs of Apache Indians led Army scouts to discover mineral traces in the Mule Mountains in 1877. By happy coincidence for those who filed the first mineral claims in what would be called the Warren mining district, the removal of the Chiricahua Apaches to a reservation farther north occurred as the electrification of America was gaining momentum. The use of electricity as a power source created an ever-growing demand for copper—and for miners to extract the ore. By 1880, the fledgling mining camp of Bisbee was beginning to dig out the red metal in ever-increasing amounts. Young men from all over the country and all over the globe flocked to the new camp to find steady work. And when they were not working hard, they played hard.

Base ball—two words in those days—was played in Bisbee and around southeastern Arizona long before Warren Ballpark opened in 1909. The game was not played in Bisbee itself during the town's earliest years simply because there was no place to lay out a field in the steep and rugged mountain canyons, where level ground, or any ground suitable for constructing buildings, was at a premium.

Bisbee's home games were played in Don Luis, a neighborhood between Bisbee and the border town of Naco. A covered wooden grandstand provided shade and comfortable seating for fans, who rode a special train from Bisbee and back for a 25¢ fare.

When the suburb of Warren was platted four miles south and west of Bisbee in 1906, a level piece of ground in the southern part of the suburb was reserved as a place to build a ballpark. Grandstands and a fence were constructed with lumber from the Warren Company, a subsidiary of the Calumet and Arizona Mining Company, one of the three biggest copper producers in the area at the time. Built for a total price of $3,600, the facility's purpose was to provide recreation and entertainment for copper miners and other townspeople.

A streetcar line linked Warren and its ballpark to the nearby communities of Bisbee, Lowell, Upper Lowell, Jiggerville, Bakerville, Johnson Addition, and South Bisbee. From 1909 until the late 1920s, the park was most commonly used by town teams subsidized by the copper companies or business organizations, which played similar teams from other towns. It was also regularly used for other sporting activities and outdoor recreational events.

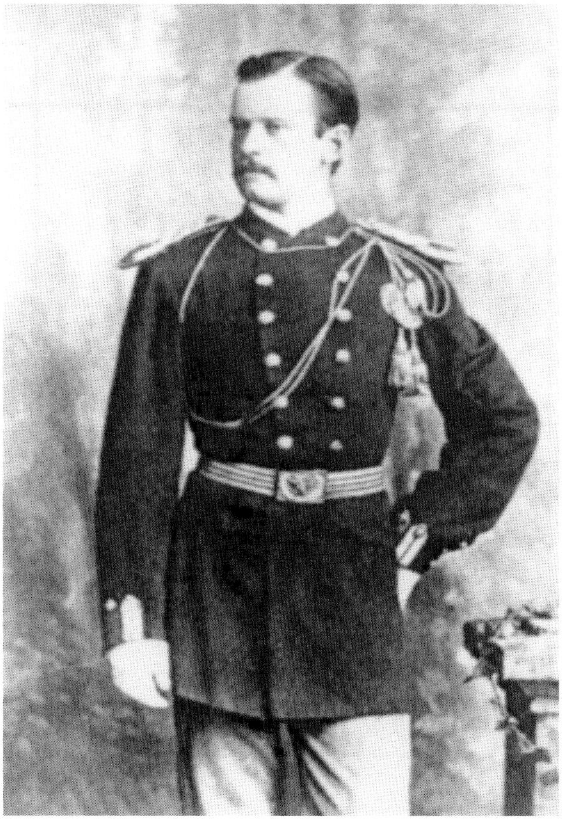

The Army patrol that 1st Lt. John Anthony Rucker of the 6th US Cavalry led into the rugged canyons of the Mule Mountains in May 1877 was on the hunt for signs of renegade Apaches. No Apaches were found, but the scouting party did make a discovery that would prove far more profound in its impact. A little over a year later, Rucker drowned along with a fellow officer after a flash flood.

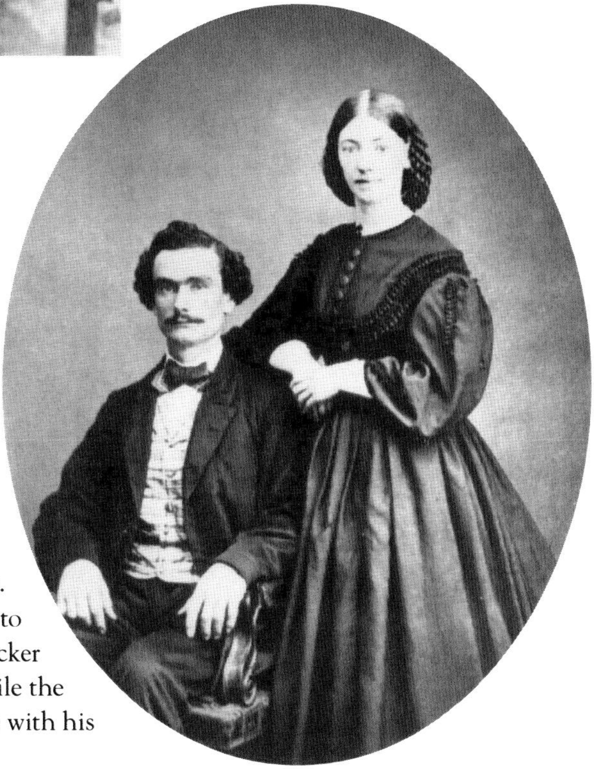

Civilian scout Jack Dunn, who guided Rucker's patrol into the Mule Mountains, went looking for water in a canyon deep in the rugged range. He found spring water and traces of copper in nearby rocks. Unable to travel to Tucson on their own to file mining claims on their discoveries, Rucker and Dunn employed George Warren to file the claims in their names. Dunn is seen here with his wife, Mary.

George Warren did file the first mining claims in what would be named the Warren mining district, but in his own name, rather than for Rucker and Dunn. An alcoholic and a drifter, Warren squandered his one-ninth ownership of the fabulously rich Copper Queen Mine on a bet that he could outrun a horse in a footrace, which he promptly lost. His name was given to a planned suburb in the hills southwest of Bisbee and also to the ballpark that was built at Warren's southern end.

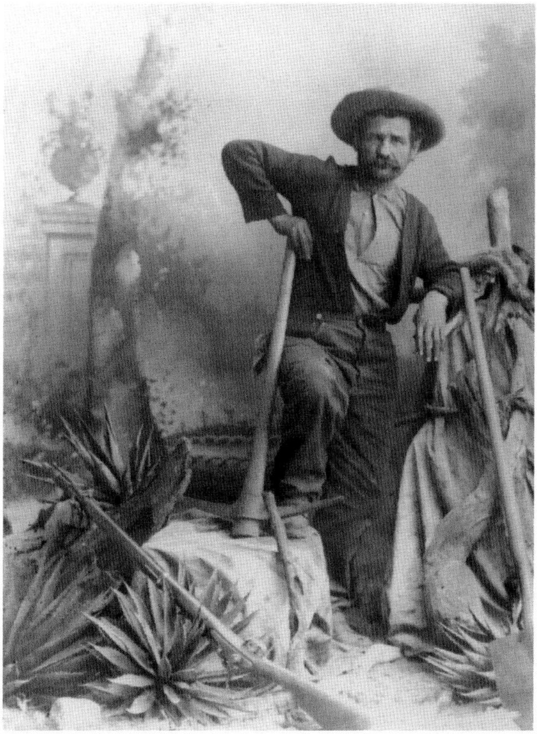

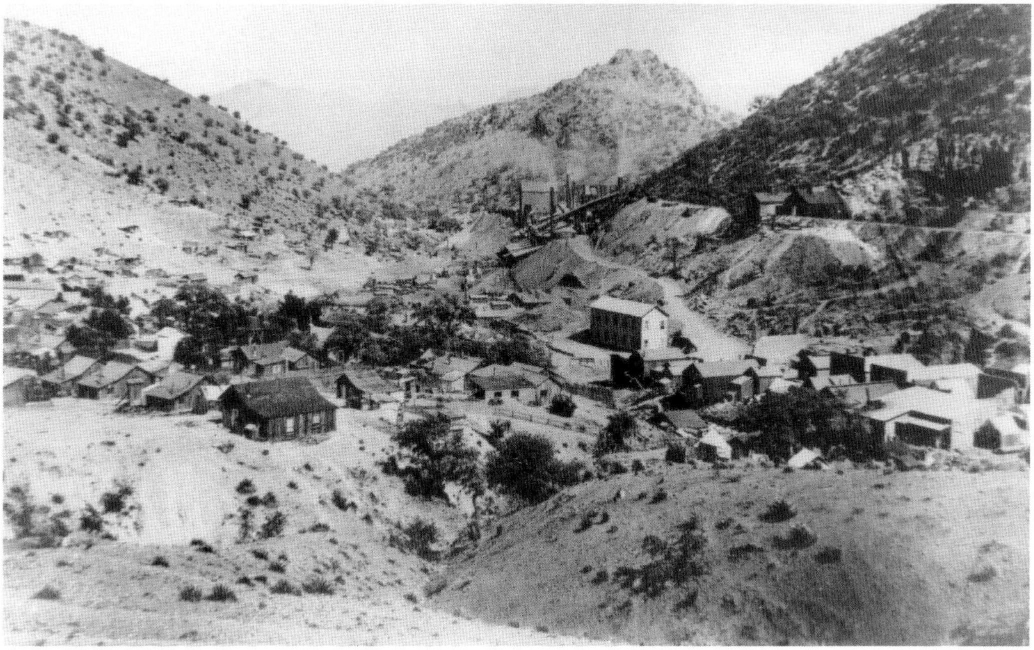

The mining camp of Bisbee was located in two steep, narrow canyons, Tombstone Canyon and Brewery Gulch. The lack of flat terrain meant that homes, businesses, schools, and churches were built on whatever ground was available, including precipitous slopes. Therefore, a location for a ballpark had to be found outside of Bisbee.

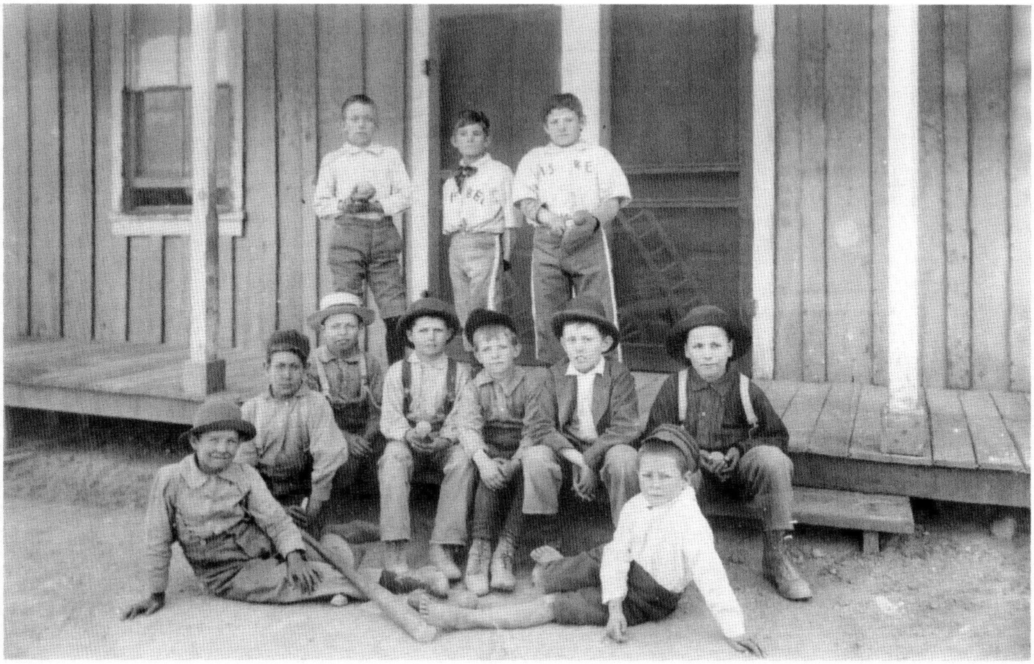

Men and boys formed baseball teams as the town grew in size and sophistication. In 1899, the Copper King Mining Company sponsored a team fittingly named the Copper Kings. In this late-1890s photograph, a team of Bisbee boys pose in front of a miner's cabin. Equipment was scarce—only one of these boys, possibly the catcher, has a glove.

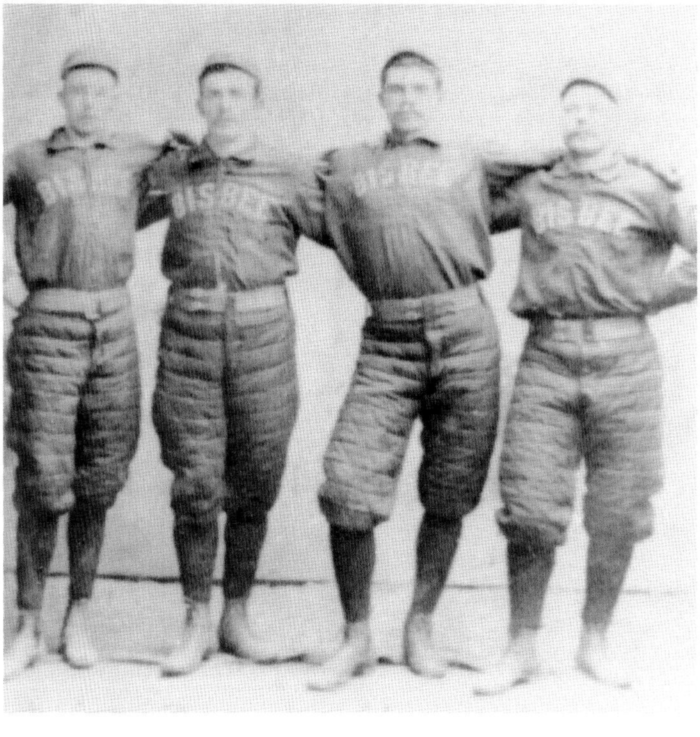

Town teams in the 1880s and 1890s were sponsored by Bisbee businesses and mining companies. Games were scheduled between teams from nearby towns on holidays. This quartet of Bisbee players, Jim Munch, Mike Delaney, Charles Lockling, and Elmore Crouch, were members of a town team that played in 1893. The quilted pants protected the runner's legs while sliding.

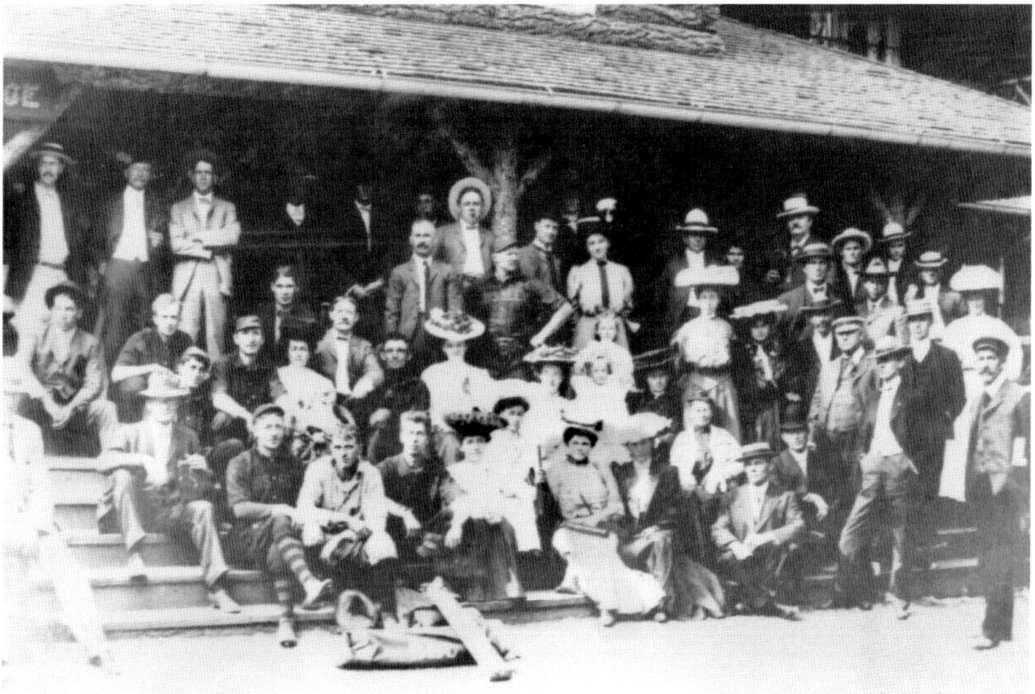

As travel conditions improved in southern Arizona and the vicinity, Bisbee town teams ventured farther abroad to play opponents. Teams traveled by train with families and friends on holiday excursions that included a match with the host team on a local field. Here, Bisbee teammates pose with family and friends before a game in Cloudcroft, New Mexico, in 1905.

Regular opponents of Bisbee teams came from Fort Huachuca, an Army post 25 miles west of town. Army teams provided an opportunity for soldiers to alleviate the boredom and hardship of service at a frontier fort. The 5th Cavalry regiment fielded a team that played other Army teams and civilian teams, including those from Bisbee. (Courtesy Fort Huachuca Museum.)

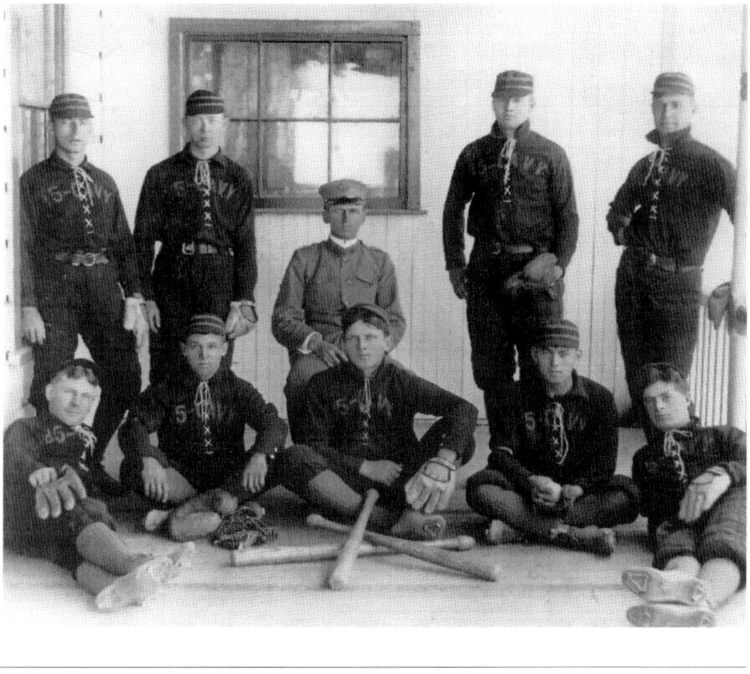

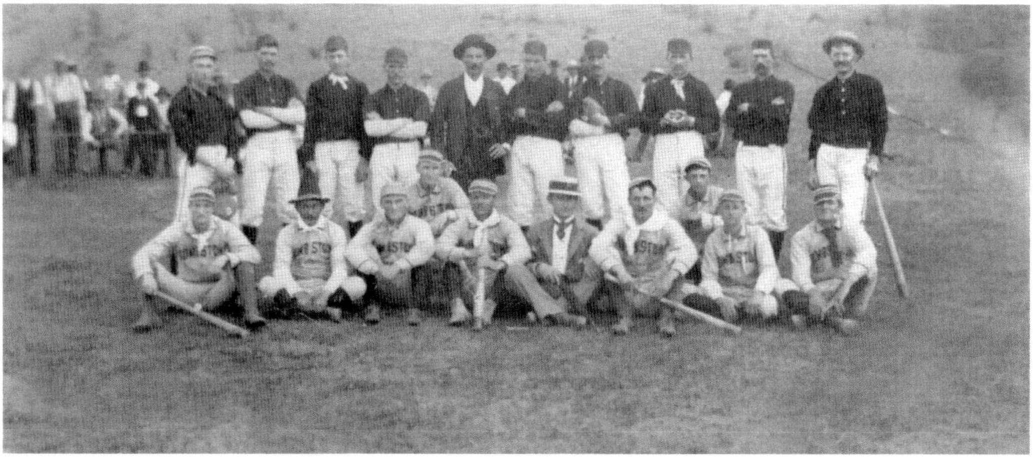

Tombstone was another familiar foe for Bisbee on the baseball diamond in the late 1800s and early 1900s. Although its silver mines declined in production in the late 1880s, Tombstone continued to serve as the county seat until 1929 and was a hub of activity for the surrounding area until then.

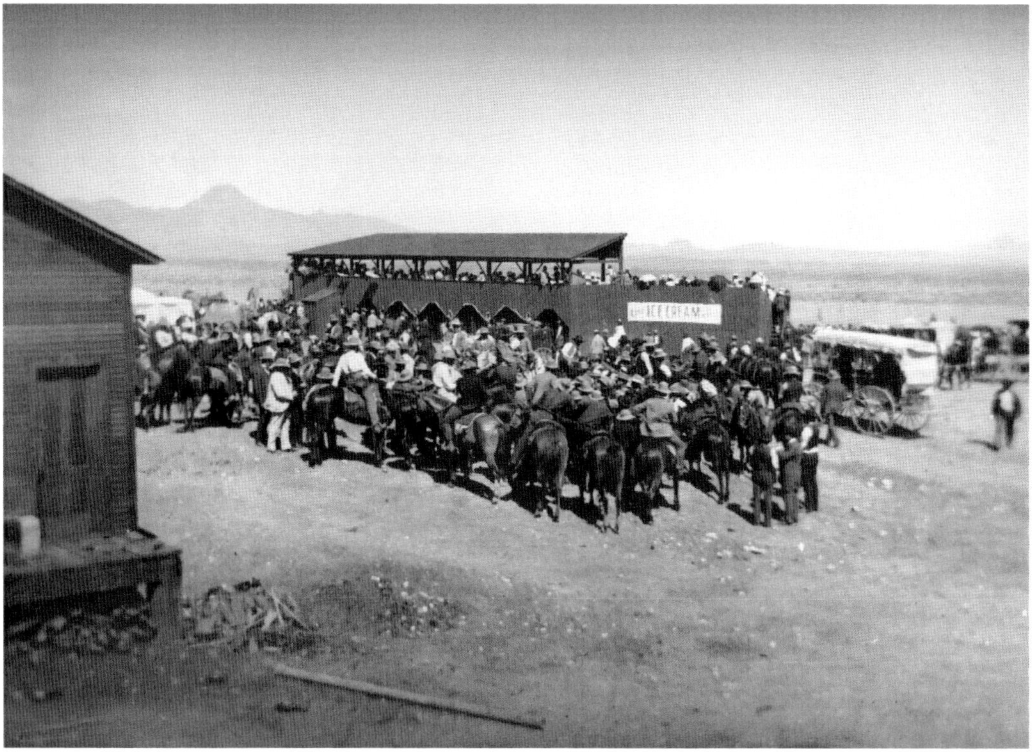

Games staged between town teams in early Bisbee were played on a cleared-off piece of nearby ground that might receive a perfunctory grading. No grass adorned a baseball field in Bisbee until the 1930s. A small wooden baseball grandstand and field was constructed in 1906 on level ground in Don Luis (pronounced "Don Looey"), a small community between Bisbee and the Mexican border.

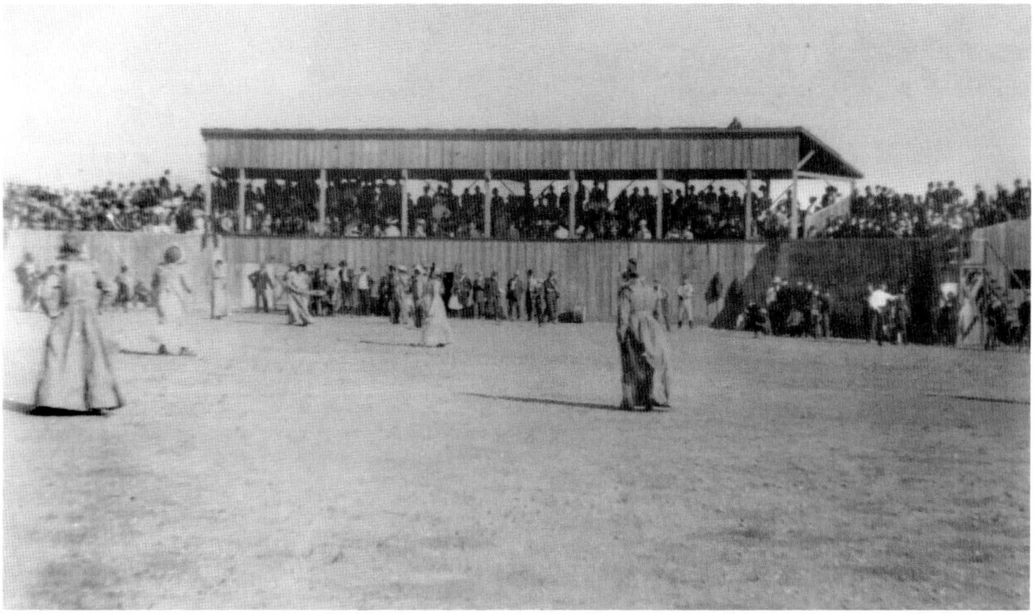

The Don Luis ballpark, built near the rail line that connected Bisbee to the outside world, was used for special events, when a special commuter train could be chartered to carry spectators out from town to watch a game. Special events at the Don Luis ballpark included exhibition games, such as this unusual contest played on July 5, 1906, by Elks Club members dressed as women.

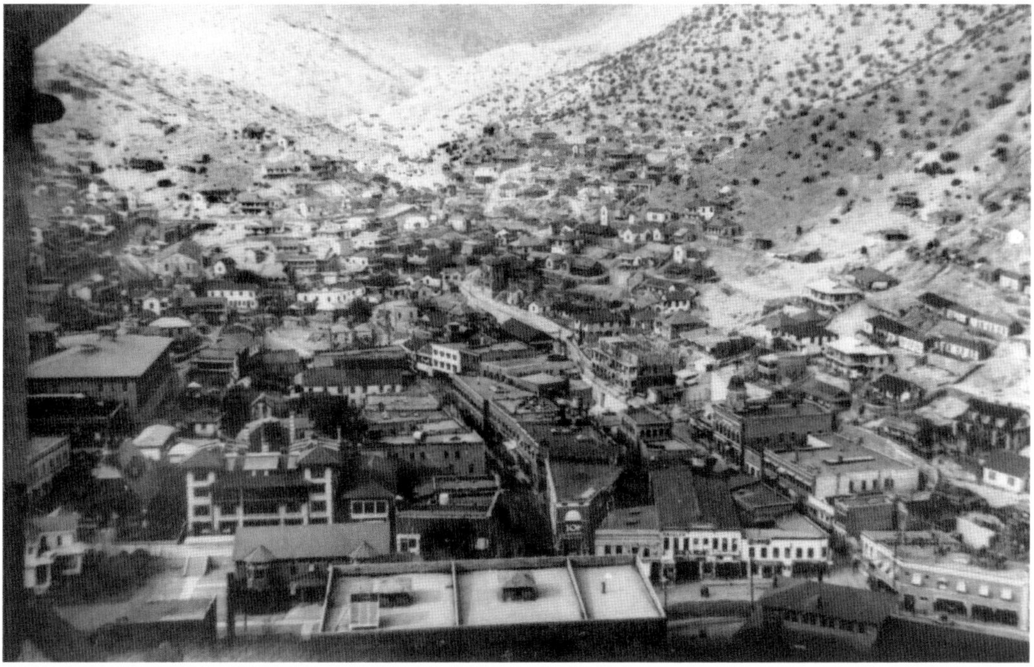

Congestion, filth, disease, and pollution made life in Bisbee increasingly unpleasant as the city grew in density and size due to the growing need for copper and the labor force to mine it. By 1910, Bisbee was bursting at the seams, with a population of approximately 25,000.

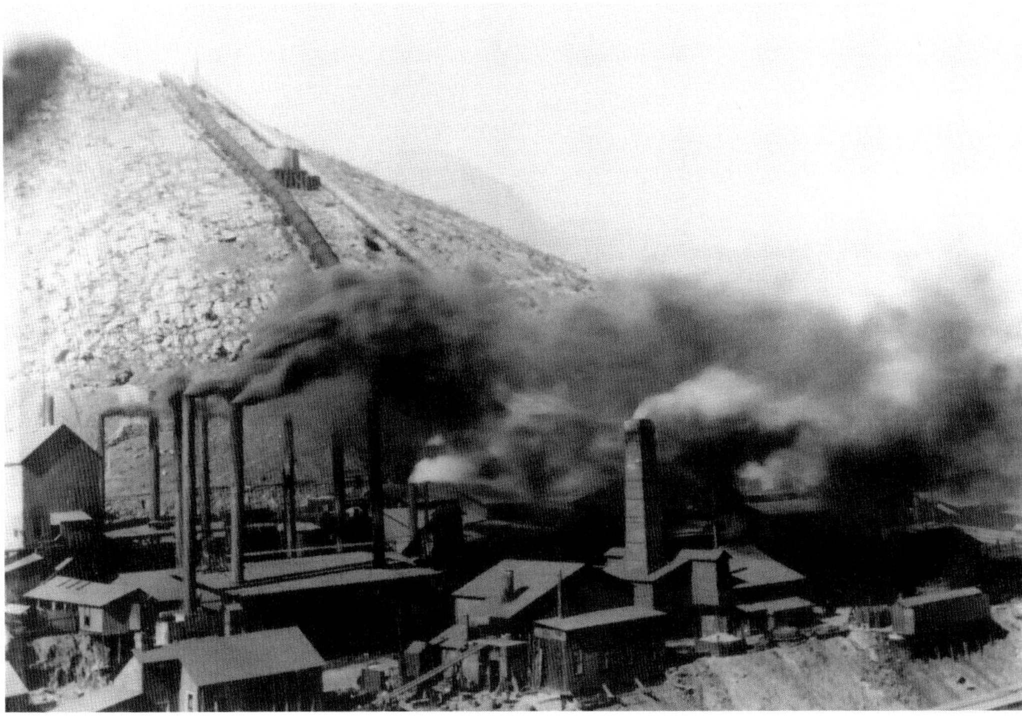

Although the Copper Queen smelter was dismantled by 1906, air pollution from coal- and wood-burning mining machinery in constant operation continued to make the quality of life in Bisbee less than desirable for those who lived in the dense urban canyons.

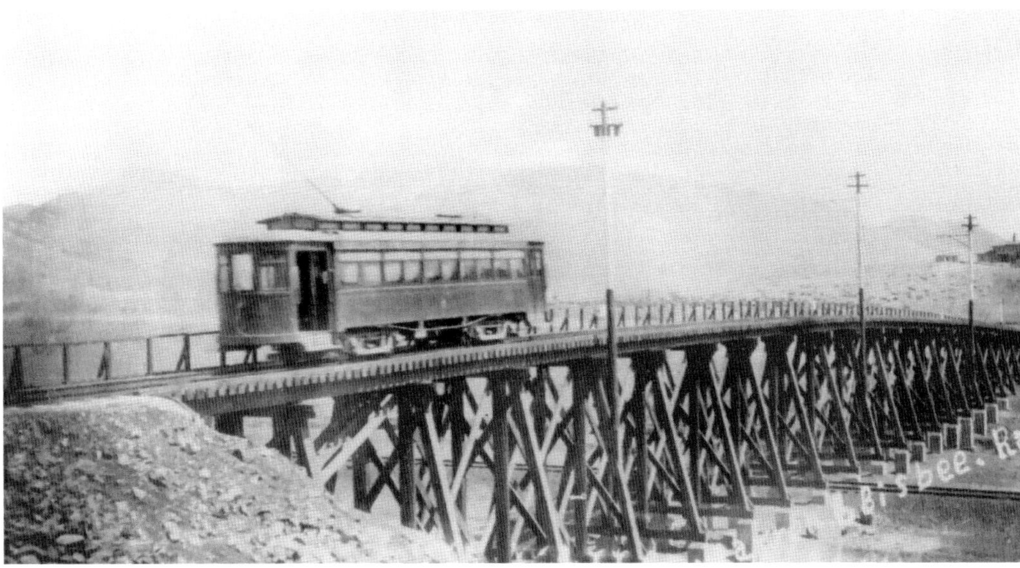

In 1906, the Calumet and Arizona Mining Company began an ambitious project to build a suburb—the first planned community in Arizona. An interurban rail line was constructed, making the necessary connection between Bisbee and the new suburb, Warren, a practical reality. The cars ran every 30 minutes for 20 hours of the day.

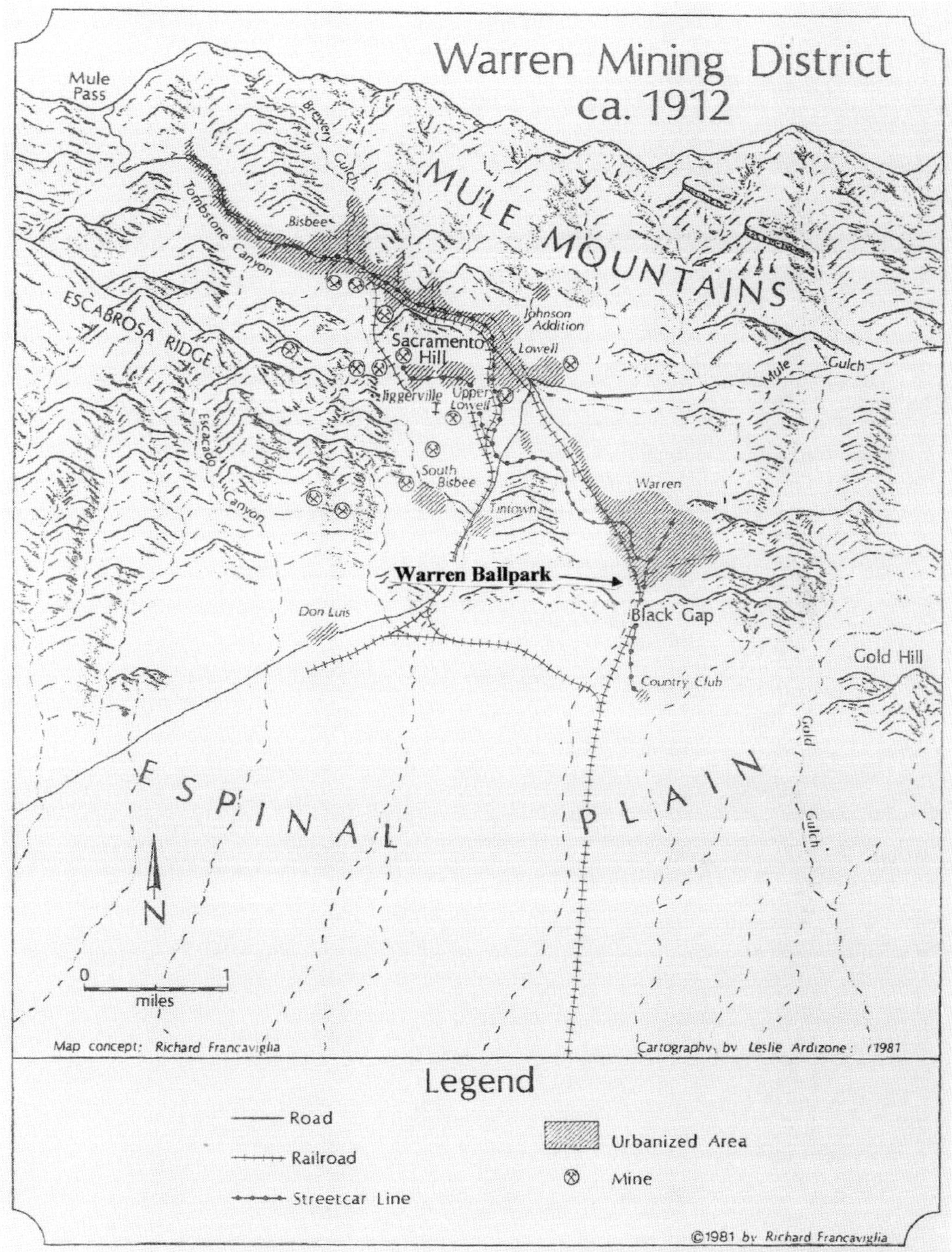

This map of the Warren mining district shows the various communities in the Mule Mountains. Bisbee was founded in 1880 around the original mineral discovery. As new mines were located, additional communities sprang up. Bisbee, Lowell, Johnson Addition, and Jiggerville were all built on the bottoms and sides of steep, narrow canyons and on hillsides. (Courtesy Richard Francaviglia.)

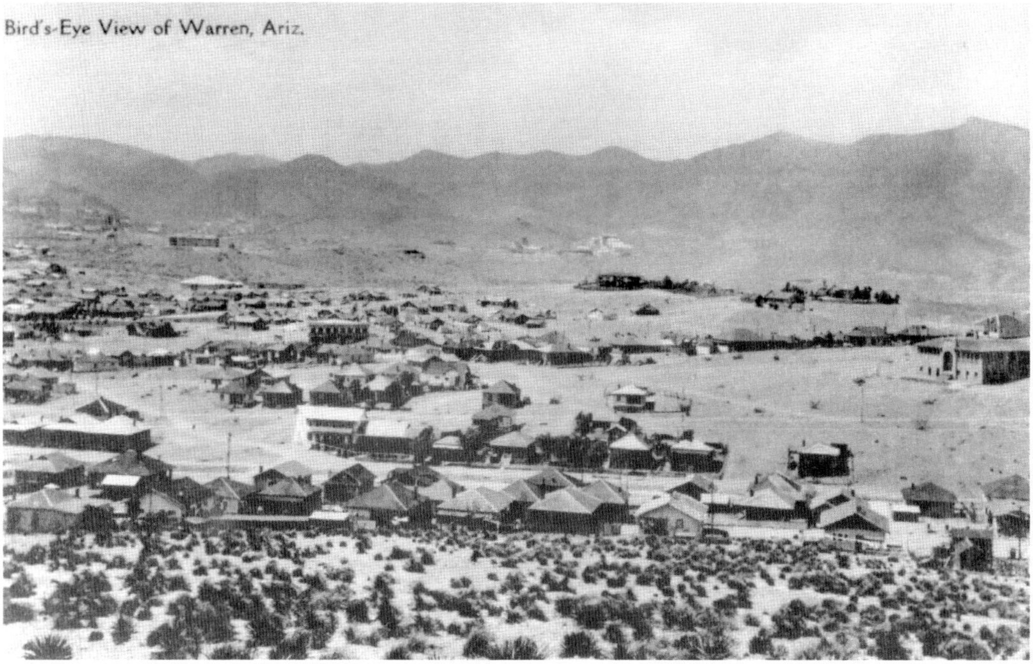

Located in a bowl surrounded by the foothills of the southern end of the Mule Mountains, Warren was laid out in a pattern of streets similar to that of Washington, DC. It was a family-oriented community of broad streets, single-family homes, churches—and no saloons. It remains that way today.

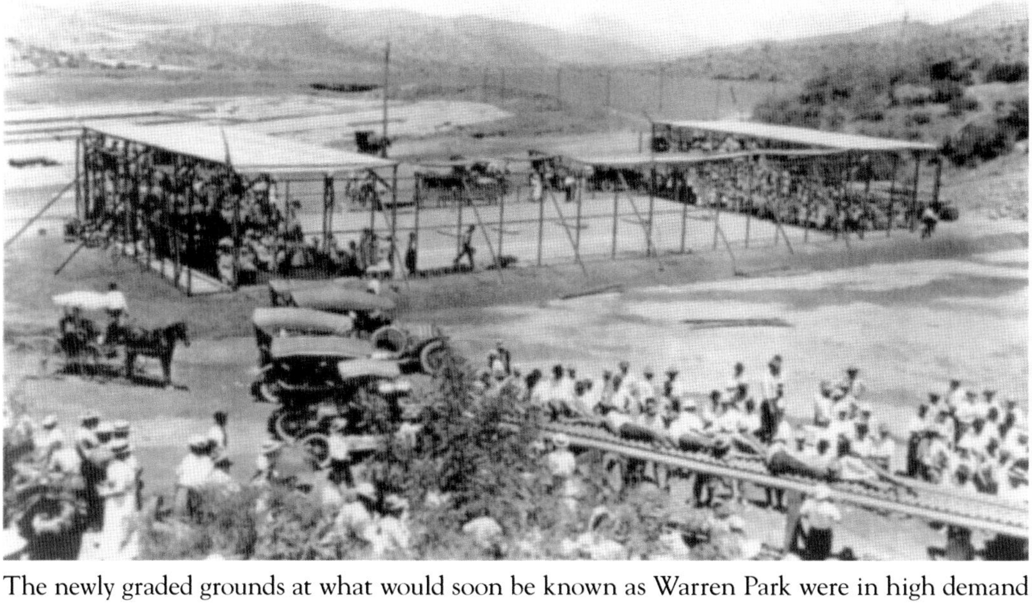

The newly graded grounds at what would soon be known as Warren Park were in high demand even before the ballpark infrastructure was completed. A conveyor belt tug-of-war contest was one of several activities held at the site before it was finished.

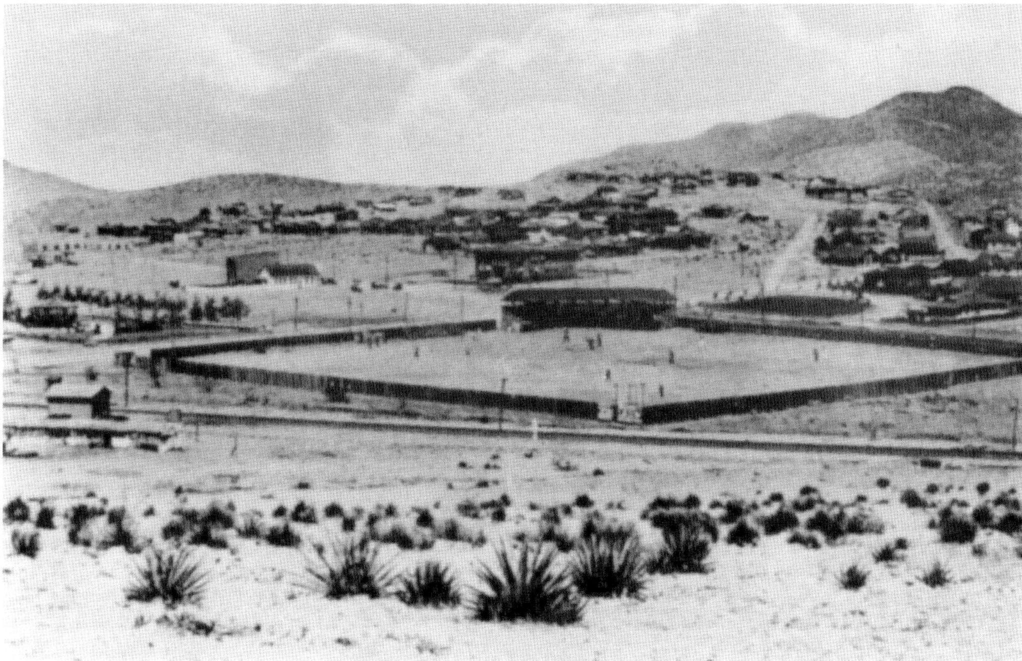

Warren Ballpark was built by the Warren Company, a subsidiary of the Calumet and Arizona Mining Company, in the spring of 1909. It was constructed for $3,600 and its wooden grandstands and dirt field were first used on June 27, 1909, when the Bisbee team hosted the visiting El Paso Browns. The home team defeated El Paso 8-3.

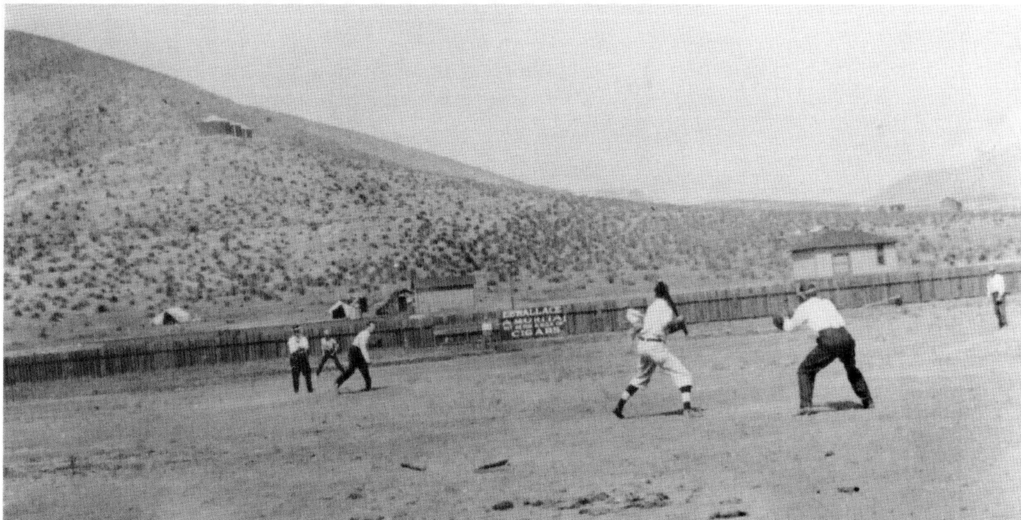

The ballpark field in its early years was bare dirt. A wooden fence surrounded the grounds. All games, except for ones held during holidays, such as the Fourth of July, Labor Day, and Christmas, were played on Sunday afternoons to avoid conflicting with the six-day workweek. Fans were charged 25¢, 35¢, or 50¢ to watch a game, depending on its importance. Ladies were often admitted for free.

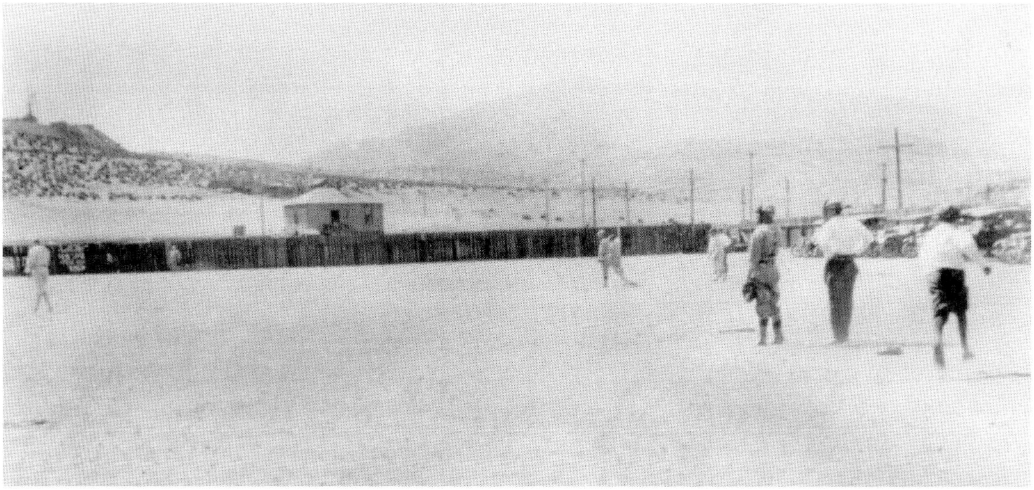

The first teams to play at Warren Ballpark were semiprofessional and sponsored by businesses or civic organizations. Although the players were ostensibly amateurs, many were actively recruited and given soft jobs that would not interfere with baseball. Others were willing to put in practice time on the baseball diamond after working a long, hard shift as a miner, a mucker, or a machinist.

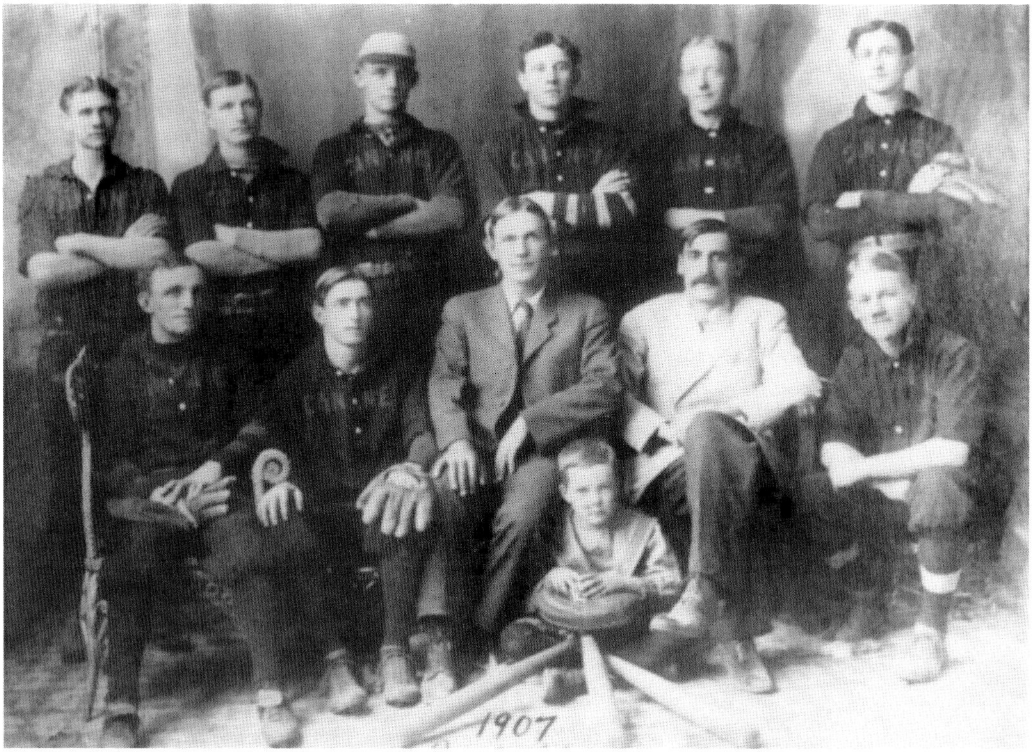

Visiting teams came to Bisbee from El Paso, Clifton, and Tucson. One team that regularly visited Warren Ballpark came from Cananea, a copper-mining town in northern Sonora. The 1907 Cananea team included Chick Gandil (back row, third from left), who went on to a successful career in the major leagues until he was implicated in the 1919 "Black Sox" scandal.

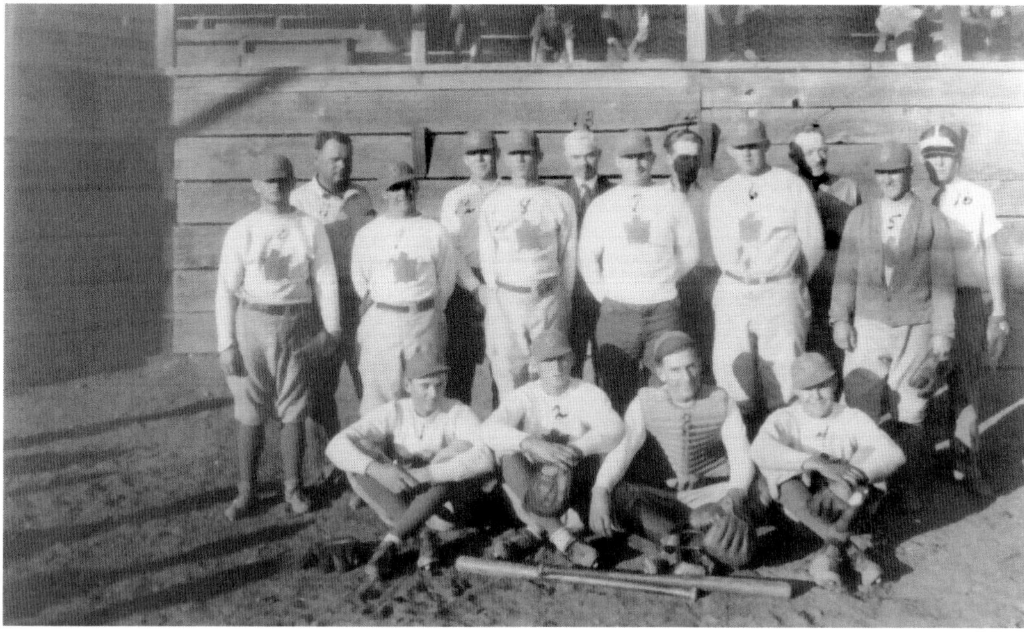

Douglas, founded in 1901 as a location to process the ore dug out of Bisbee's mines, was one of the closest cities to Bisbee. It was and still is its chief sports rival. Games between adult or youth teams from the two communities have always been well attended. This Douglas semiprofessional baseball team visited Warren Ballpark in the 1920s.

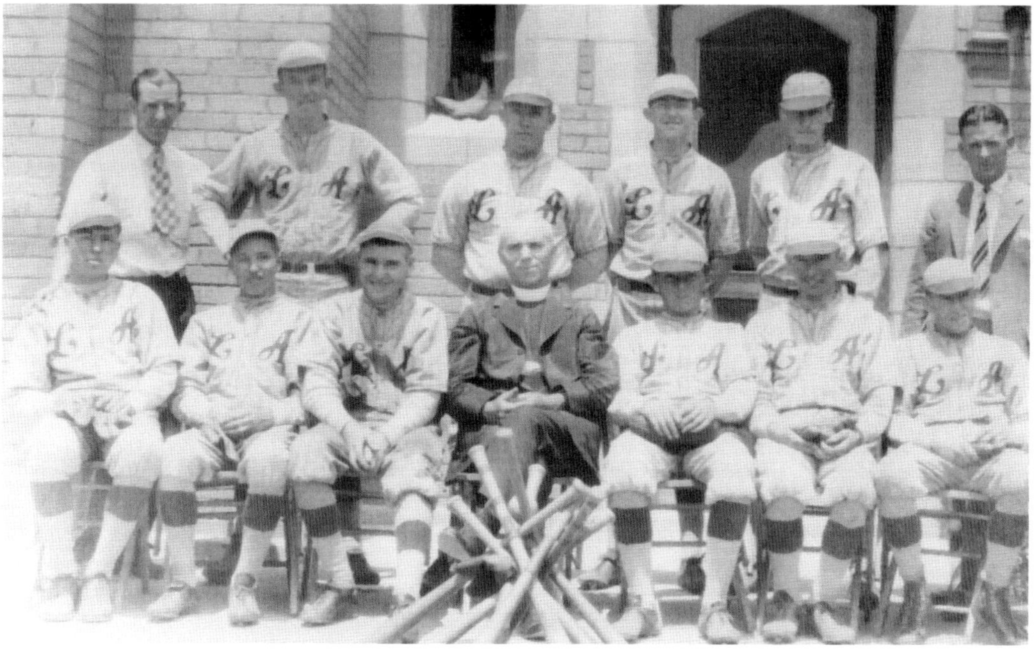

Church teams and fraternal teams also used the ball diamond at Warren. Loreto Academy, a Catholic School, fielded its own team. The Loyal Order of Moose also sponsored a local team, and the Knights of Columbus sponsored an adult soccer team.

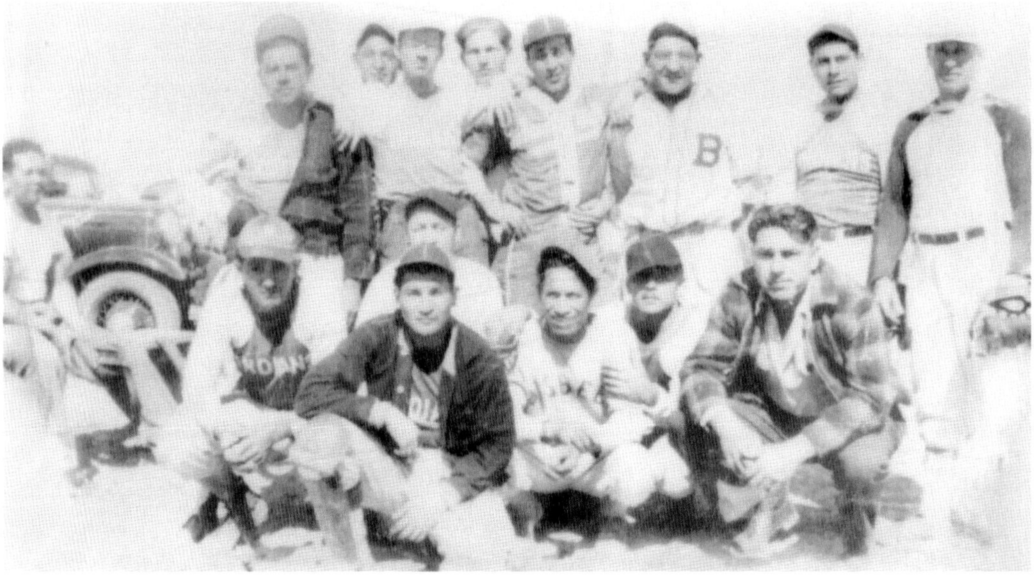

This undated photograph of two Bisbee teams appears to exclusively include Hispanic men, underscoring an important aspect of life in the Warren mining district. There was a strong line between "whites" and "nonwhites." Hispanics and blacks were not allowed into Warren Ballpark as fans or players until the mid-1920s. (Courtesy Arizona Historical Society.)

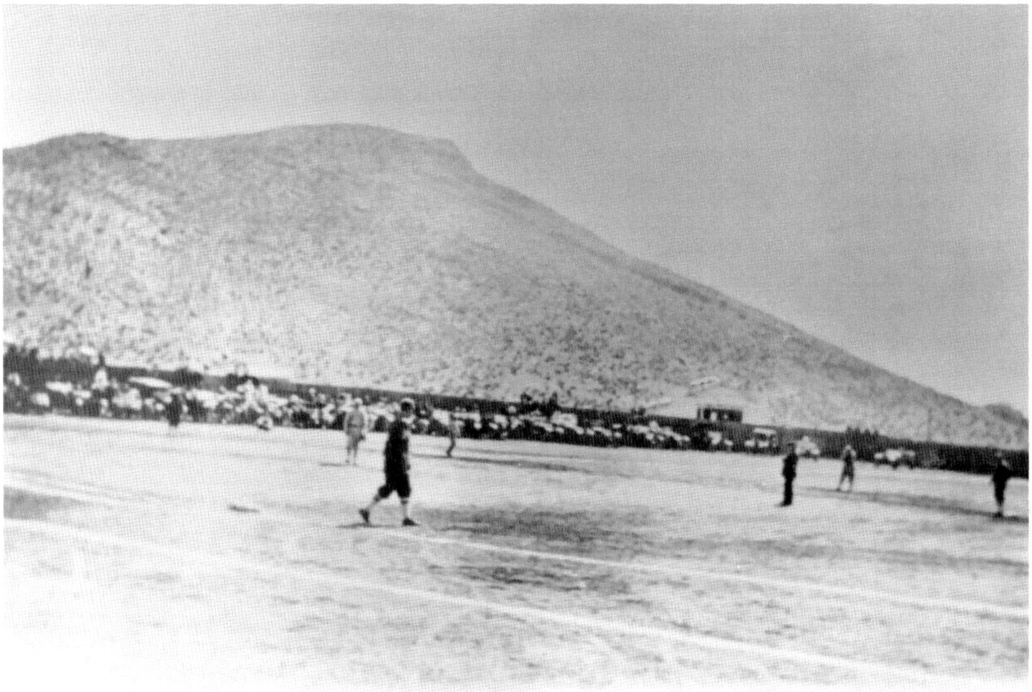

One curious policy during the early days at Warren Ballpark was the establishment of "auto bays" along the first- and third-base lines. Motorists parked their vehicles inside the fence and hired boys to catch foul balls that might damage their vehicles.

Ball Park Or Auto Park?

With a club in the Arizona State league, playing organized baseball, Bisbee has taken on the responsibility of keeping apace with other cities in the league. Some of them may have larger grandstands and better diamonds, but none of them allow motor cars and motorists to trespass on the confines of the baseball field, which is for baseball players and baseballs.

In the five State league games played at Warren park a number of men have reached base because it was physically impossible for outfielders to field fly balls which dropped among automobiles parked near the west fence. An equal number of players have been forced to be content with a two-base hit because their long drives reposed under somebody's car.

However, it is not the extra bases or the loss of bases which brings forth this comment. It is the player's welfare that interests us, primarily. Bisbee, Miami, Tucson and Phoenix have willing ball players and an outfielder chasing fly balls is watching those balls, rather than the automobiles parked inside the players' territory.

A petition is being circulated among fans of Bisbee, requesting the directors of the local club to abolish auto parking inside the baseball field. With the view that an ounce of prevention is worth a ball player's leg, and for the sake of baseball as a game of skill, we urge the directors to carefully consider this petition.

The problem of parked automobiles interfering with play during games came to a head in 1928, when minor league baseball came to Warren Ballpark. Strong protests by managers, players, and umpires brought an end to the odd practice shortly after the season started.

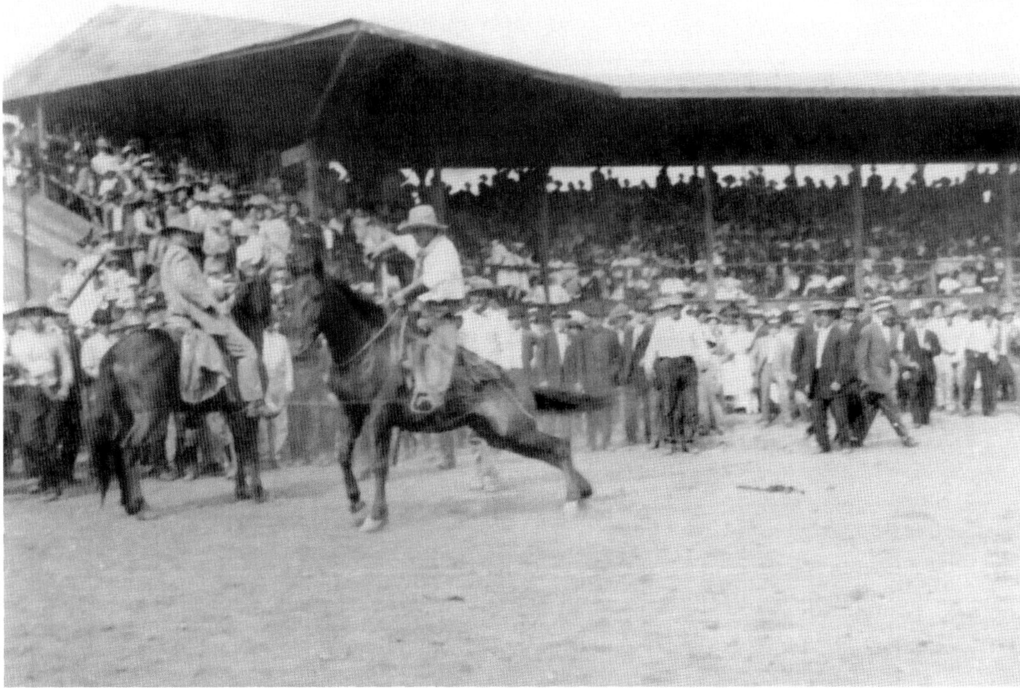

Although Bisbee prided itself on its sophistication and cosmopolitan nature, it still had a raw, frontier mining camp feeling to it. Wild West shows and rodeos were regular events at Warren Ballpark in the early 1900s. Cowboys from nearby Sulphur Springs Valley would ride into town to compete for prizes.

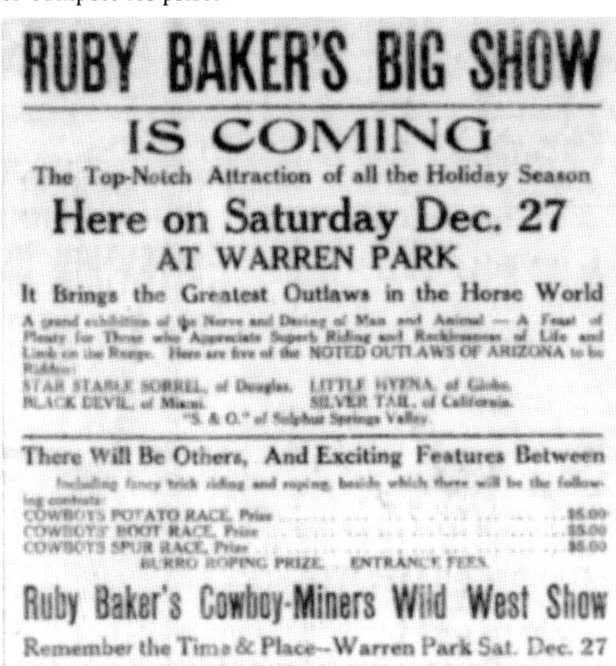

RUBY BAKER'S BIG SHOW

IS COMING

The Top-Notch Attraction of all the Holiday Season

Here on Saturday Dec. 27

AT WARREN PARK

It Brings the Greatest Outlaws in the Horse World

A grand exhibition of the Nerve and Daring of Man and Animal — A Feast of Plenty for Those who Appreciate Superb Riding and Recklessness of Life and Limb on the Range. Here are five of the NOTED OUTLAWS OF ARIZONA to be Ridden:

STAR STABLE SORREL, of Douglas. LITTLE HYENA, of Globe.
BLACK DEVIL, of Miami. SILVER TAIL, of California.
"S. & O." of Sulphur Springs Valley

There Will Be Others, And Exciting Features Between

Including fancy trick riding and roping, beside which there will be the following contests:

COWBOYS POTATO RACE, Prize $5.00
COWBOYS' BOOT RACE, Prize $5.00
COWBOYS SPUR RACE, Prize $5.00
BURRO ROPING PRIZE. ENTRANCE FEES.

Ruby Baker's Cowboy-Miners Wild West Show

Remember the Time & Place—Warren Park Sat. Dec. 27

Ruby Baker's Big Show came to Warren Ballpark right after Christmas in 1913. According to newspaper reports, the show was well attended. Displays of trick riding and roping were intermixed with contests featuring participants from Bisbee and outlying communities.

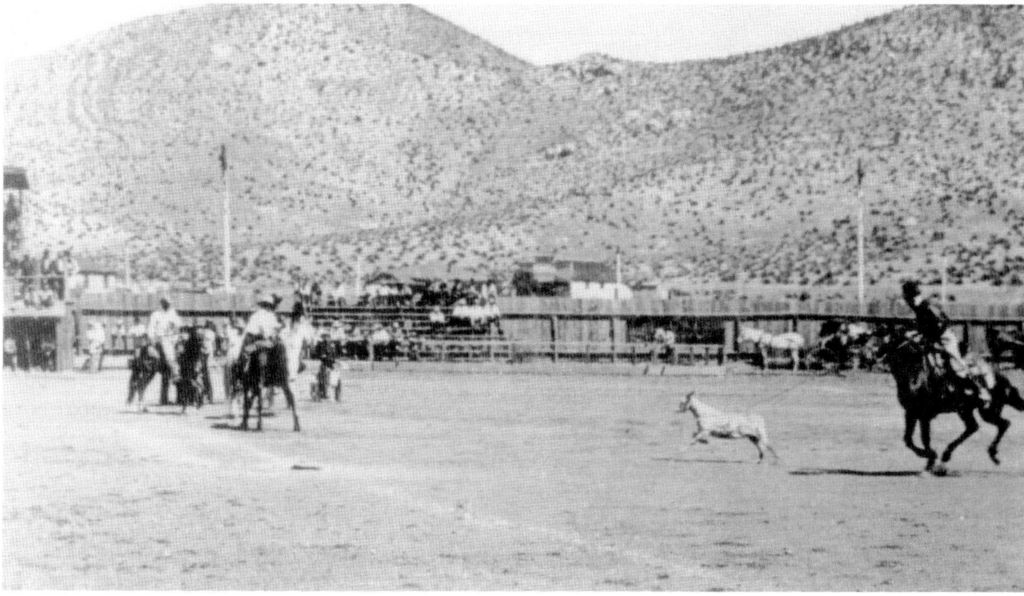

Rodeo events such as goat-roping, steer-roping, and bronco-riding provided crowds, many of whom were recent immigrants from Serbia, Great Britain, and other far-off places, with a vivid reminder that Bisbee was still a part of the Old West. Other events held at the park included circuses and blockbuster silent movies.

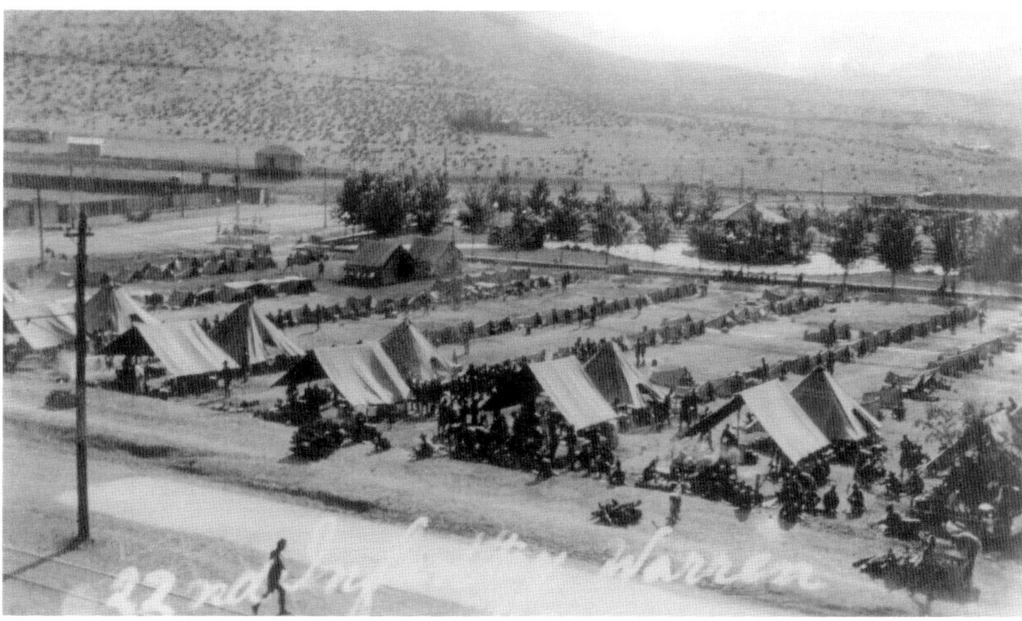

Bisbee's proximity to Mexico made life stressful after the Mexican Revolution erupted in 1910. Warren, only a few miles from the border, was garrisoned by soldiers who were bivouacked across the street from Warren Ballpark. The ballpark fence is seen here at the upper left. In March 1915, a US army machine gun squad set up its weapons on the diamond at Warren Ballpark and fired at known points on nearby hills to zero in their guns.

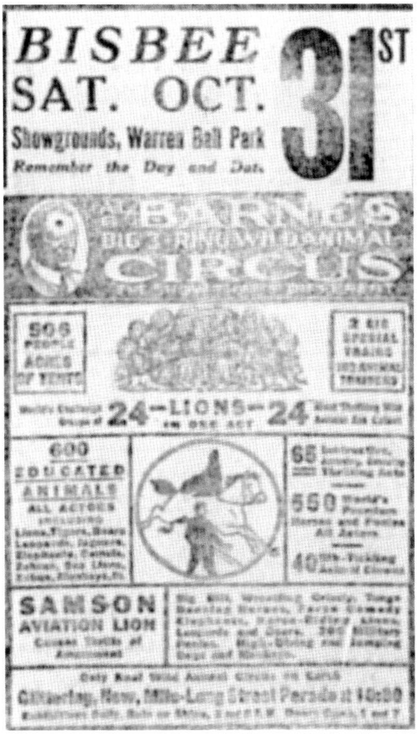

Traveling circuses such as Al Barnes's three-ring wild-animal circus came by special train to Bisbee to perform at Warren Ballpark. The railroad tracks running north from Bisbee Junction to Bisbee passed through Warren a few yards west of the ballpark, making the unloading of animals and equipment convenient.

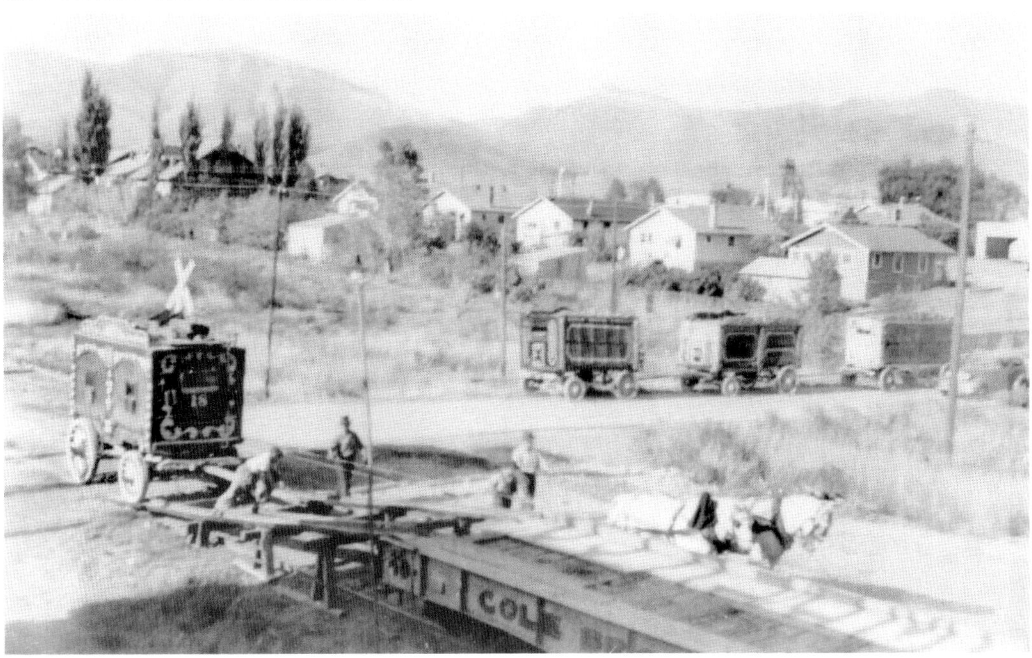

Circus workers unload wagons from flatbed cars parked on the rail line immediately west of Warren Ballpark. The wagons were hitched to teams of horses and paraded through town to drum up enthusiasm and publicize the event at the ballpark. It was just as easy to load up the circus equipment and leave town after the shows were over.

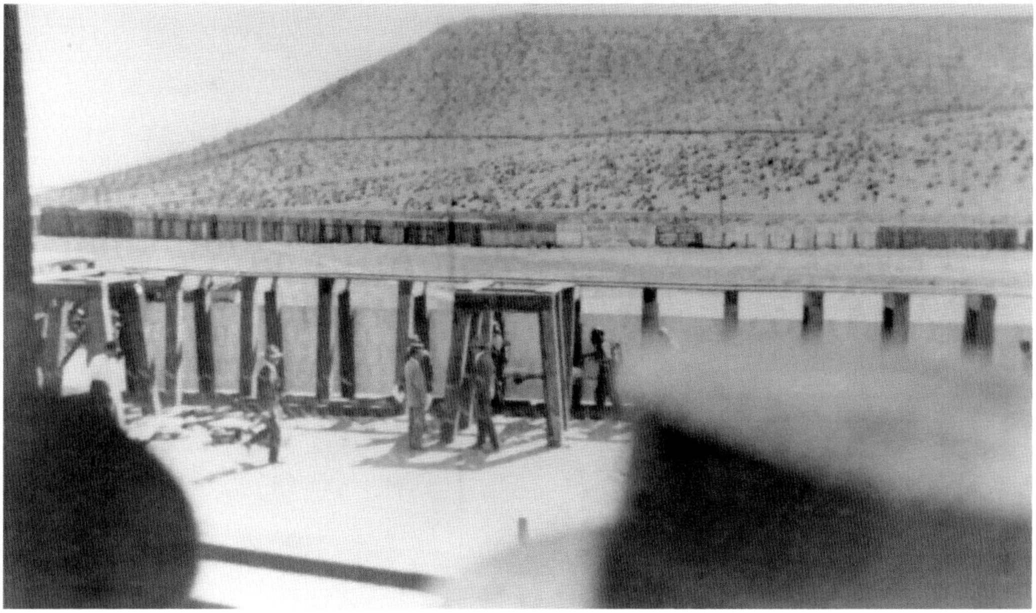

Mine Safety First Days also featured first-aid competition. Miners wearing self-contained breathing equipment carried a simulated injured miner to a first-aid station for treatment while judges evaluated and graded their actions. Mine safety became a priority when state mine-safety regulations were enacted and mine inspectors were hired.

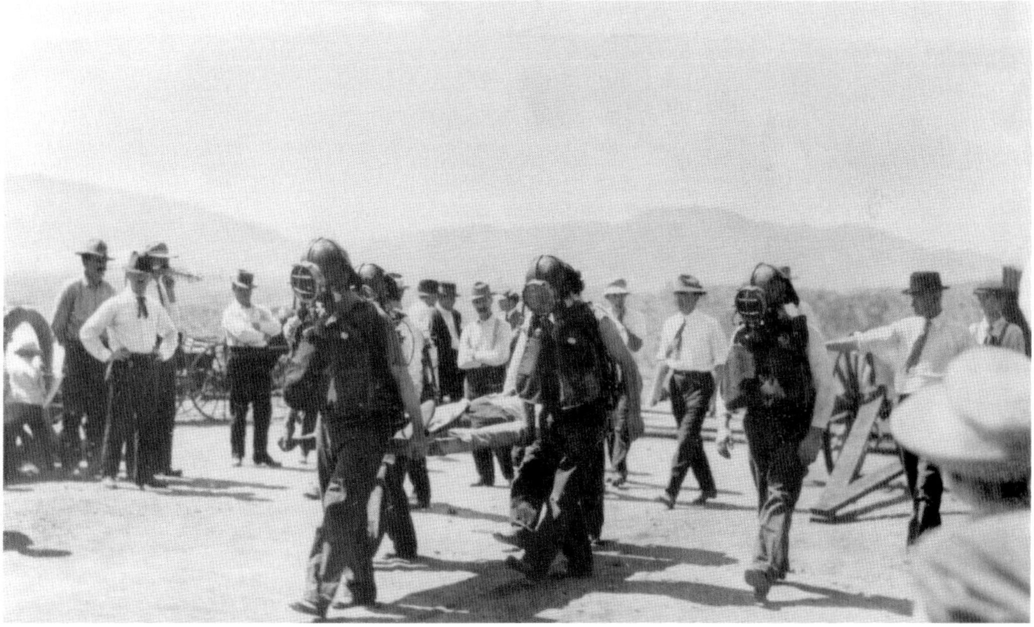

Events were sponsored by the mining companies to promote workplace safety and to provide competition between rival companies and mining towns. A typical Safety First Day at Warren Ballpark featured timed events simulating the rescue of miners trapped in underground fires by a team wearing self-contained oxygen systems and helmets.

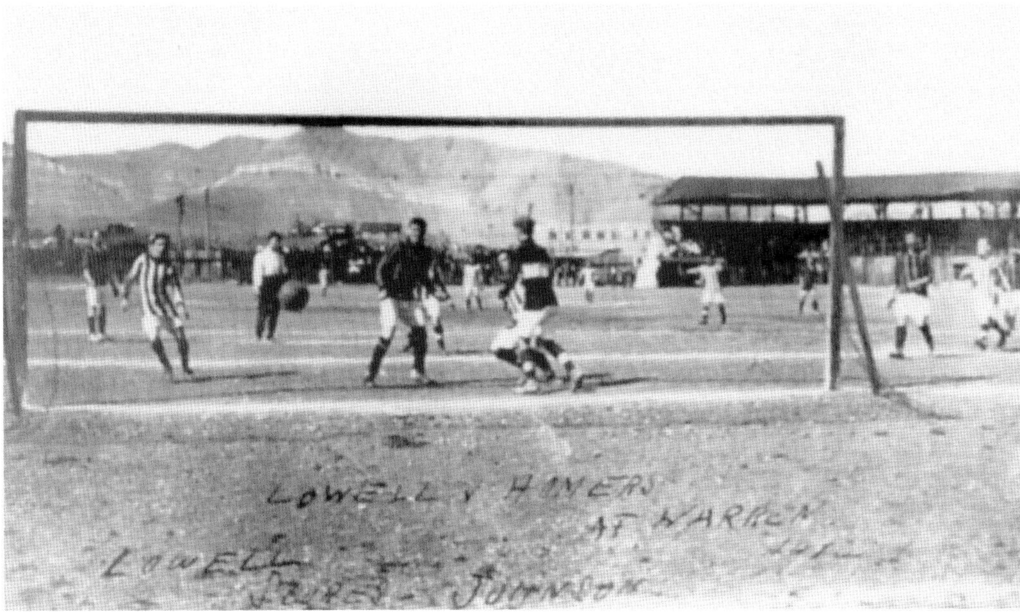

With some 40 percent of Bisbee's workforce being foreign-born, it was not surprising that immigrants from England, Scotland, Ireland, Canada, Australia, and South Africa organized leagues to play a regular schedule of their favorite games. Here, a forward for the Lowell United soccer team scores a goal against the Bisbee Homers.

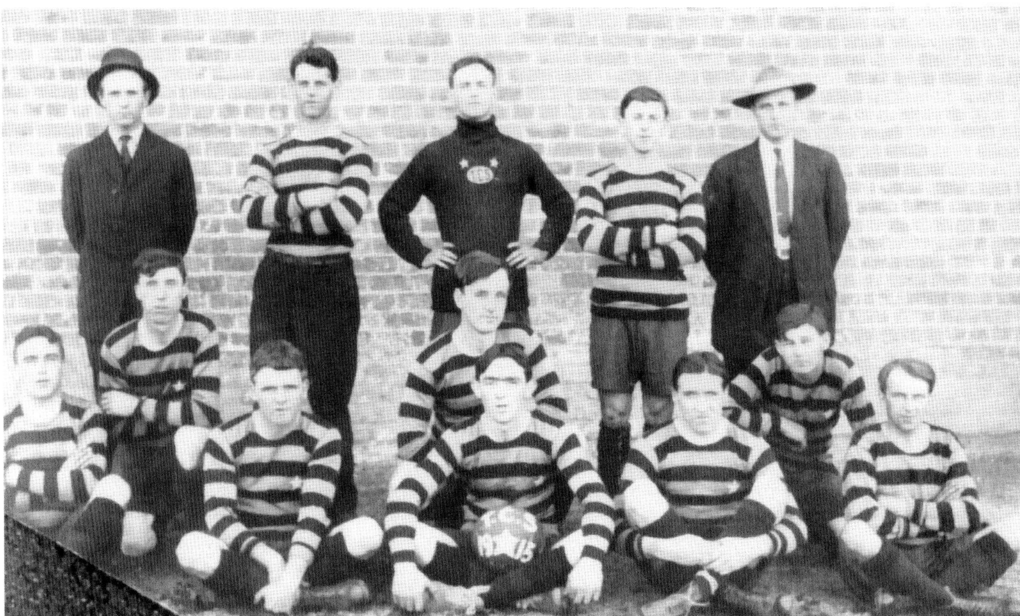

The Tombstone Canyon Stars line up for a postseason photograph at Warren Ballpark. Other adult soccer teams included the Graham Colts and the Knights of Columbus. Soccer season began in October after the baseball season and continued through March, with all matches being played on Sunday afternoons.

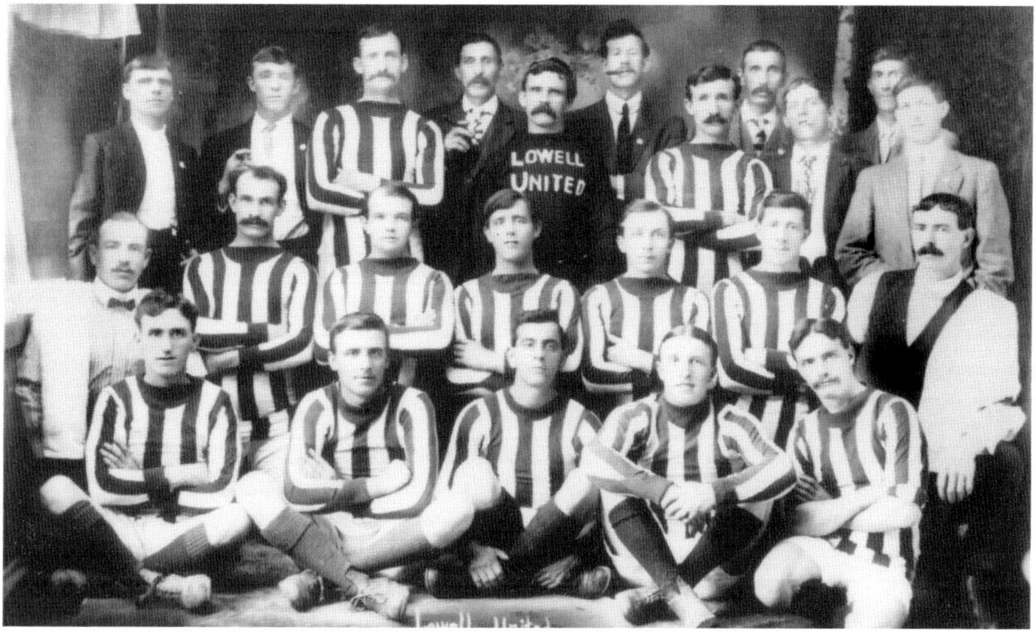

The lads of Lowell United pose triumphantly after completing the 1912–1913 soccer season undefeated. As the league became larger and the game more popular in Bisbee, all-star soccer teams offered challenges to other communities like Clifton. Adult soccer matches were well attended and results were reported in the local newspaper.

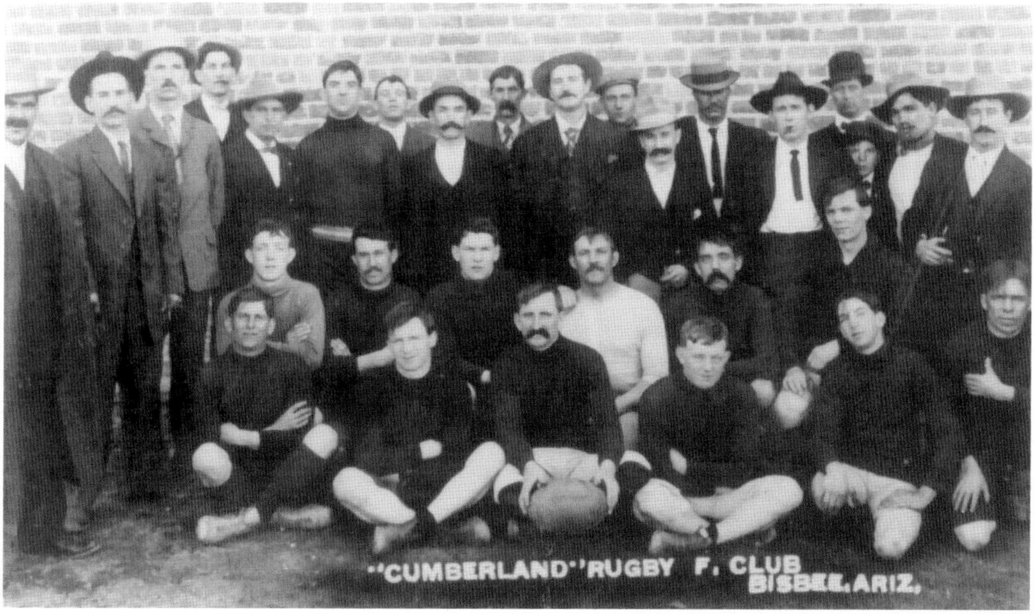

English-speaking immigrants desiring more physical contact on the field organized a rugby league in the Warren mining district. Among the teams that played rugby at Warren Ballpark were the Cumberlands and the Bisbee Reds. Like the other English sports, rugby's popularity waned as the immigrants aged and lost interest.

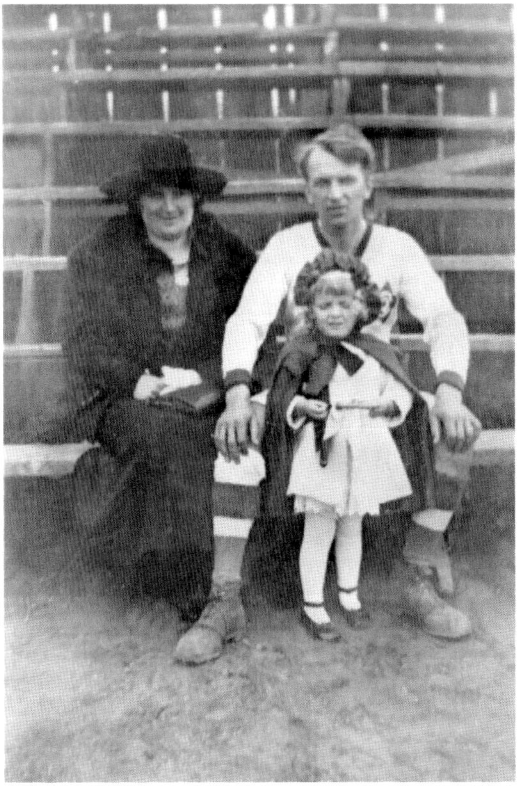

Whatever the sport—soccer, rugby, or cricket—the families of the players and their friends attended the matches at Warren Ballpark on winter Sunday mornings and afternoons. Here, William and Esther White posed with their daughter for a photograph after a match. White, an immigrant from England, was an engineer for the Calumet and Arizona Mining Company.

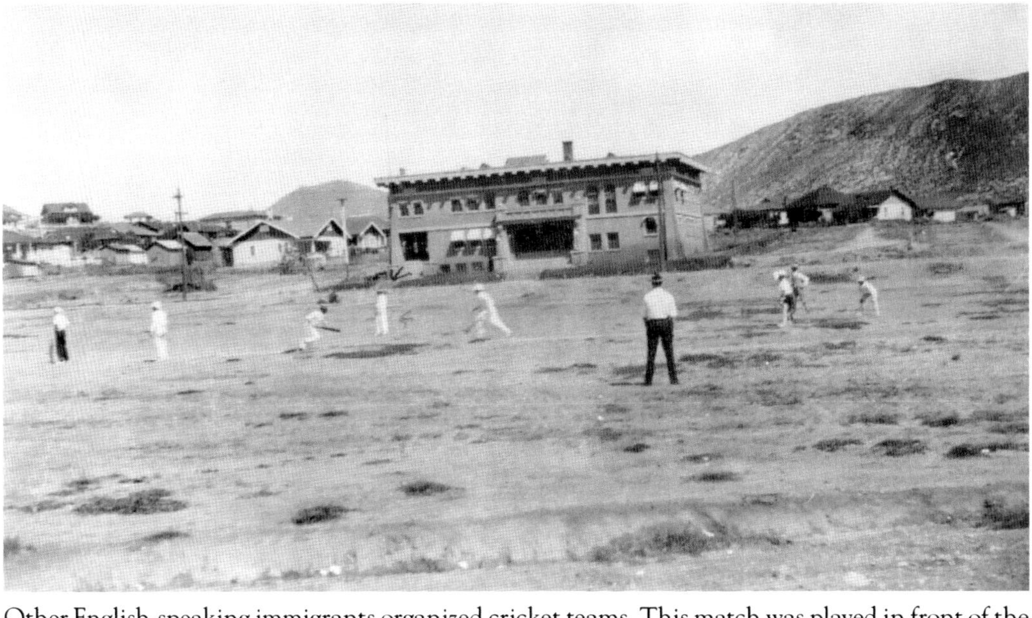

Other English-speaking immigrants organized cricket teams. This match was played in front of the Calumet and Arizona Mining Company offices (now Bisbee's city hall). The *Bisbee Daily Review* dutifully reported the results of the weekly cricket matches each week, undoubtedly confusing many of the paper's American-born readers

2

Barnstormers and Outlaws

Before television, most Americans who lived outside the northeast part of the nation only saw major league players on the field if a "barnstorming" team visited their town by train before or after the regular season to play an exhibition game. As a wealthy, politically influential city located on the Southern Pacific Railroad, Bisbee was frequently visited by barnstorming teams over a 34-year period.

A postseason game played on November 7, 1913, between John "Mugsy" McGraw's New York Giants and the Chicago White Sox was the first played by barnstorming teams. It was one stop on the 13-nation world tour through which McGraw and White Sox owner Charlie Comiskey intended to introduce baseball across the globe. That day, six future Hall of Famers and legendary Olympic athlete Jim Thorpe took the field.

Other major league teams that stopped to play exhibition games at Warren Ballpark were the Chicago Cubs, the Philadelphia Athletics, the Pittsburgh Pirates, and the Cleveland Indians. At least 16 inductees into the Hall of Fame are known to have played, coached, or managed exhibition games at Warren Ballpark.

Although not major league organizations, colorful and well-known barnstorming teams such as the Chinese University of Hawaii and the House of David also visited Warren Ballpark to play local teams before capacity crowds.

While outlaw leagues operated in the southwest before World War I, outlaw players did not make their appearance at Warren Ballpark until the mid-1920s. Two leagues, the Frontier and Copper Leagues, provided employment for players banned from organized baseball. Several former members of the Chicago White Sox joined the league after being accused of accepting bribes from gamblers to throw the 1919 World Series. "Black Sox" Chick Gandil, Buck Weaver, and Lefty Williams played on visiting teams at Warren Ball Park, as did ex–New York Giant Jimmie O'Connell and Cincinnati Reds first baseman Hal Chase, who were also banned for "throwing" ball games.

At the urging of baseball commissioner Kennesaw Mountain Landis, the Copper League was disbanded after the 1927 season, setting the stage for the introduction of organized baseball to Bisbee and the rest of the southwest.

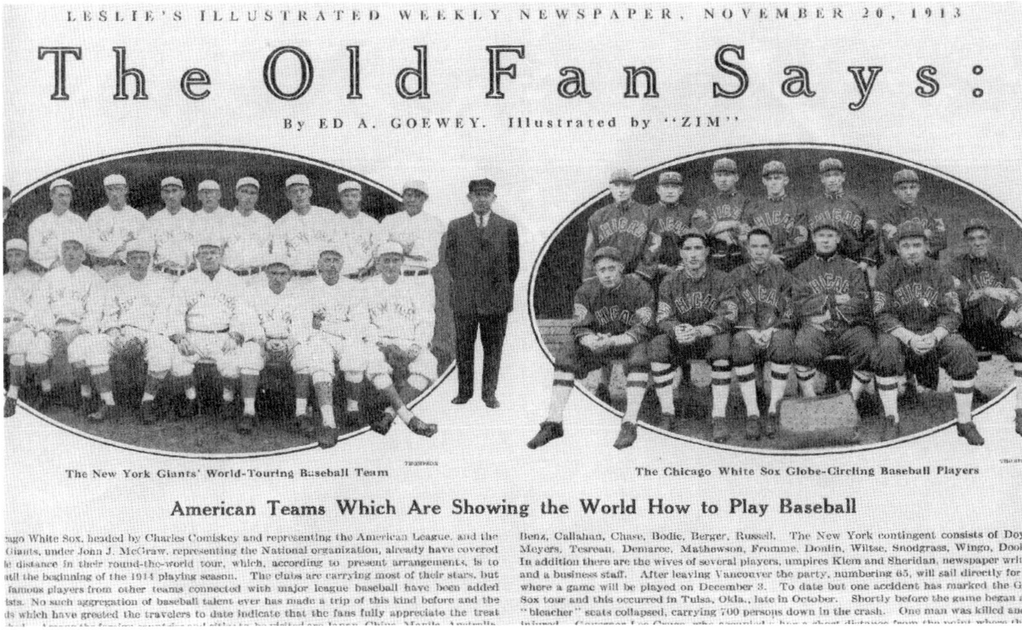

LESLIE'S ILLUSTRATED WEEKLY NEWSPAPER, NOVEMBER 20, 1913

The Old Fan Says:

By ED A. GOEWEY. Illustrated by "ZIM"

The New York Giants' World-Touring Baseball Team

The Chicago White Sox Globe-Circling Baseball Players

American Teams Which Are Showing the World How to Play Baseball

ago White Sox, headed by Charles Comiskey and representing the American League, and the Giants, under John J. McGraw, representing the National organization, already have covered le distance in their round-the-world tour, which, according to present arrangements, is to ntil the beginning of the 1914 playing season. The clubs are carrying most of their stars, but famous players from other teams connected with major league baseball have been added ists. No such aggregation of baseball talent ever has made a trip of this kind before and the ds which have greeted the travelers to date indicate that the fans fully appreciate the treat

Benz, Callahan, Chase, Bodie, Berger, Russell. The New York contingent consists of Doyle Meyers, Tesreau, Demaree, Mathewson, Fromme, Donlin, Wiltse, Snodgrass, Wingo, Doolan In addition there are the wives of several players, umpires Klem and Sheridan, newspaper writer and a business staff. After leaving Vancouver the party, numbering 65, will sail directly for Y where a game will be played on December 3. To date but one accident has marked the Gia Sox tour and this occurred in Tulsa, Okla., late in October. Shortly before the game began a "bleacher" seats collapsed, carrying 700 persons down in the crash. One man was killed and

The first barnstorming major league teams to visit Warren Ballpark were the New York Giants and the Chicago White Sox. The two teams, consisting of regular team members and players picked up from other major league teams to fill out the rosters, stopped at Bisbee on November 7, 1913, to play a game while on their way around the world by train and steamship. (Author's collection.)

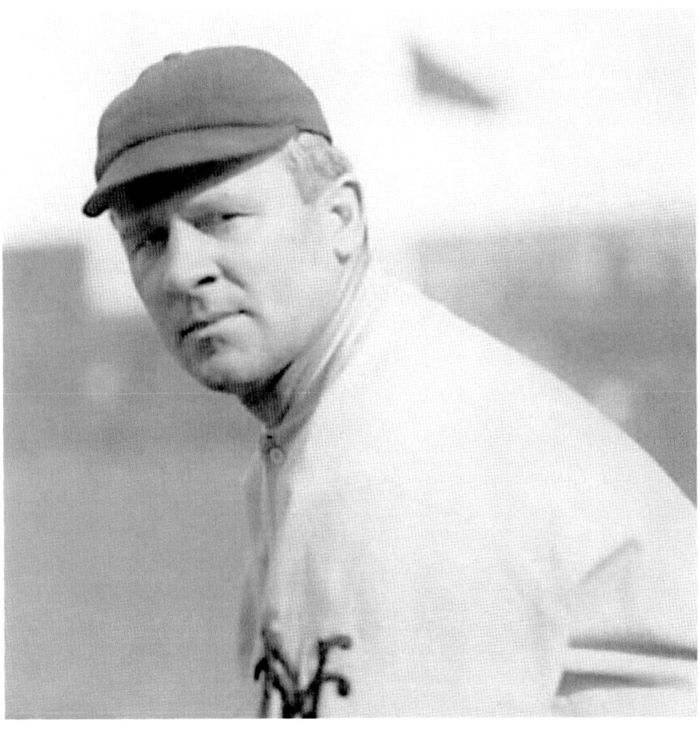

Arguably the greatest manager of all time, John McGraw led the New York Giants from 1902 to 1932, winning 10 National League pennants and three World Series championships along the way. Bisbee went all-out to entertain McGraw, his wife, Blanche, and the rest of the "World Tourists" during their visit to Warren Ballpark. (Courtesy Library of Congress.)

While he was not a great baseball player, Jim Thorpe was already known to the world as its greatest all-around athlete when he played center field for the Giants at Warren Ballpark. The 1912 Olympic pentathlon and decathlon star thrilled the Bisbee crowd when he smashed a home run over the center field fence. (Courtesy Library of Congress.)

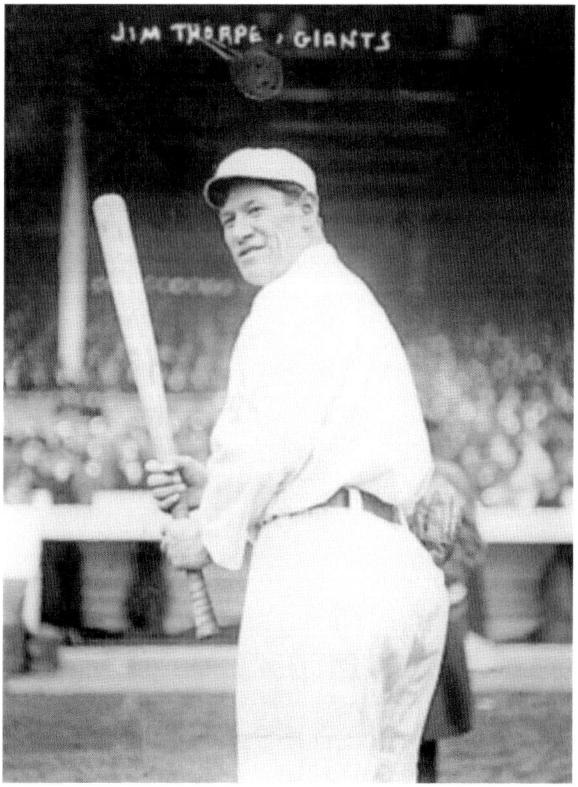

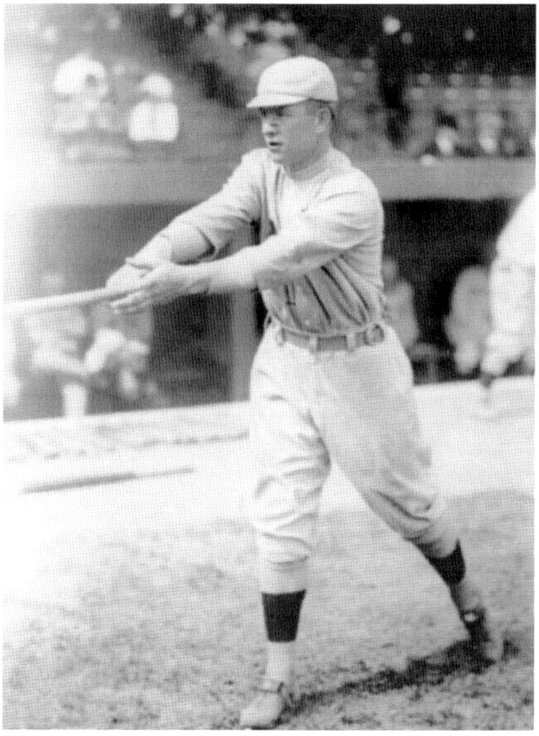

Tristam "Tris" Speaker, the stellar center fielder for the 1913 Boston Red Sox, signed on with Charlie Comiskey's White Sox traveling team to play on the world tour. Speaker had a lifetime .345 batting average and was a superior fielder. (Courtesy Library of Congress.)

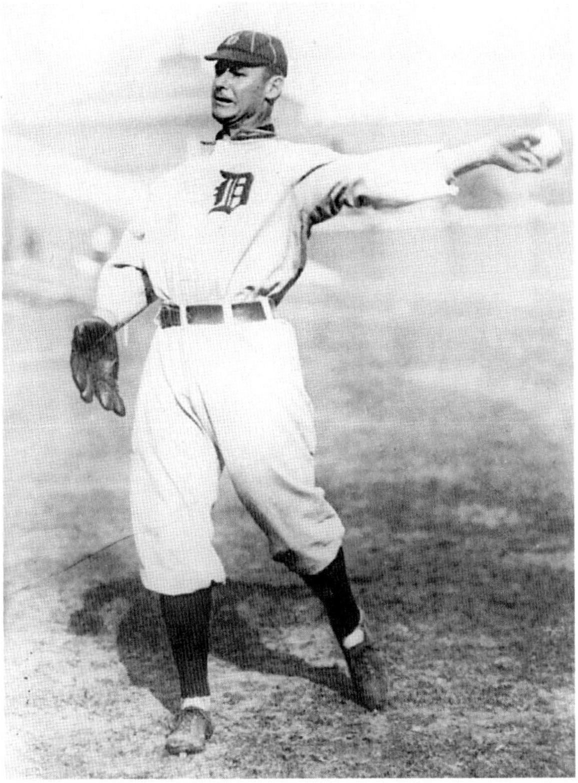

An outfielder with the Detroit Tigers and a teammate of Ty Cobb's at the time of the world tour, "Wahoo" Sam Crawford signed up to play with the White Sox as they circled the globe with the New York Giants. A powerful hitter with a lifetime batting average of .309, Crawford went hitless against Art Fromme at Warren Ballpark. He was inducted into the Baseball Hall of Fame in 1957. (Photograph courtesy Library of Congress.)

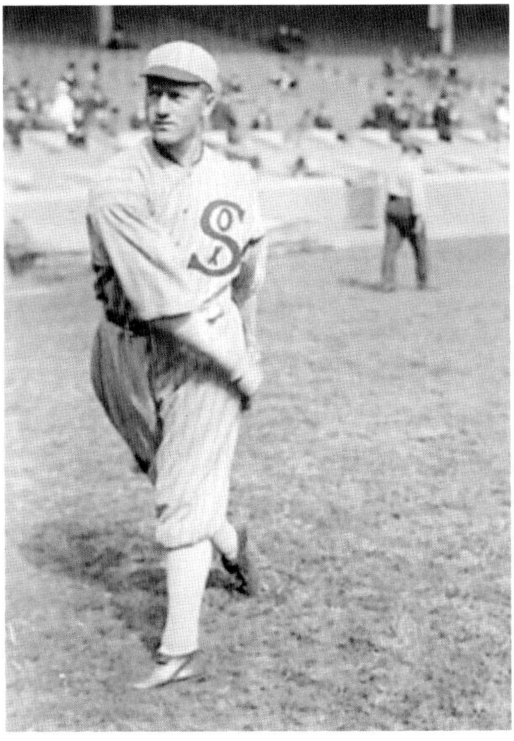

Urban "Red" Faber had yet to throw a single pitch in the big leagues when Charlie Comiskey invited him on the world tour. Faber took the mound for the White Sox when they played the Giants at Warren Ballpark, losing 9-1 to Giants hurler Art Fromme. Faber would be the last pitcher to use the spitball legally in the American League. He was inducted into the Hall of Fame in 1964. (Courtesy Library of Congress.)

White Sox catcher Ray Schalk had been a big league catcher for only a year when he worked behind the plate for the Chicago White Sox at Warren Ballpark during the world tour. A superb defensive player and adequate hitter, he was untainted by the 1919 "Black Sox" scandal and ended up getting inducted into the Hall of Fame in 1953. (Courtesy Library of Congress.)

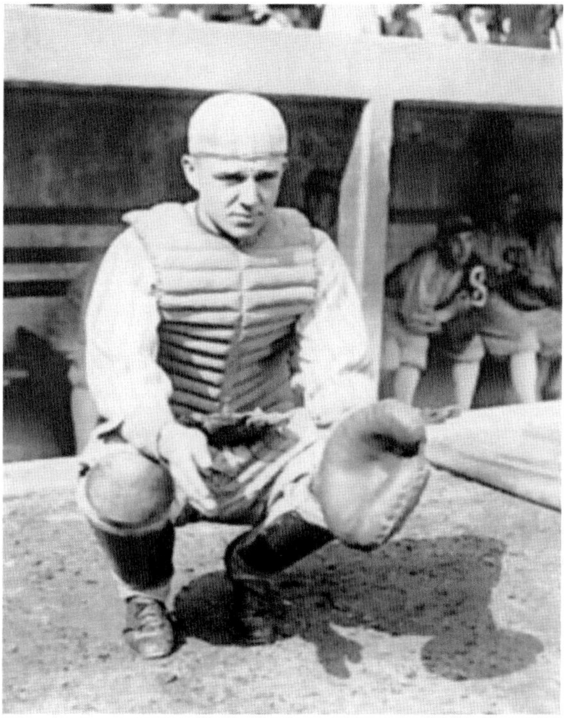

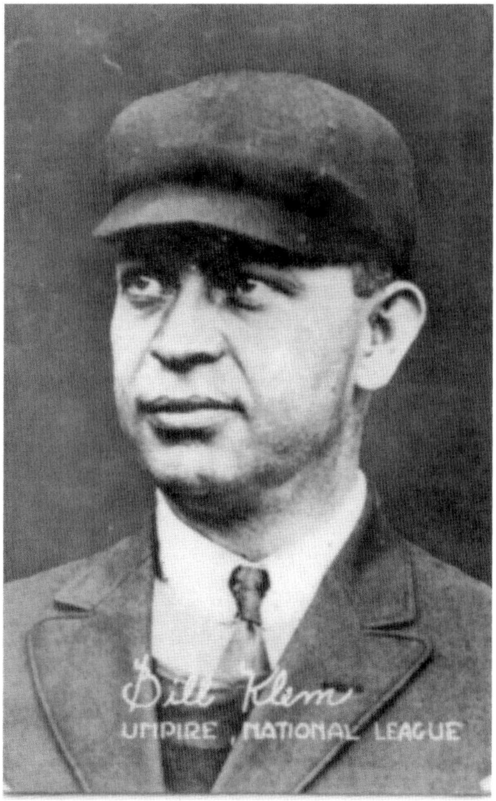

Bill Klem, also elected to the Hall of Fame in 1953, is considered the finest umpire to call games in the National League. He worked behind the plate at Warren Ballpark when the Giants and White Sox came to Bisbee. Klem and John McGraw despised each other, which must have made the trip around the world together a memorable experience for both of them. (Author's collection.)

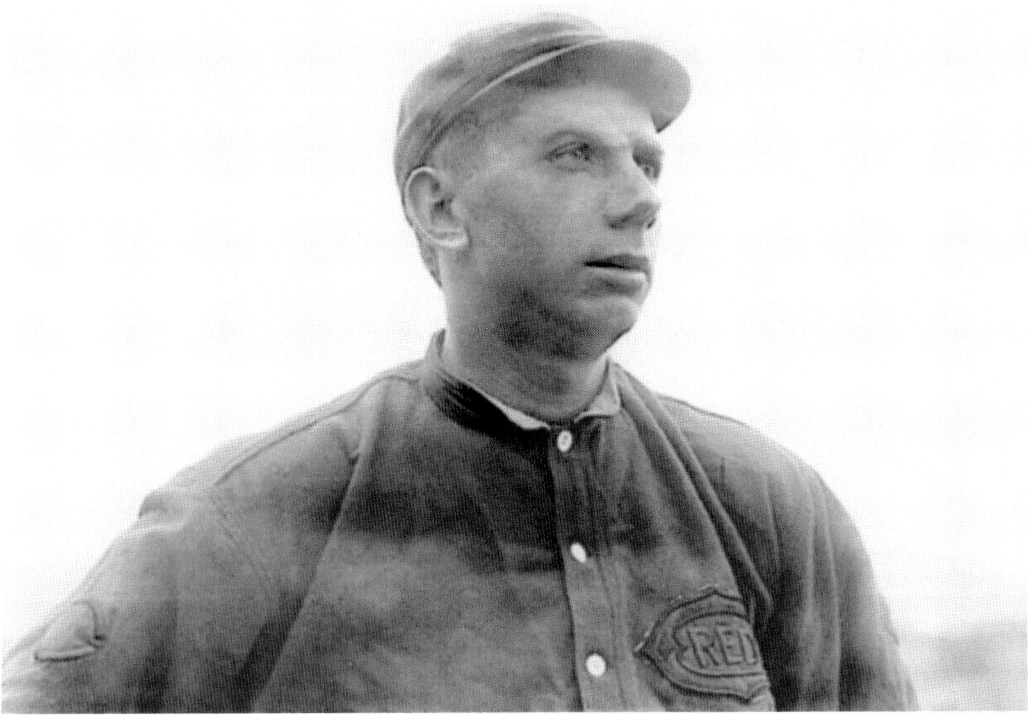

A right-handed pitcher, Art Fromme handcuffed the White Sox, throwing a complete game at Warren Ballpark. He held Chicago to a single run and nine hits over nine innings. Fromme spent 10 years in the National League, pitching for the Cardinals, Reds, and Giants. (Courtesy Library of Congress.)

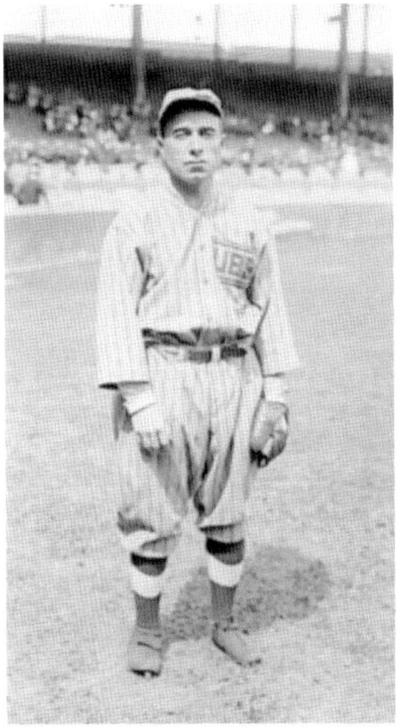

Fred Mitchell was the manager of the 1918 National League champion Chicago Cubs when they stopped at Warren Ballpark on a barnstorming tour to play a local team in April 1919. The Cubs were rumored to have "thrown" the 1918 World Series to the Boston Red Sox, predating the 1919 Black Sox scandal by a year. (Courtesy Library of Congress.)

James "Hippo" Vaughn was considered to be the best left-handed pitcher in the National League when the Cubs stopped at Warren Ballpark in 1919, but he was chased from the mound by the Warren District Grays in the first inning. His nickname came from his large size and lumbering gait. Vaughn was a 22-game winner for Chicago in 1918 and won 20 games or more in five seasons with the Cubs. (Courtesy Library of Congress.)

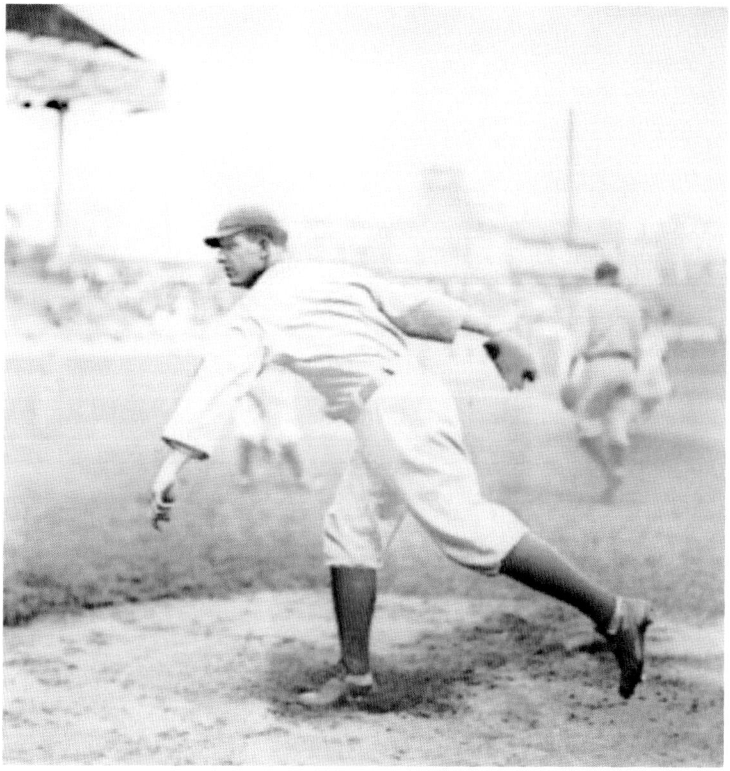

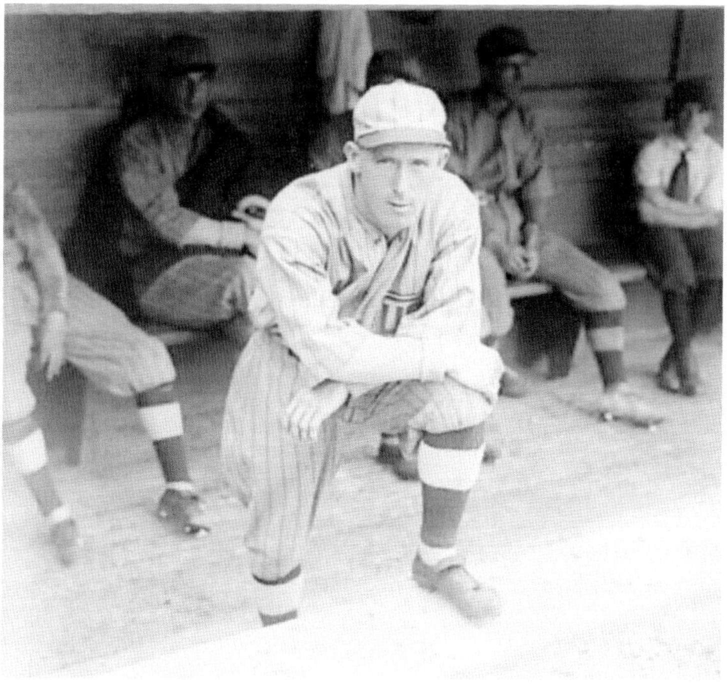

Max Flack, Chicago's right fielder, went 2-4 and scored three runs as the leadoff hitter in the Cubs' exhibition game at Warren Ballpark. Flack's throwing errors and poor baserunning in the 1918 World Series against the Red Sox created suspicion that he had been paid by gamblers to "throw" the series. (Courtesy Library of Congress.)

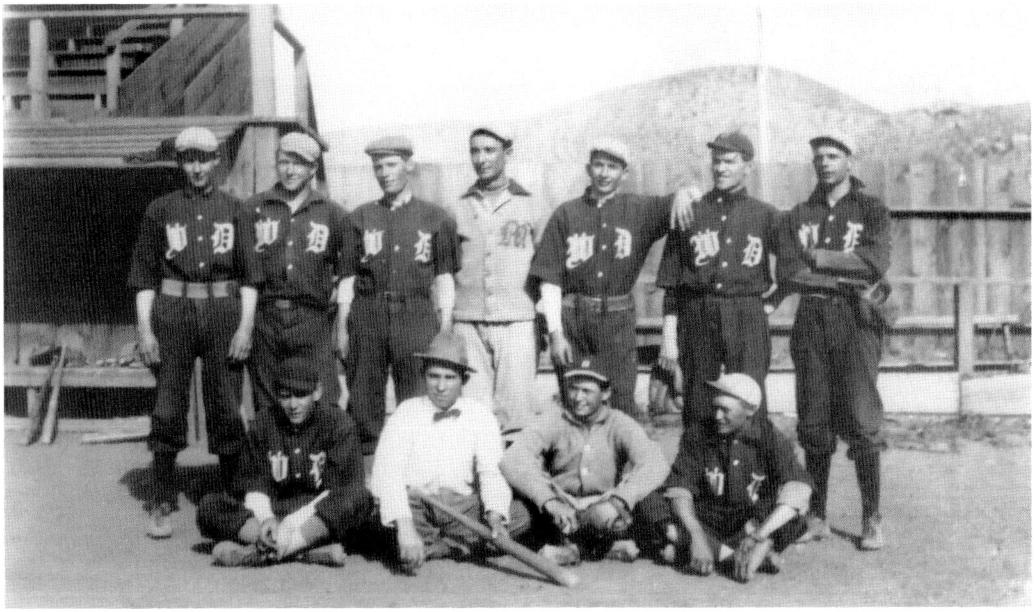

The semiprofessional Warren District Grays gave the National League champion Chicago Cubs a scare when the Cubbies stopped at Warren Ballpark on April 12, 1919, to play an exhibition game on their way from California back to the Windy City. The Cubs were the last barnstorming major league team to play an exhibition game in Bisbee until the late 1930s.

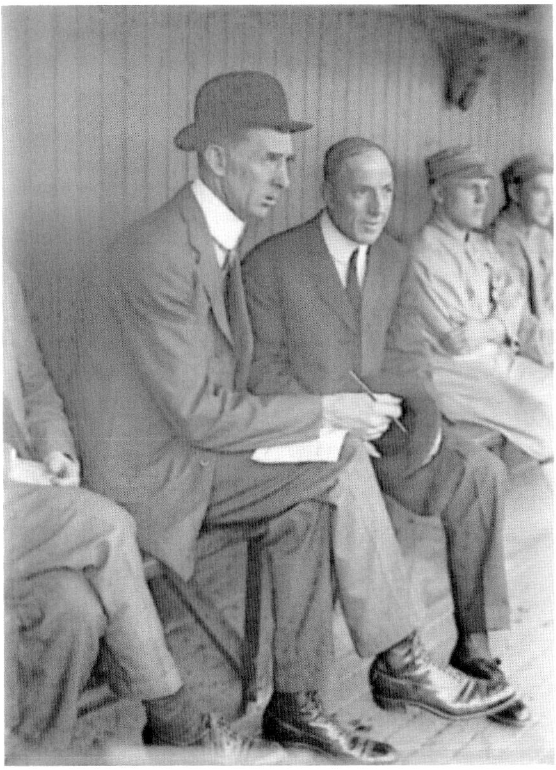

Cornelius McGillicuddy, better known as Connie Mack, had already managed the Philadelphia Athletics for 39 years when he brought his team to Warren Ballpark on April 2, 1940, to play the Pirates. Inducted into the Baseball Hall of Fame in 1937, Mack managed the Athletics for half a century. (Courtesy Library of Congress.)

Honus Wagner, the "Flying Dutchman," considered to be the game's finest shortstop, was long past his playing time when he arrived at Warren Ballpark as a coach with the barnstorming Pittsburgh Pirates in April 1940, but he still thrilled Bisbee fans. He returned to Bisbee again in March 1946, when the Pirates played the White Sox. Wagner was one of the three original inductees into the Hall of Fame in 1936. (Courtesy Library of Congress.)

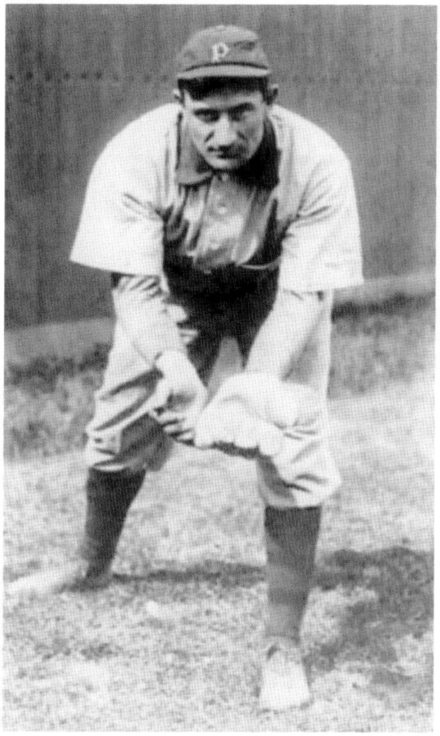

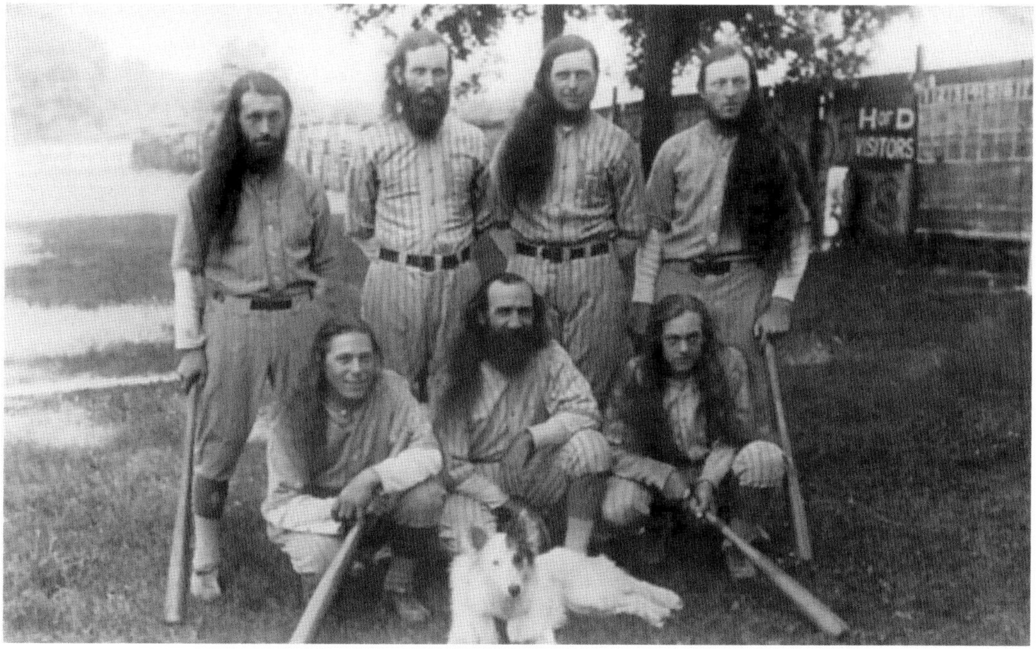

The House of David, a religious commune in Michigan, sponsored a barnstorming team of ballplayers who were famous for their long hair and beards. In April 1928, the House of David team defeated the Bisbee Bees 11-9 in an exhibition game at Warren Ballpark. It was the Bees' first appearance on their new home field. (Courtesy House of David Museum.)

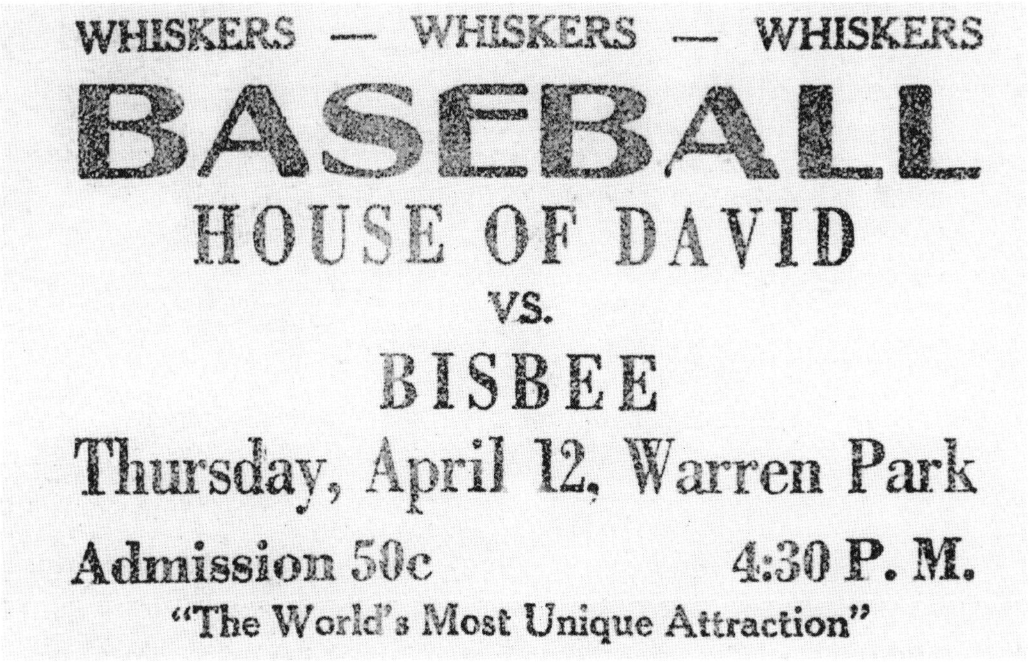
WHISKERS — WHISKERS — WHISKERS
BASEBALL
HOUSE OF DAVID
VS.
BISBEE
Thursday, April 12, Warren Park
Admission 50c
4:30 P. M.
"The World's Most Unique Attraction"

This advertisement appeared in the *Bisbee Daily Review* before the April 12, 1928, exhibition game between the House of David and Bisbee's new minor league team, the Bees. The beards and long hair worn by the commune members and the ringers who played for them were good for drawing crowds.

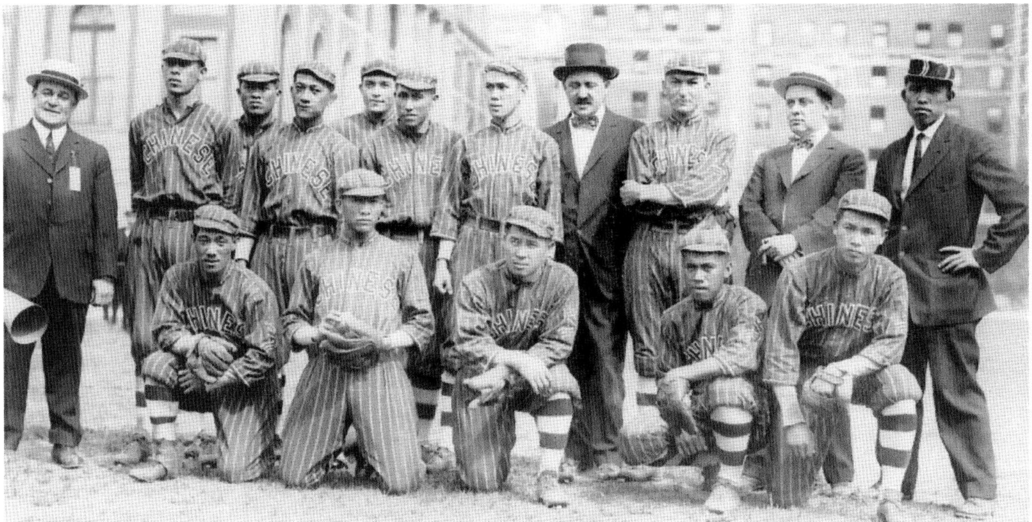

The Chinese University of Hawaii traveling team was not really a university team—nor was it an all-Chinese team—when it visited Warren Ballpark in March 1915. Sponsored by Chinese American businessmen in Hawaii, the players were of Chinese, Japanese, Hawaiian, Portuguese, and Haole descent. The boys from Oahu defeated the Warren District Grays. (Courtesy Library of Congress.)

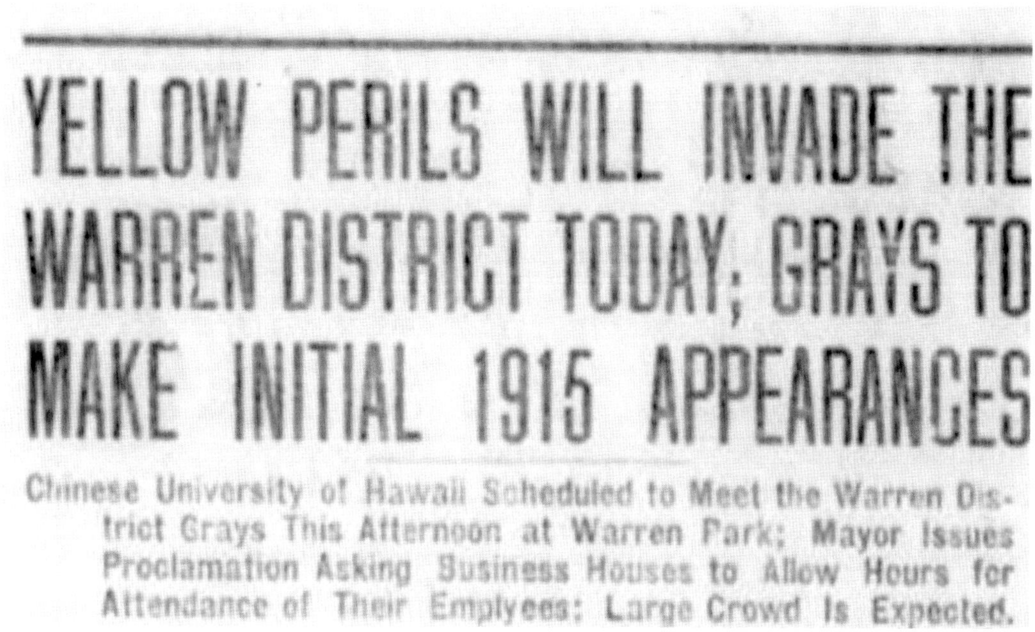
YELLOW PERILS WILL INVADE THE WARREN DISTRICT TODAY; GRAYS TO MAKE INITIAL 1915 APPEARANCES

Chinese University of Hawaii Scheduled to Meet the Warren District Grays This Afternoon at Warren Park; Mayor Issues Proclamation Asking Business Houses to Allow Hours for Attendance of Their Emplyees; Large Crowd Is Expected.

Bisbee was not a friendly place to Asians in the early 1900s. References to "celestials" and "yellow peril" were reflective of the racial stereotypes then commonly held in America. While some Anglos believed Asians to be weak and effeminate, that belief was put to rest when they lost to their guests from Hawaii.

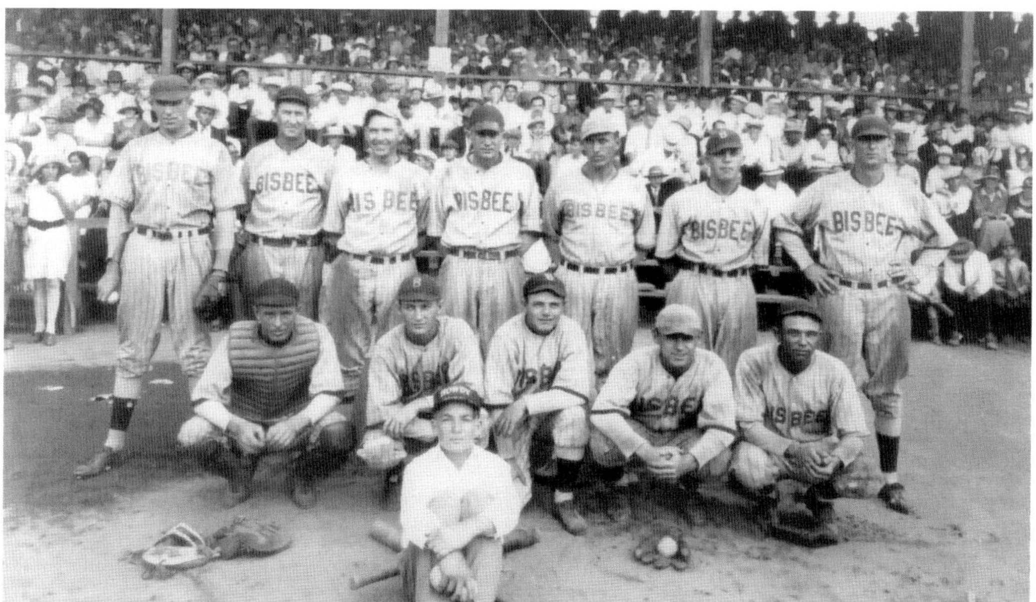

The 1927 Bisbee Miners were a team in the outlaw Copper League, which included teams from southwestern New Mexico and southeastern Arizona. The Miners, who played in Bisbee during the 1926 and 1927 seasons, never used players who had been officially banished from baseball, but the team's manager, Tom Seaton, had been blackballed from organized baseball.

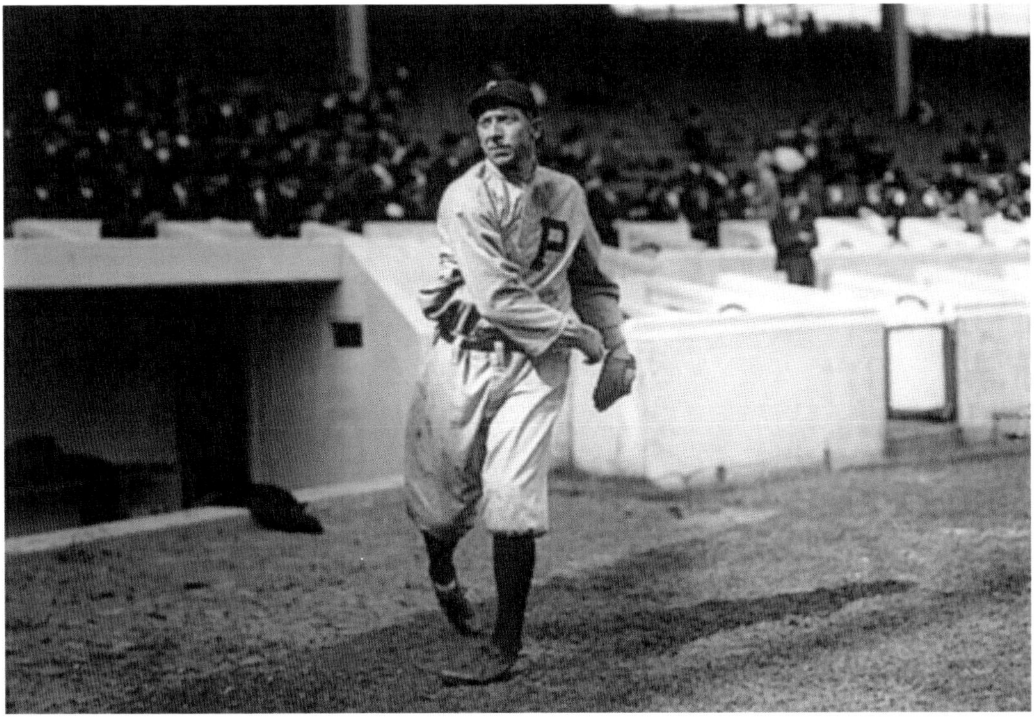

A former ace pitcher for the Philadelphia Phillies, Tom Seaton returned to the Pacific Coast League after the 1917 season. Suspected of throwing games in the PCL and released from the San Francisco Seals, Seaton moved around trying to find a spot in organized baseball, without success. By 1926, he was playing and managing in Bisbee. (Courtesy Library of Congress.)

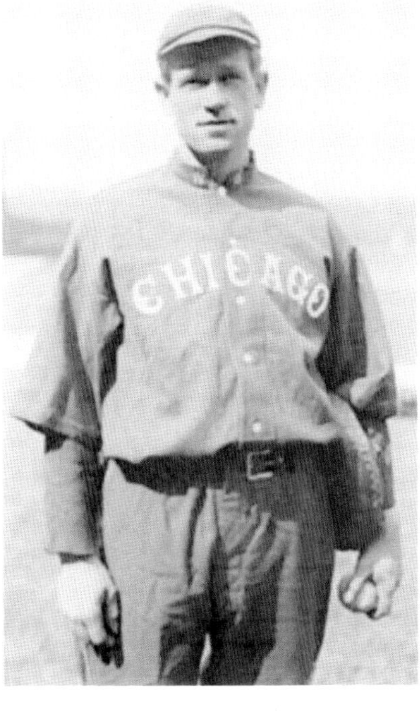

Hal Chase had many talents and few scruples. Recognized as one of the finest first basemen in the game during the dead ball era, Chase was banished from organized baseball in the early 1920s for fixing games. He played for and managed teams in the outlaw Frontier and Copper leagues, primarily in Douglas. He also encouraged other outlaw players to join teams in the league.

A star shortstop and third baseman with the Chicago White Sox, George "Buck" Weaver was banned from organized baseball in 1920 after being implicated in the 1919 "Black Sox" scandal. He steadfastly maintained his innocence. In the mid-1920s, he played in the outlaw Copper League. (Courtesy Hall of Fame.)

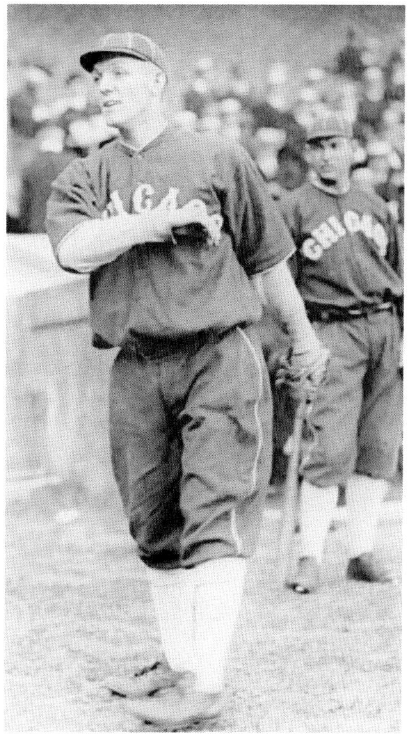

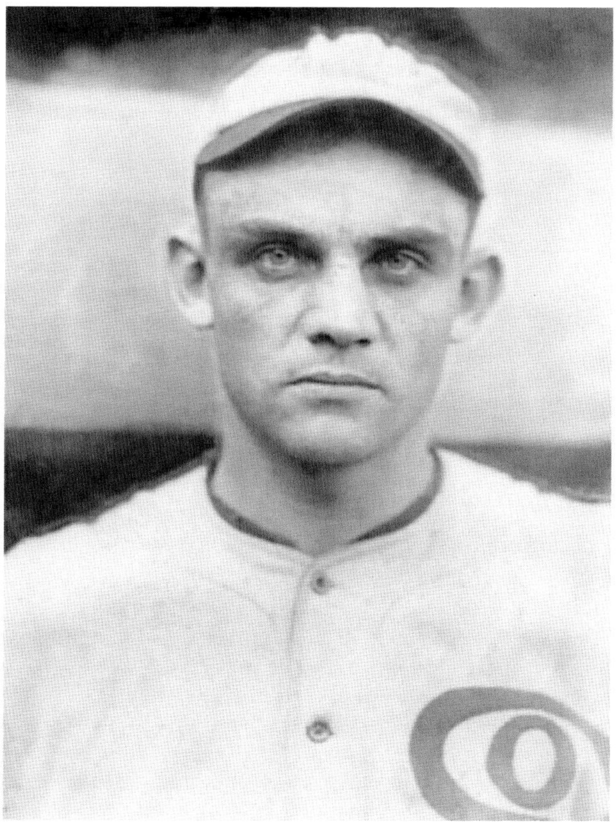

A hard man on and off the field, White Sox first baseman Chick Gandil was a leader of the 1919 "Black Sox" scandal. Banned from playing in organized baseball, Gandil drifted west to play in the outlaw Frontier and Copper Leagues from 1925 through 1927. He had appeared at Warren Ballpark twice previously, in 1907 with the Cananea team and in 1913 on the world tour. (Courtesy Hall of Fame.)

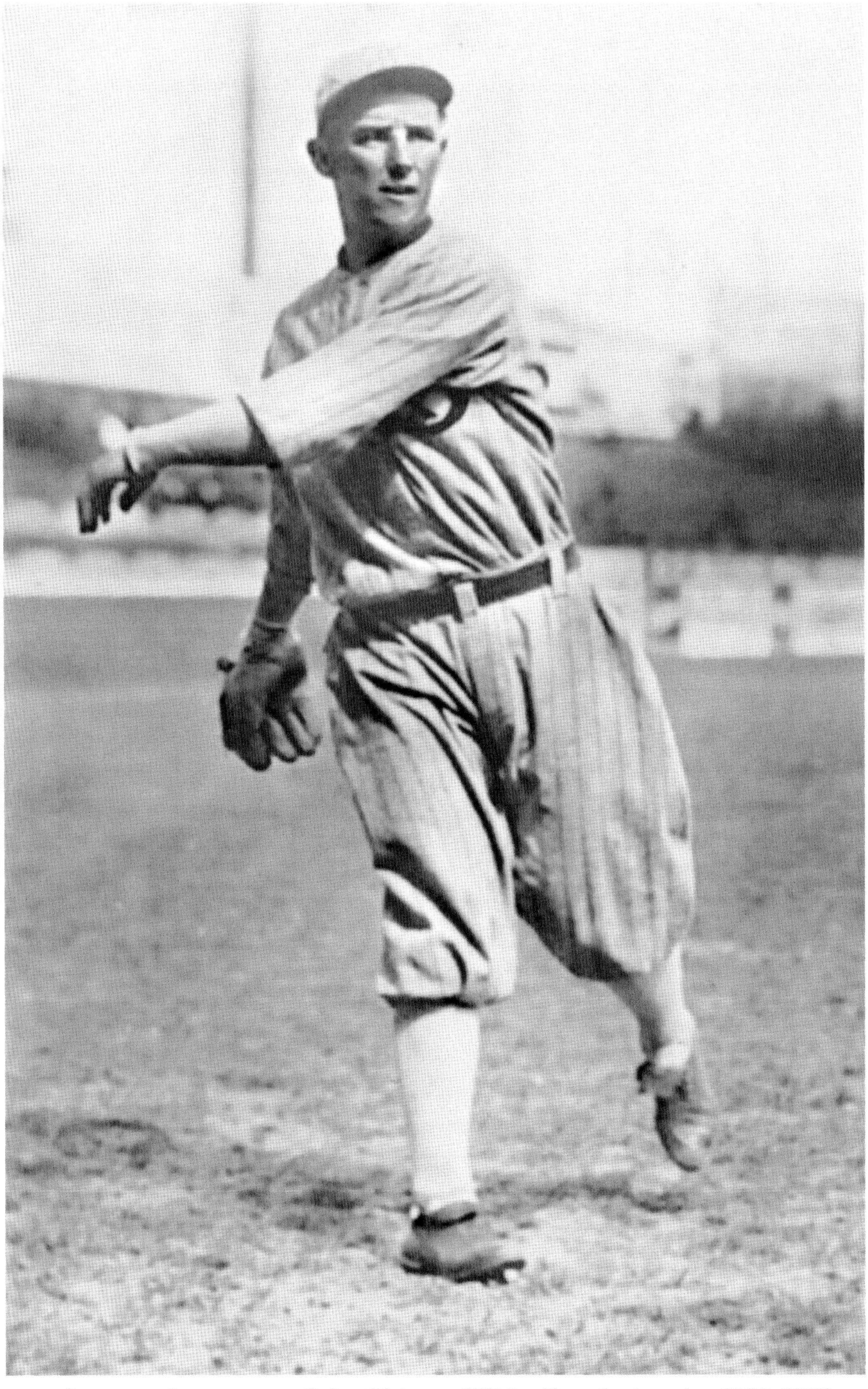

A key contributor to the success of the Chicago White Sox during the 1917, 1919, and 1920 seasons, pitcher Claude "Lefty" Williams threw his reputation away when he deliberately "threw" three games during the 1919 World Series. Williams joined other banished Black Sox players in the outlaw Frontier and Copper Leagues in the mid-1920s. (Courtesy Library of Congress.)

3

DARK DAY IN JULY

America's neutrality in World War I came to an end in April 1917 when war was declared against Germany. For most Americans, however, the war was still a far-off distraction. Life went on much as before, although the country was gearing up to send a rapidly mobilizing army of doughboys "over there" to fight the Germans and "make the world safe for democracy," as Pres. Woodrow Wilson explained.

A copper-mining town such as Bisbee always had its share of tensions between labor and management. Strikes had been organized in Arizona and management had been compelled to make concessions, to an extent, only a year before. Walter Douglas and other ranking leaders of the state's copper-mining industry had not forgotten or forgiven and had learned valuable lessons in the setback. But for now, all was quiet on the home front, including Bisbee.

Baseball as a recreational and spectator pastime was encouraged and supported by the copper companies. The ballpark was considered neutral ground, where white-collar workers, bosses, foremen, merchants, muckers, and drillers could all mingle, drink a little beer, and forget their differences as they rooted for the home team, whether it be baseball, football, soccer, rugby, or cricket.

That neutrality was shattered in 1917 when a heavily armed posse of some 2,000 men led by Cochise County sheriff Harry Wheeler rounded up more than 1,500 striking Bisbee copper miners and their sympathizers in a well-planned operation.

Within a short time, Bisbee's main venue for pleasure and recreation had become something else entirely. To many Americans, the images of men being herded into Warren Ballpark at gunpoint mirrored their beliefs that drastic acts were necessary to protect the nation from internal subversion and sabotage during wartime. To others, the deportation represented one more act in a long series of injustices perpetrated by capital upon labor.

Although many participants in the deportation were initially charged with crimes related to the kidnapping of the strikers and the denial of their civil rights, only one stood trial, and he was immediately acquitted by a local jury. No matter how each resident of Bisbee felt about or was affected by the deportation, the Warren mining district and its ballpark would never be quite the same.

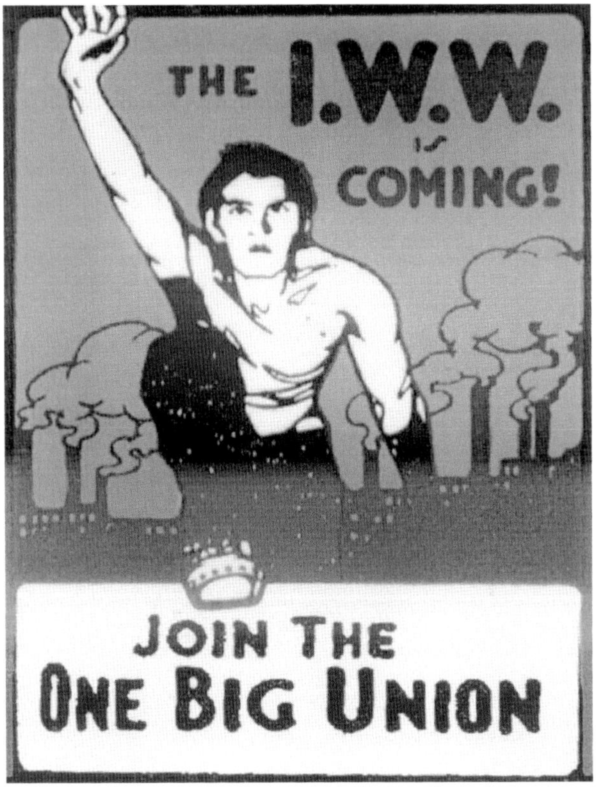

The Industrial Workers of the World (IWW) became the symbol of radical labor in America in the early 1900s. Founded in 1905, the IWW was an anarchist labor movement that believed in direct confrontation through general strikes and work slowdowns. Although its rhetoric was inflammatory, the IWW committed few overt acts of violence.

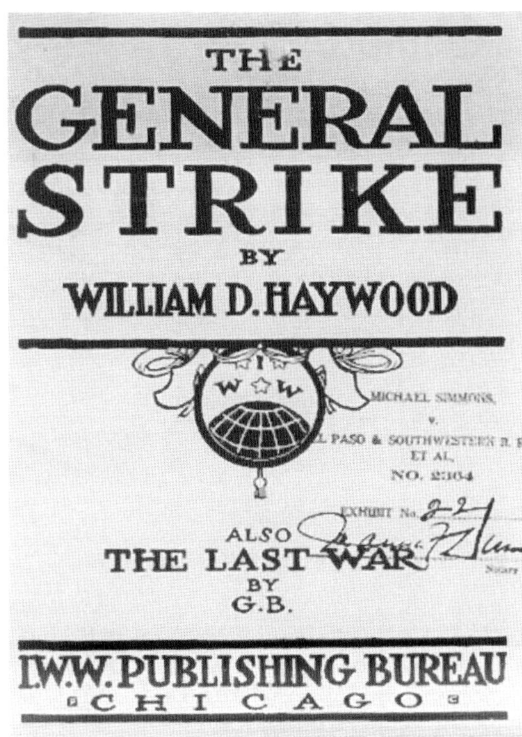

Prior to 1916, the IWW had been active organizing factories and mills in the eastern United States. That year, the union decided to focus its attention on organizing mining and lumber camps in the southwest. Its aggressive recruiting efforts in communities that had already been organized by more moderate labor unions caused resentment.

Frank Little, an IWW organizer and board member, came to Bisbee in June 1917 to direct union activities. Originally opposed to the strike, Little was deported with the other striking miners on July 12. He went on to Butte, Montana, from Columbus, New Mexico, and was lynched there less than three weeks later. (Photograph courtesy Industrial Workers of the World.)

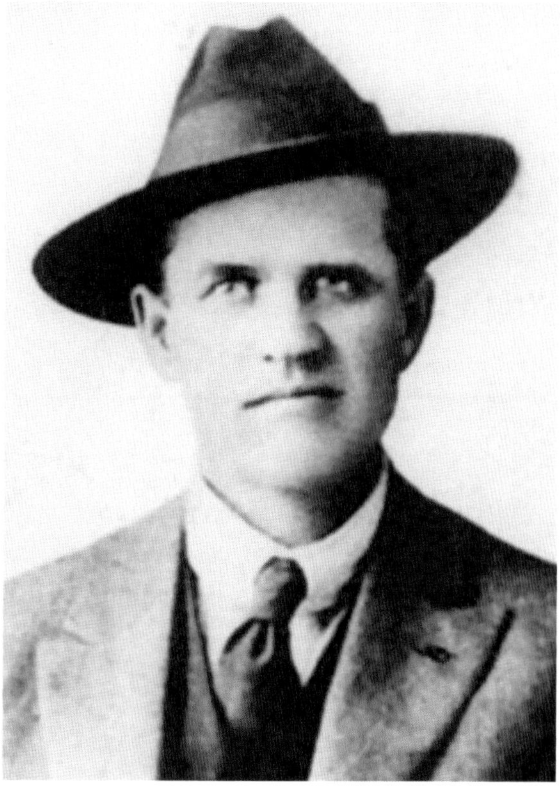

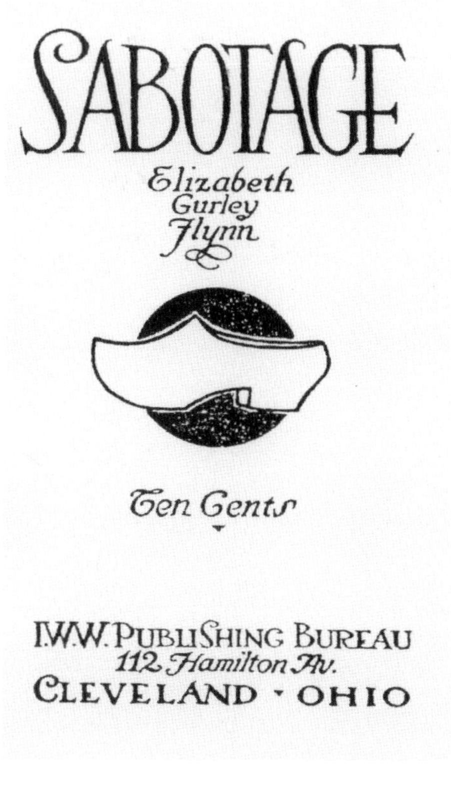

Calls by IWW leaders to resist the military draft and to conduct work slowdowns angered Americans who supported America's entry into World War I. The IWW's advocacy of disrupting industrial production to further union goals made it easy for the movement's enemies to portray the union as bomb-throwing radicals.

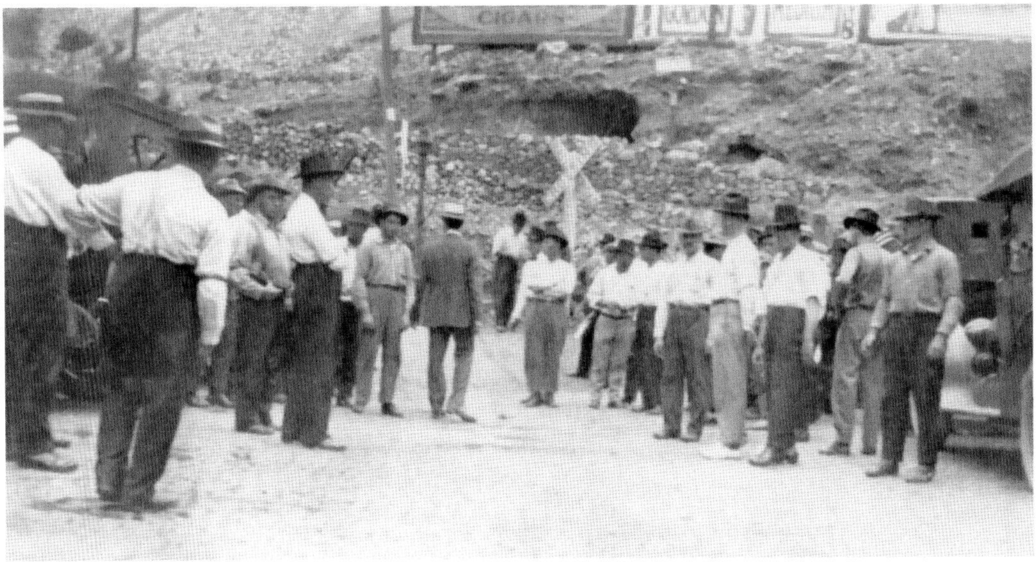

The IWW took over as the dominant union in Bisbee in June 1917 and called a strike on June 27. The demands included safer working conditions, a wage that was not tied to the price of copper, and an end to discrimination against union members. A picket line of strikers near Bisbee's post office on Main Street was very effective, and 85 percent of the labor force in the mines went out on strike.

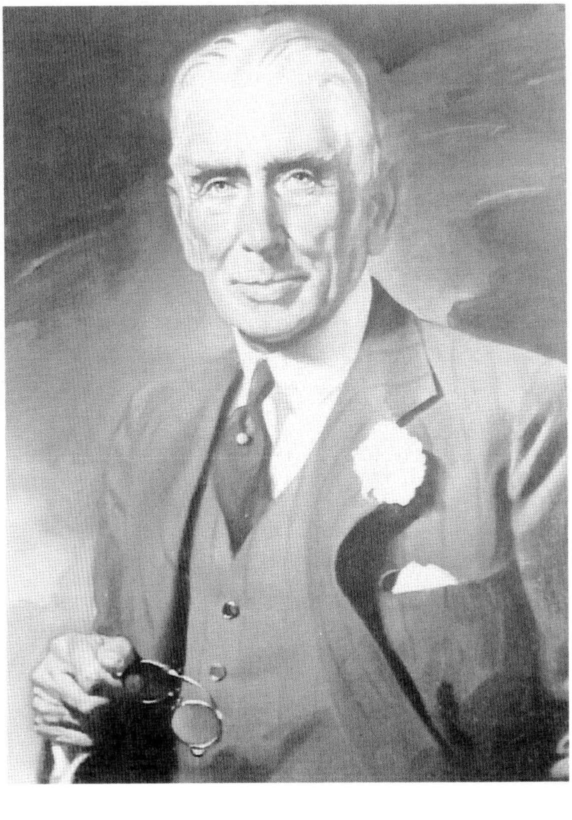

Walter Douglas, the general superintendent of the Copper Queen Mine in Bisbee, was an implacable enemy of labor unions. He and the heads of the other mining companies in Bisbee refused to accept the demands of the strikers. Douglas began to work behind the scenes to organize a response to the strike that would crush it—and all labor unions in Arizona.

John Greenway, a Rough Rider, Yale graduate, and mining engineer, was the general superintendent of the Calumet and Arizona Mining Company when the strike broke out. More moderate in his political views than Douglas, Greenway nonetheless took an active part in planning the response to the strike and was the only top mining company official to directly participate in the deportation.

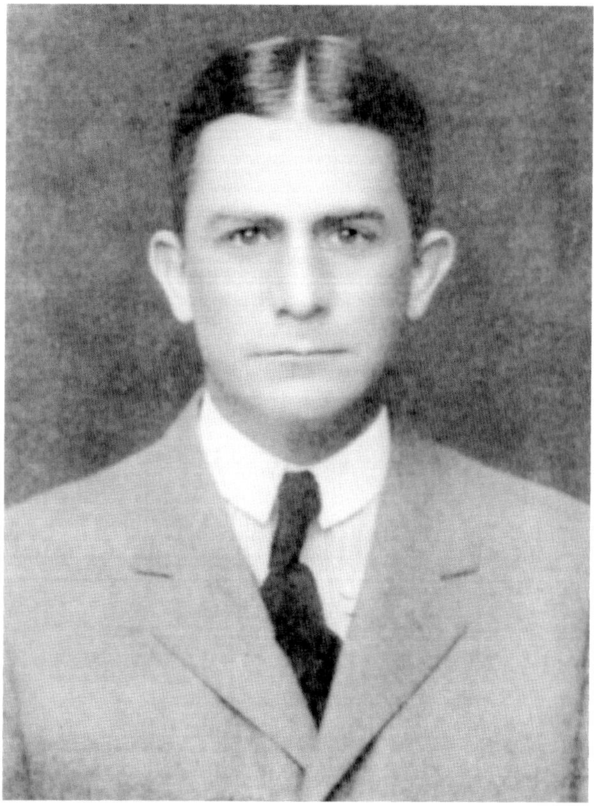

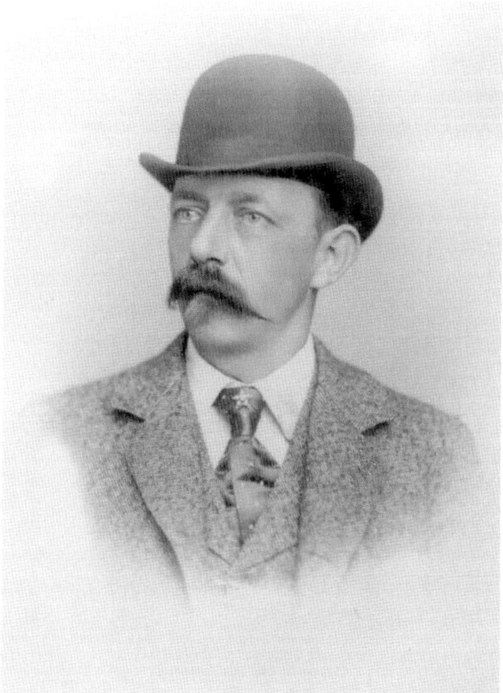

Lemuel Shattuck, the head of the Shattuck-Denn Mining Company, was a self-made man who was sympathetic to the working class. However, after openly attending IWW meetings, he came away convinced he should oppose the strike. Shattuck did not directly participate in the planning and execution of the deportation but he did support it.

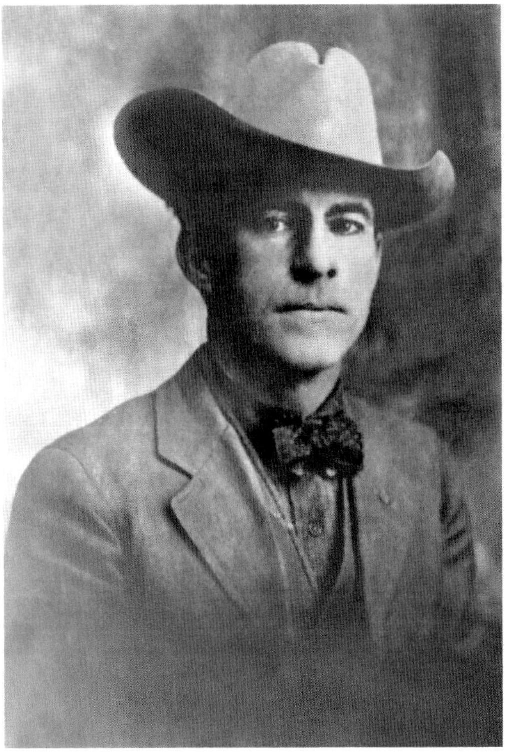

A tough, courageous man who followed a strict code of ethics, Harry Wheeler was the Cochise County sheriff when the IWW called the strike. Wheeler, who viewed wartime strikes as treasonous acts, tried to prevent violence and called for federal intervention. The US government refused to act, however, prompting Wheeler to join the mining company officials in planning a response.

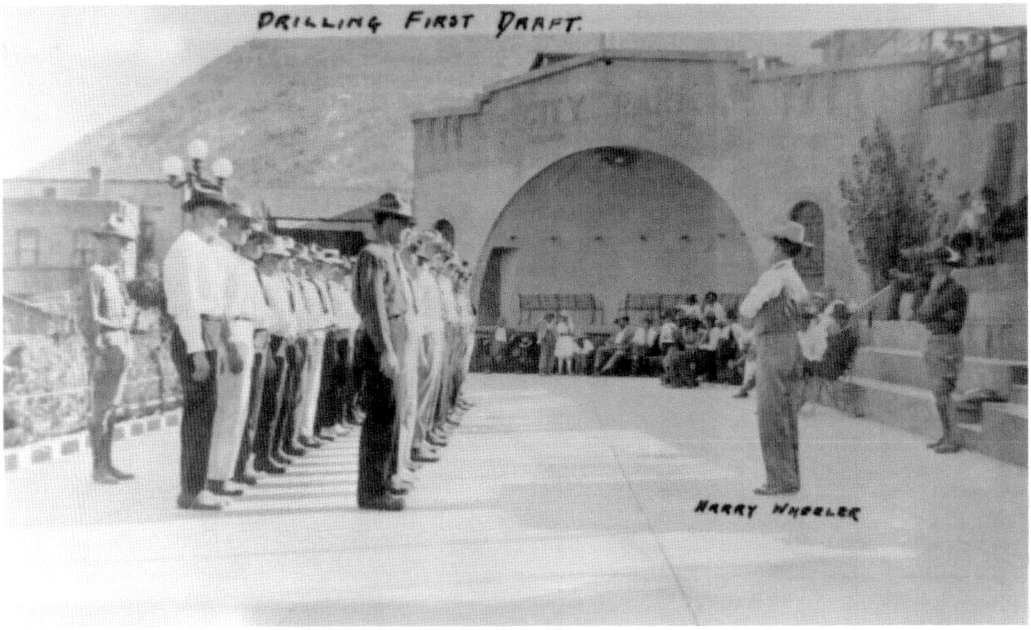

Wheeler was also a fervent patriot who wanted desperately to get into action on the Western Front in France. Unable to immediately secure an officer's commission, he settled for drilling draftees in Bisbee's city park until he could go to France and fight the Germans. He was contemptuous towards anyone who did not support America's war effort.

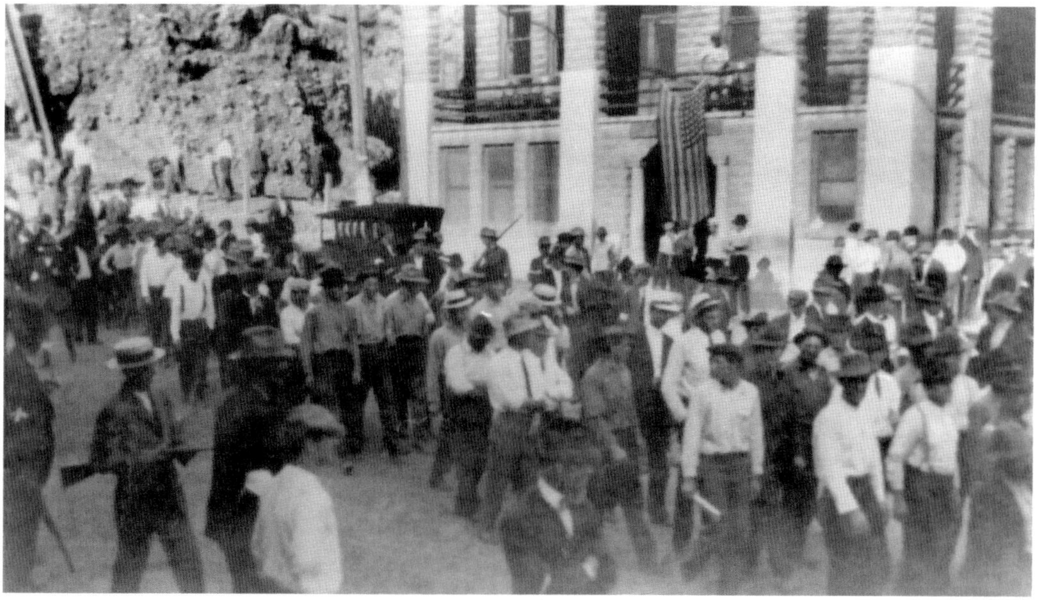

The atmosphere was tense. Newspapers whipped up sentiment against the strikers, portraying them as German agents and Bolsheviks. Walter Douglas and his lieutenants drew up lists of the strikers. Sheriff Wheeler secretly organized a posse of 2,000 men, and on the morning of July 12, Wheeler and the posse went into action. The roundup of strikers started at the picket line near the post office.

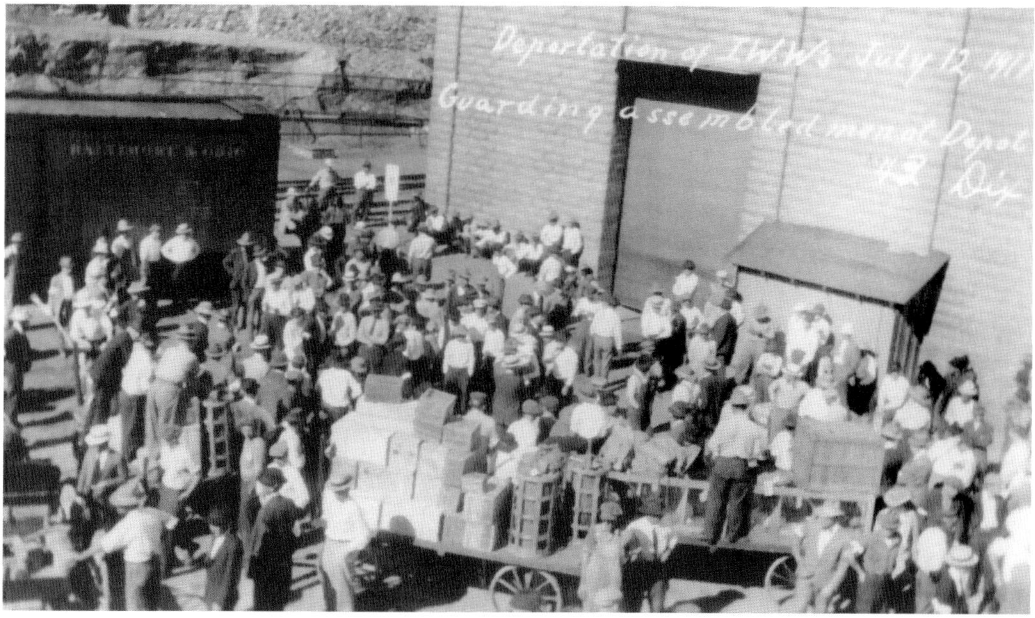

Teams of armed posse members fanned out through Bisbee neighborhoods, each team supplied with a list of strikers and their supporters. As the strikers and their sympathizers were collected and escorted to the plaza near the post office, they were cordoned off and closely guarded. Posse members wore white handkerchiefs tied around their right arms to identify themselves.

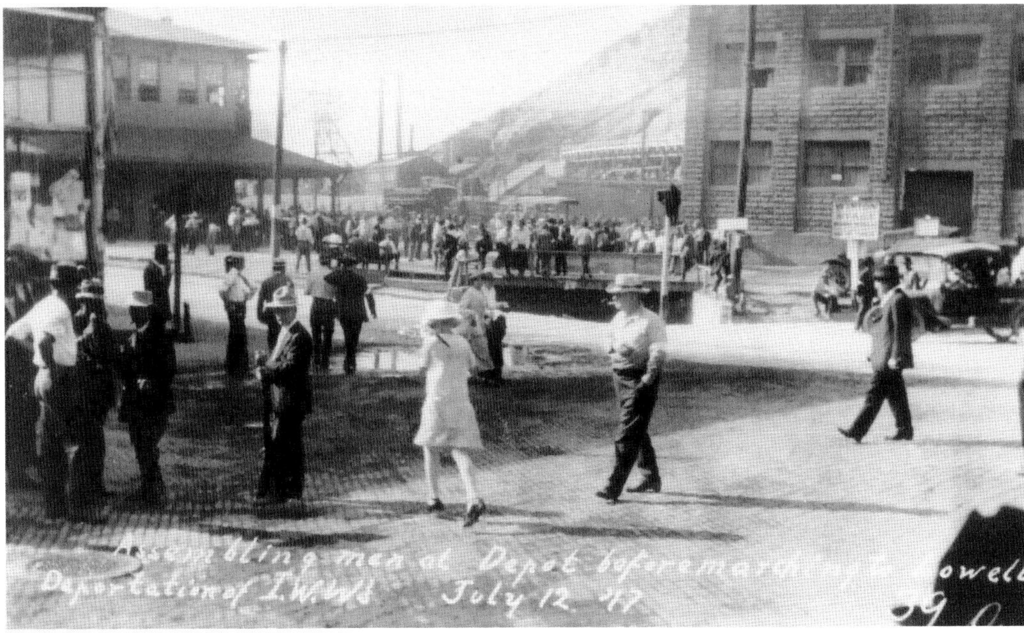

A woman dashes through armed posse members towards the train depot. In the background stands a group of strikers under guard. At first, most townspeople heeded Wheeler's warning to citizens to stay off the streets, but residents were taken by surprise to see hundreds of men patrolling the streets with rifles and shotguns.

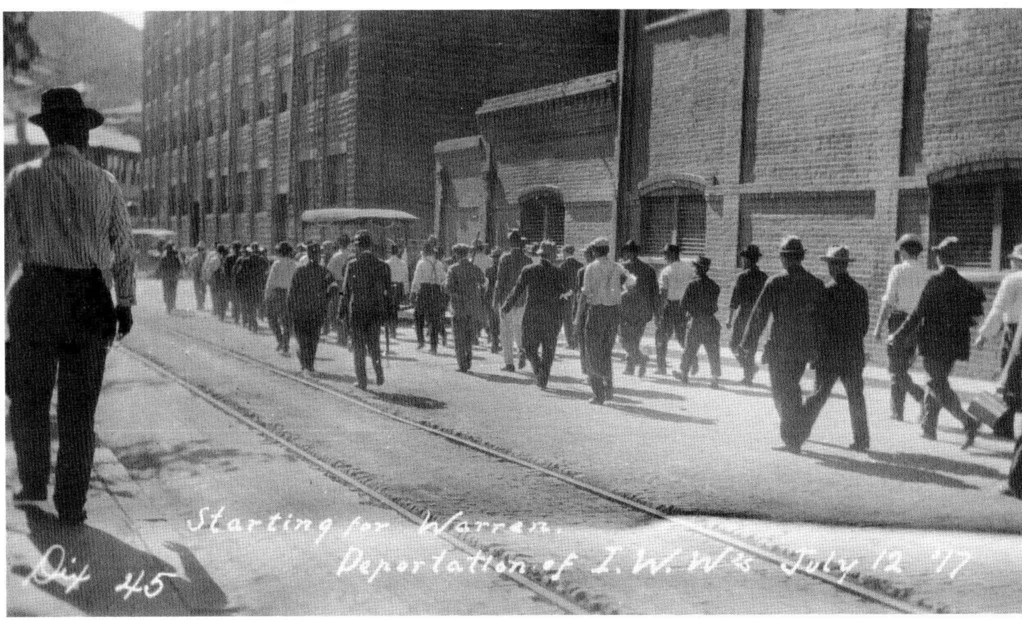

Sometime between 8:00 a.m. and 9:00 a.m., the strikers were organized into a long column escorted by rifle-bearing posse members. The four-mile walk started in downtown Bisbee and went past the Phelps Dodge company store and its adjoining warehouse to Warren Ballpark. Few spoke as the sun and the temperature rose higher.

The grim procession, watched from windows and street corners, moved out of Bisbee past the mines that had been shut down by the strike. Some of the strikers were fully dressed while others wore only what they were able to quickly put on as they were rousted from their beds.

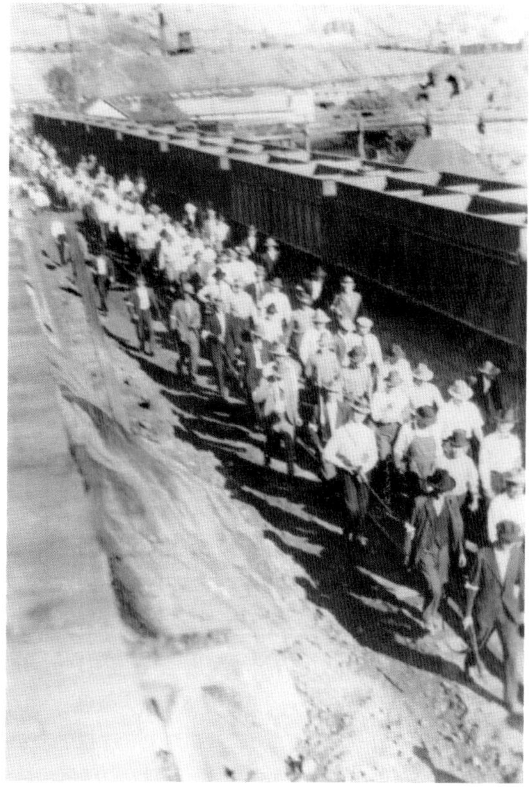

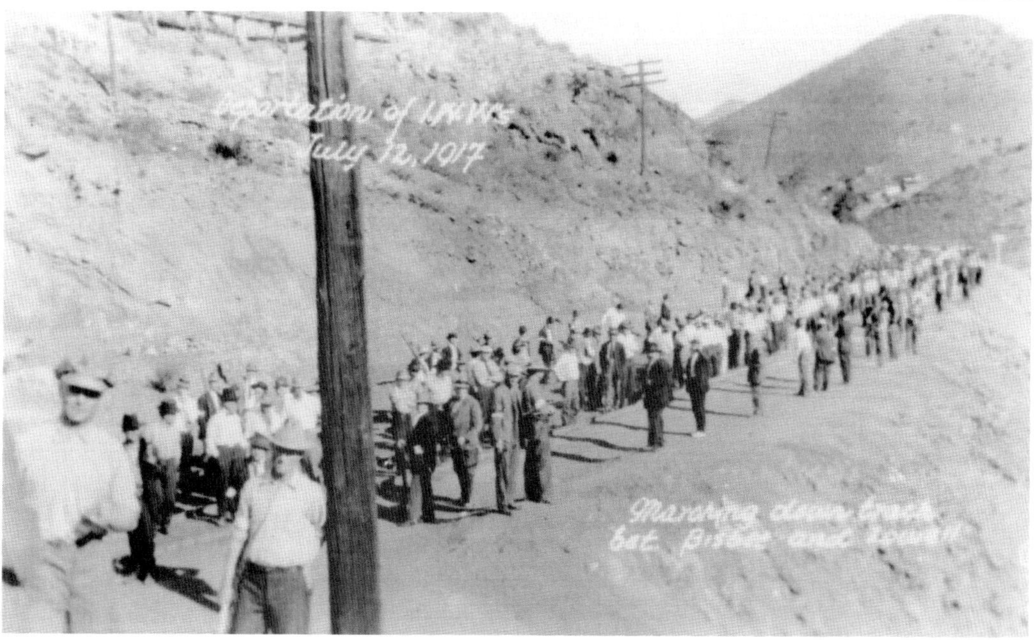

Three parallel columns of men slowly made their way along the railroad tracks that passed along the base of Sacramento Hill. The columns on the left and right were armed posse members. Between them walked the strikers.

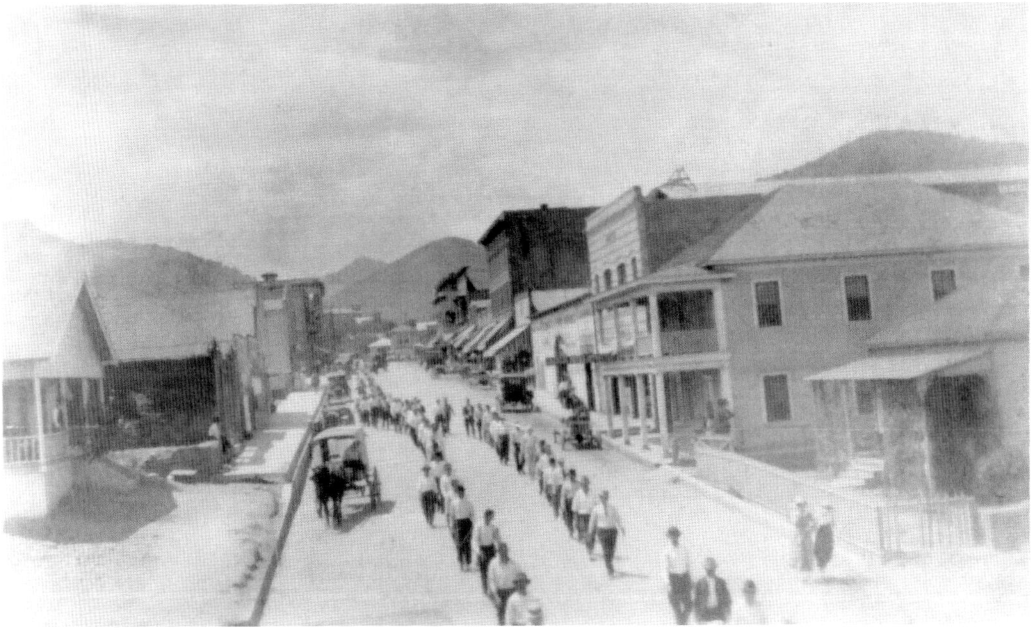

The strikers and their escorts continued down the road to Warren, passing through the community of Lowell. As they did, other posse members and the strikers they had rounded up in Lowell and Jiggerville joined the column.

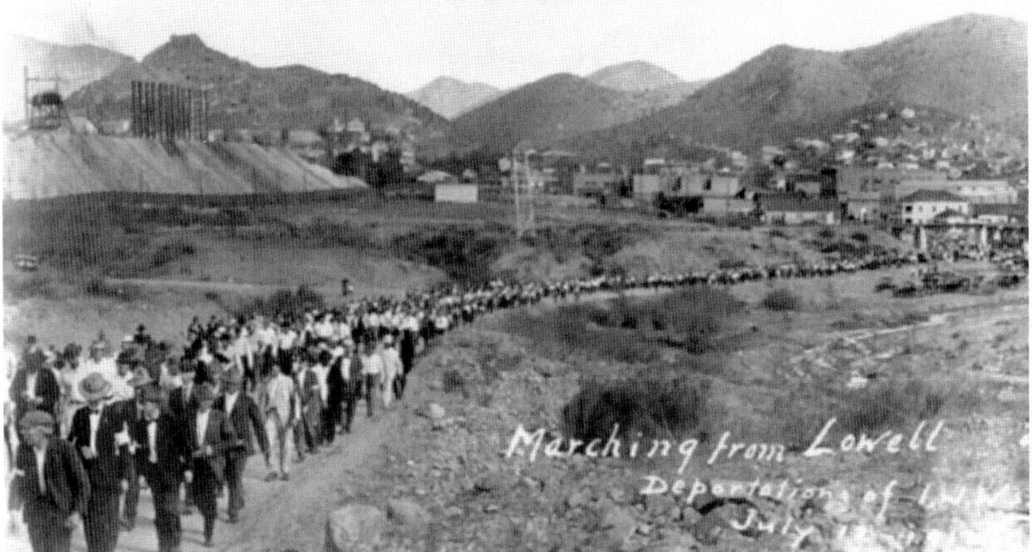

The strikers and their armed escorts left Lowell and moved on towards Warren. By then, word must have passed through the ranks of captors and captives that there had been bloodshed. Two men, a striker and a deputized posse member, had been killed. There were, fortunately, no more deaths in the well-planned operation.

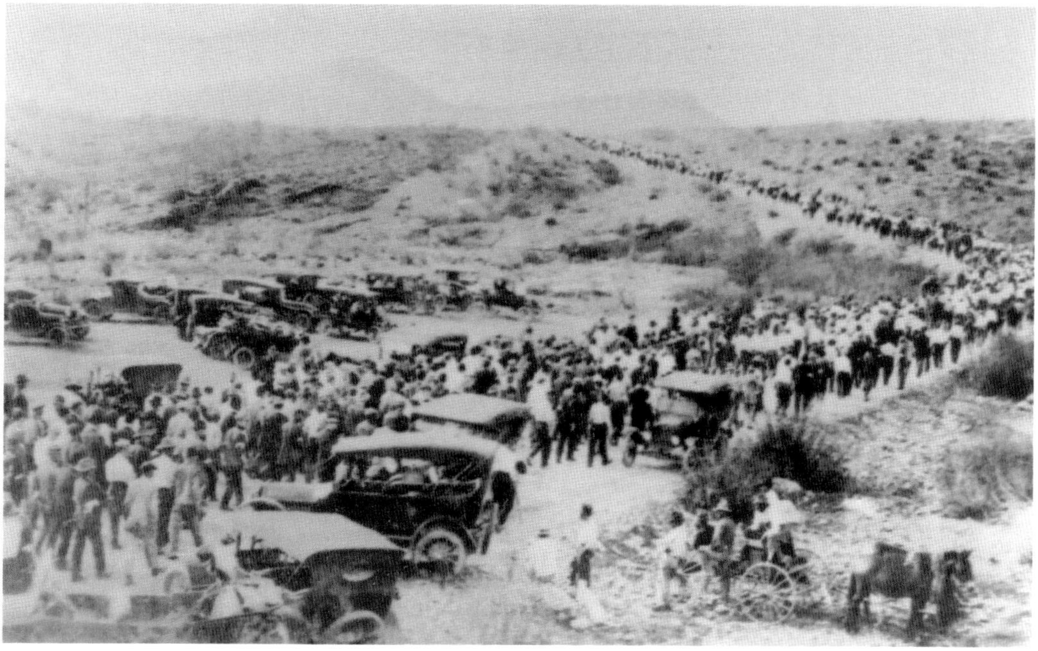

Armed posse members gathered at road junctions to direct the deportees and their guards along the road to Warren. Casual spectators, although warned by Sheriff Wheeler to stay away from the roundup, ignored the advice and stood along the road, silently watching as the files of men in sweat-stained shirts and hats shuffled by.

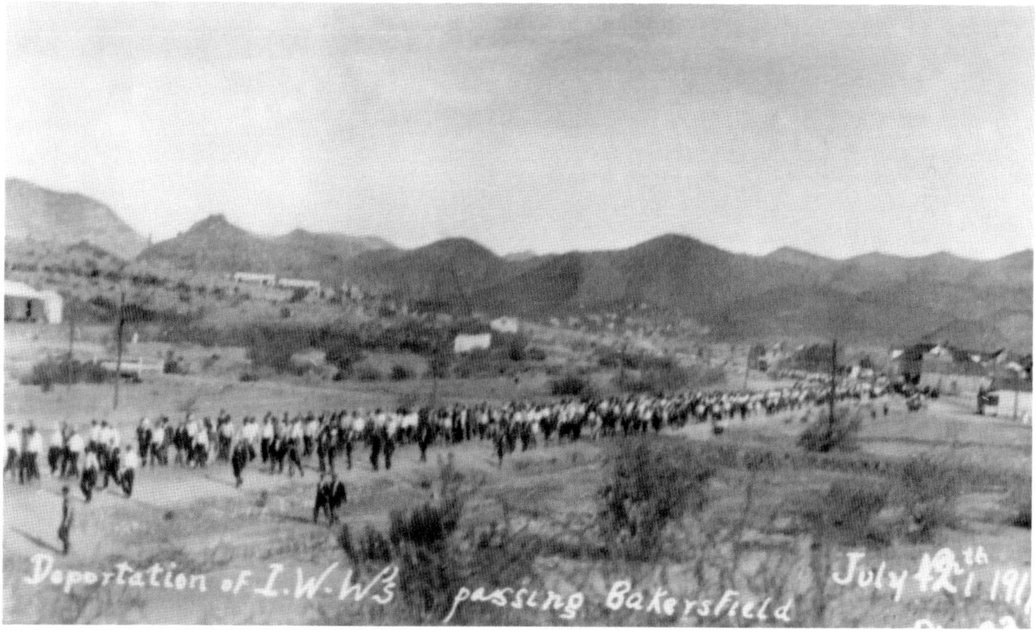

The procession, now hundreds of yards long, soon reached Bakerville, another small community only a mile or so from their destination. No effort was made by the men in the column to resist or escape.

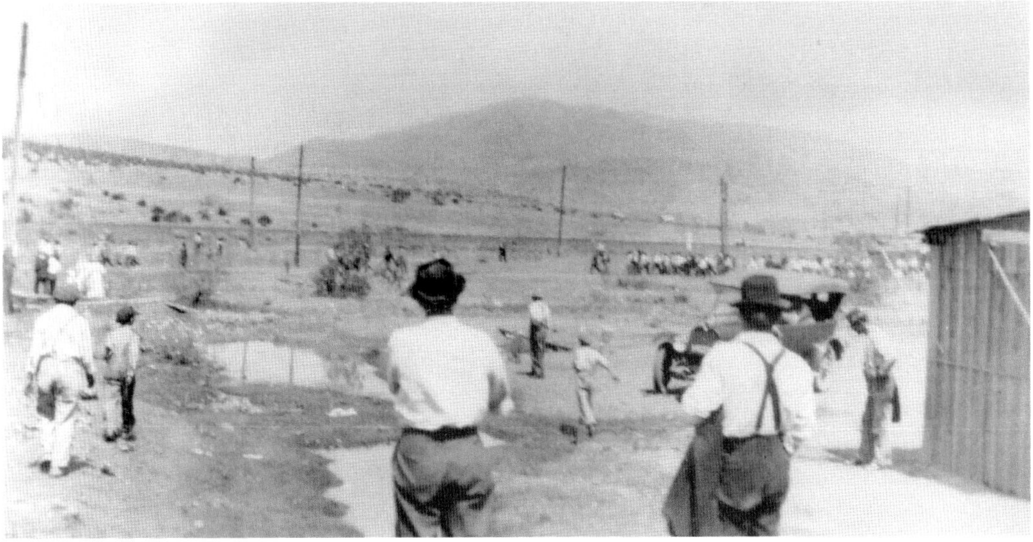

At times, the march took on a holiday atmosphere, as small children and curious adults ran up to or walked along the roadside to watch the men pass by. Some were supportive of the roundup and encouraged the posse. Others cursed the posse members as they walked by.

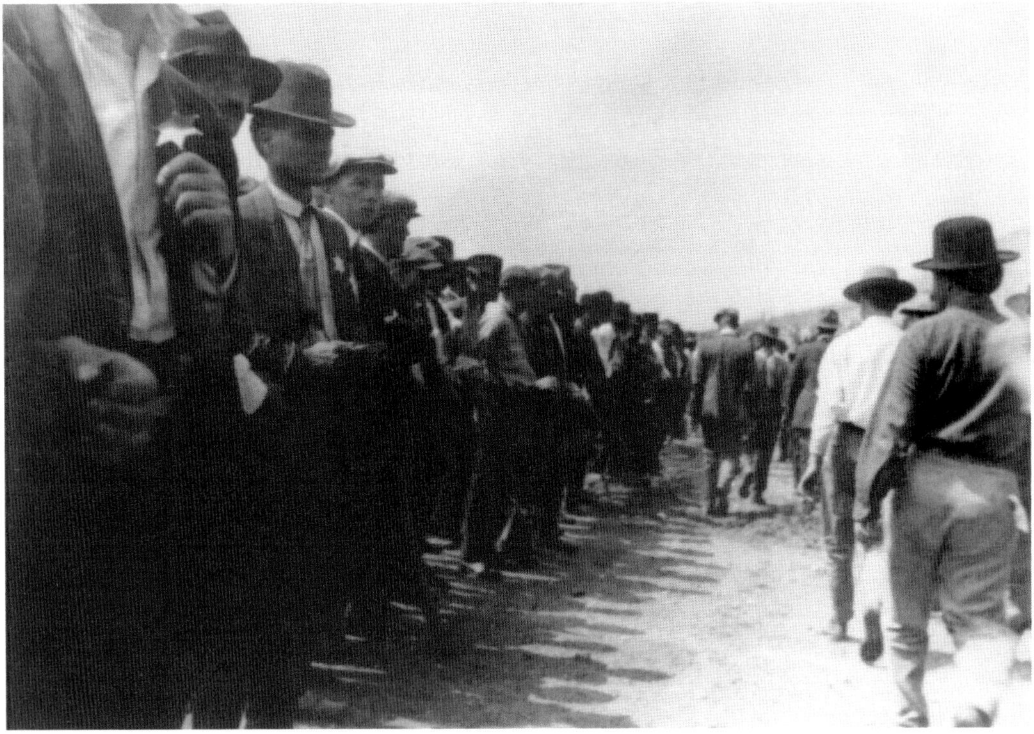

Few words were exchanged between the parallel lines of strikers and the deputized posse members during the long walk. The line had been drawn between strikers and posse members long before and there was no crossing it until the procession reached Warren Ballpark, where a final effort to convince strikers to go back to work took place.

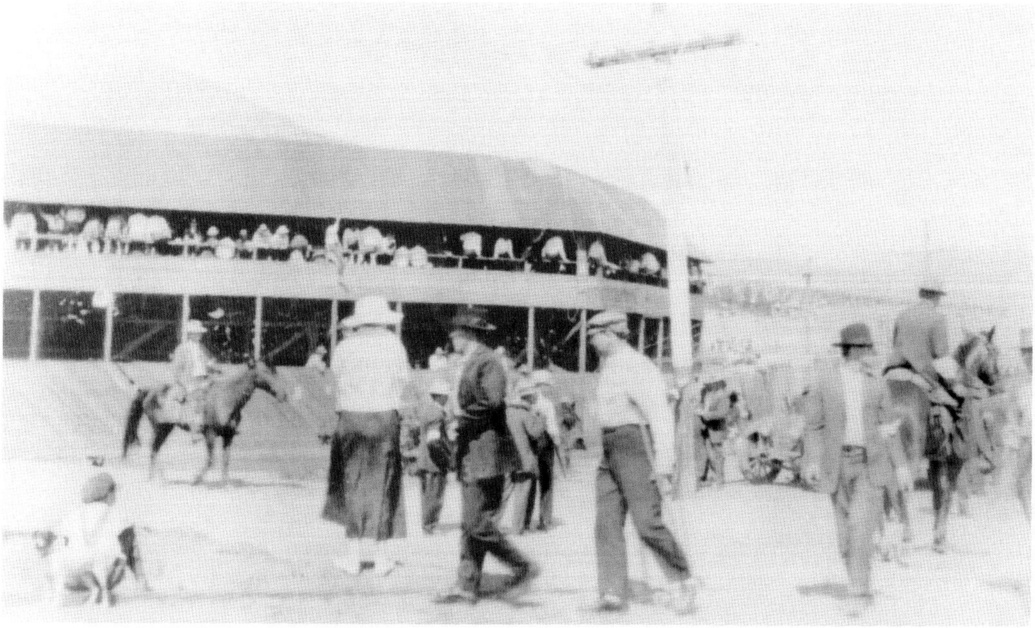

As the posse and strikers reached their destination, the northwest entrance of Warren Ballpark was opened and the strikers were herded into the grandstands. Mounted horsemen patrolled the ballpark perimeter. Loaded machine guns mounted on automobiles and on the rooftop of the Calumet and Arizona office building emphasized the deadly nature of the business at hand.

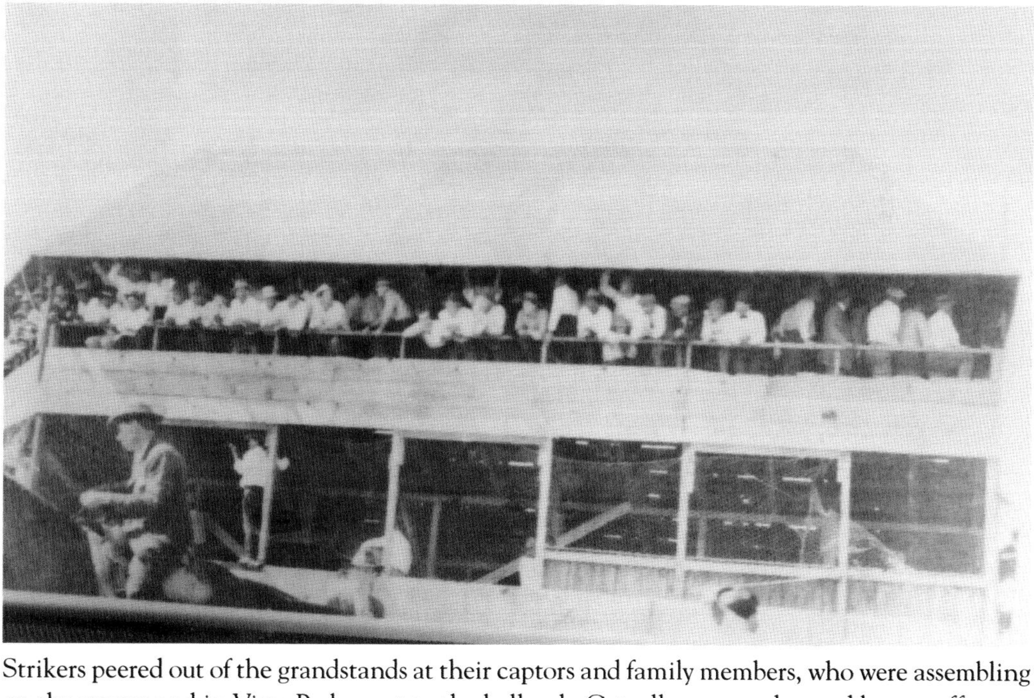

Strikers peered out of the grandstands at their captors and family members, who were assembling on the streets and in Vista Park, next to the ballpark. Catcalls were exchanged but no efforts at resistance were offered.

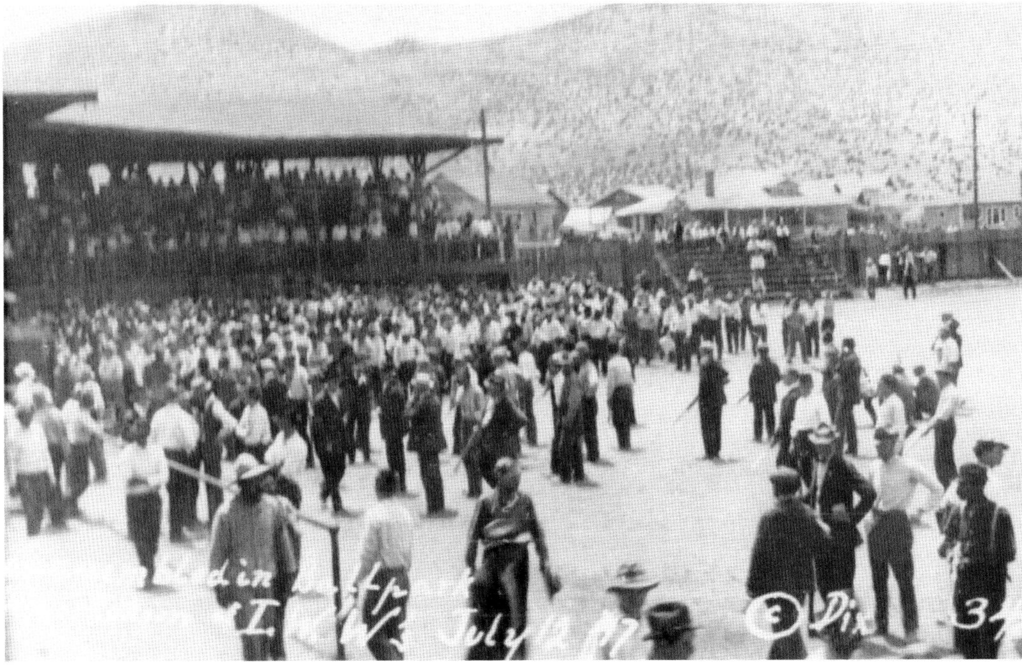

Within a short time, the grandstands were filled and the strikers were packed into the infield behind home plate. A cordon of armed posse members stood ready to maintain control over their prisoners.

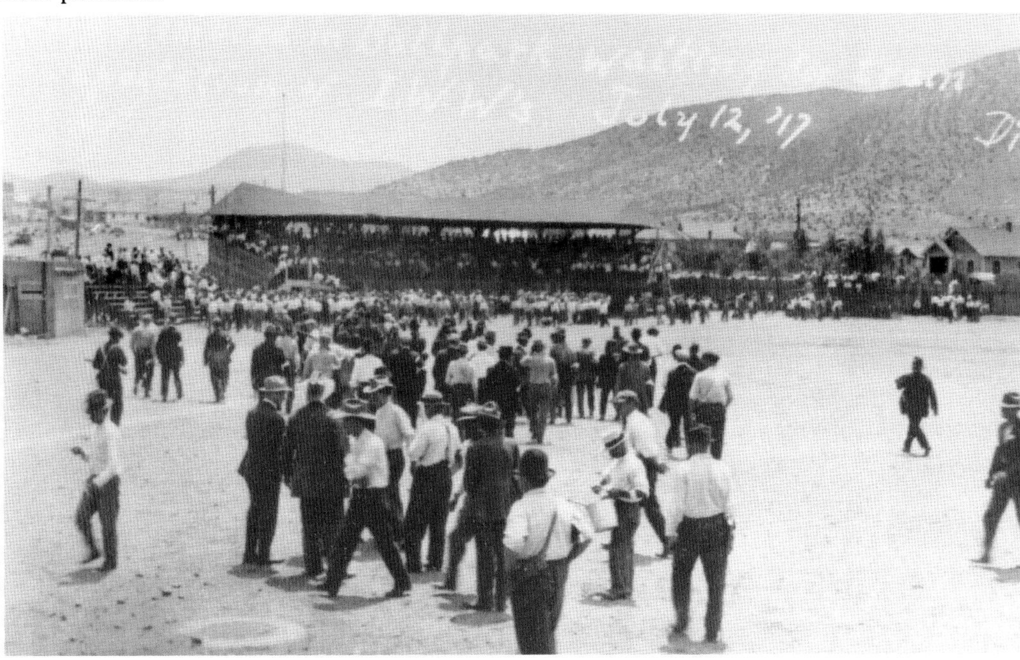

John Greenway and other leaders of the roundup pleaded with the rank-and-file strikers to promise to return to work. If they did, they would be set free. No such offer was extended to strike leaders and union organizers. Few of the strikers heeded the call to change sides.

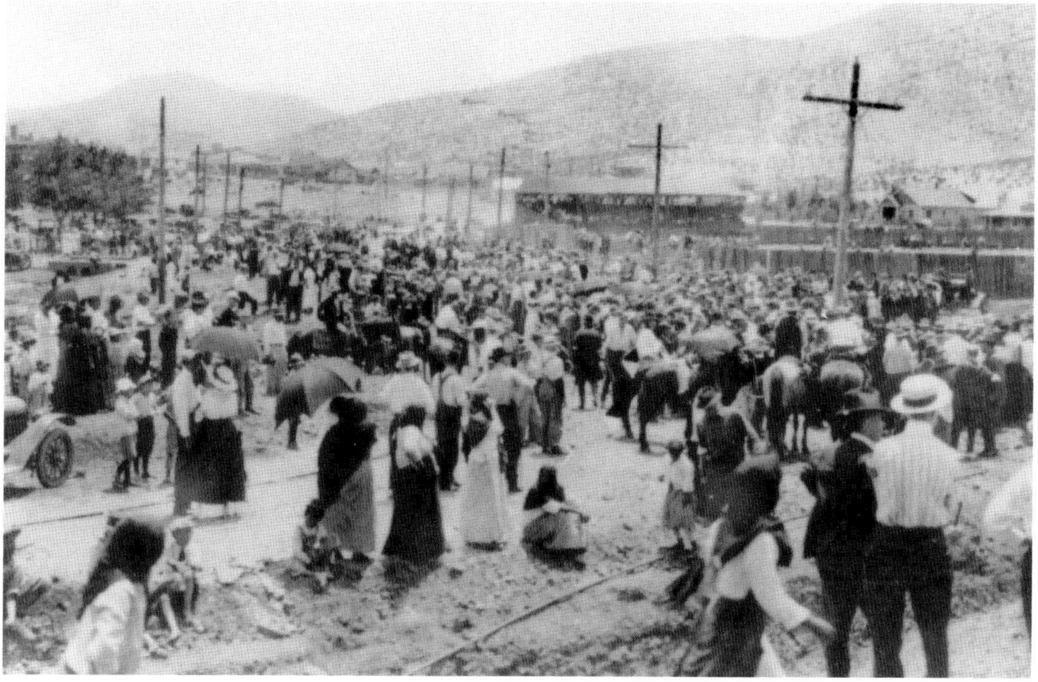

As news of the roundup and its destination circulated through Bisbee, a large crowd gathered outside Warren Ballpark. Some of them were family members or friends of the strikers. Others were there to show their support for the posse. The mood was tense but calm; no one wanted more blood to be spilled.

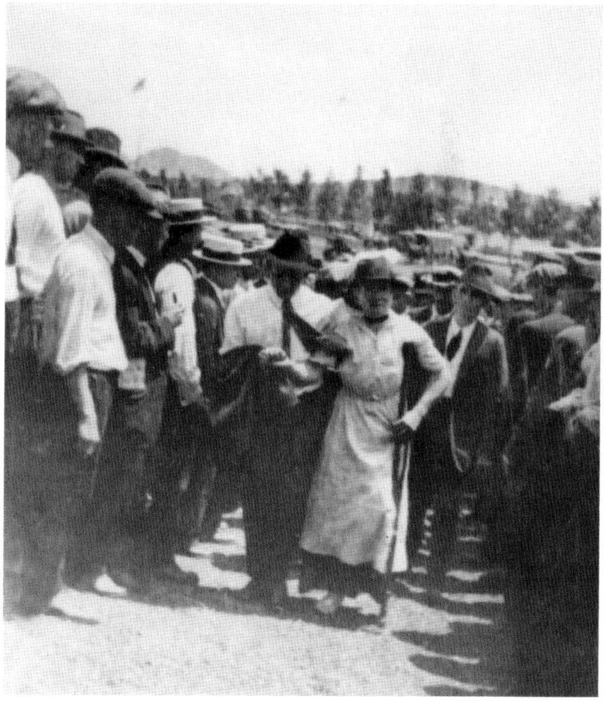

Anna Payne was one of hundreds who rushed to Warren Ballpark. Her two sons had been picked up in the roundup, and she demanded their release. After heated discussion, the two Payne boys were released to their mother, seen here, and left the ballpark.

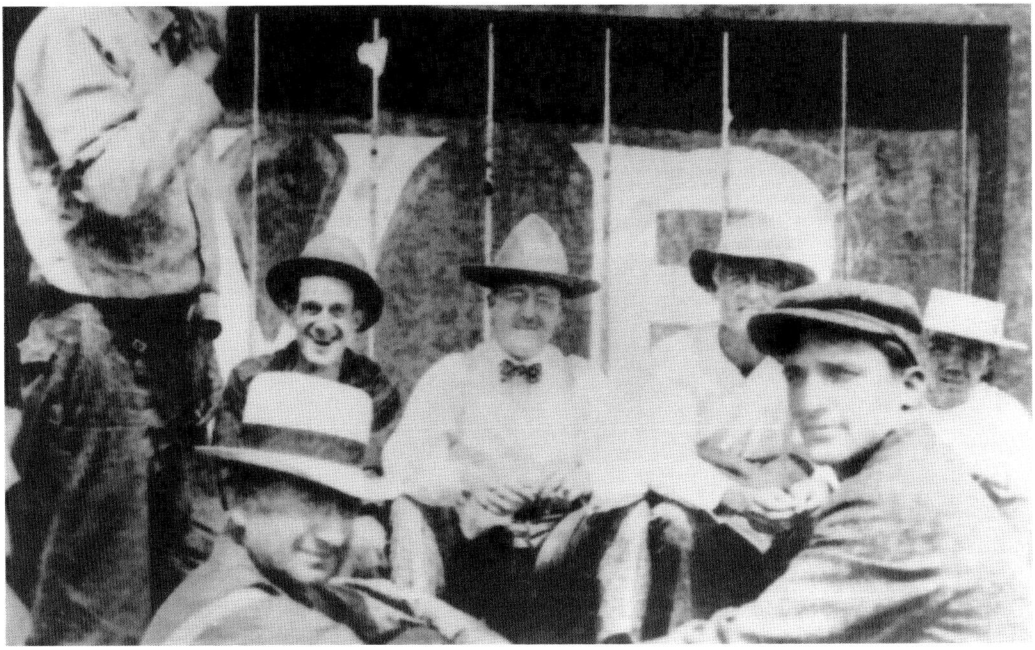

William B. Cleary (center, with peaked hat and bow tie) was legal counsel for the Industrial Workers of the World. He was also caught up in the posse's dragnet and deported. He urged the striking miners to refuse the offer to return to work.

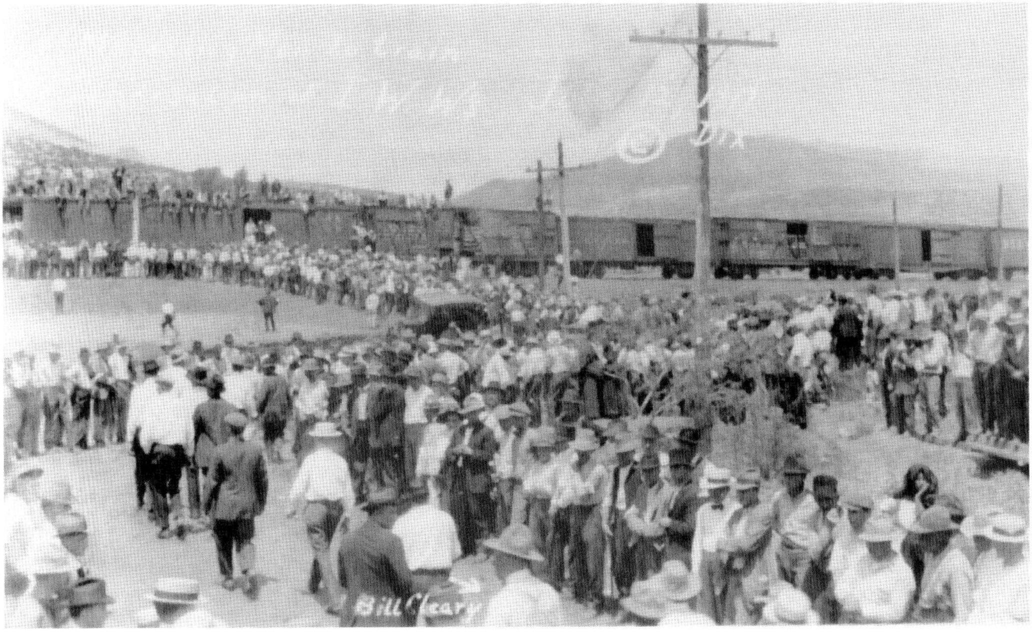

As the morning wore on, a locomotive pulling 23 boxcars came to a halt near the ballpark's outfield fence. The strikers who had refused to return to work were ordered to line up and walk between lines of armed posse members to the waiting cars.

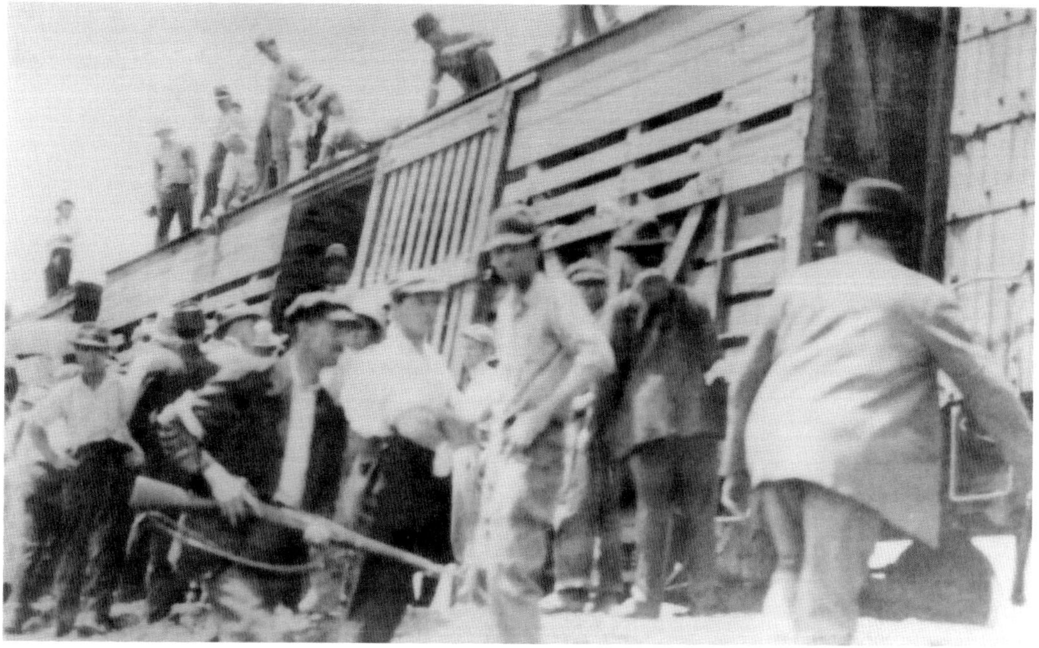

Each boxcar was packed with 50 strikers. Armed guards stood on the car's roofs. The posse members later claimed that food and water were provided for the train ride into exile, but the strikers claimed otherwise.

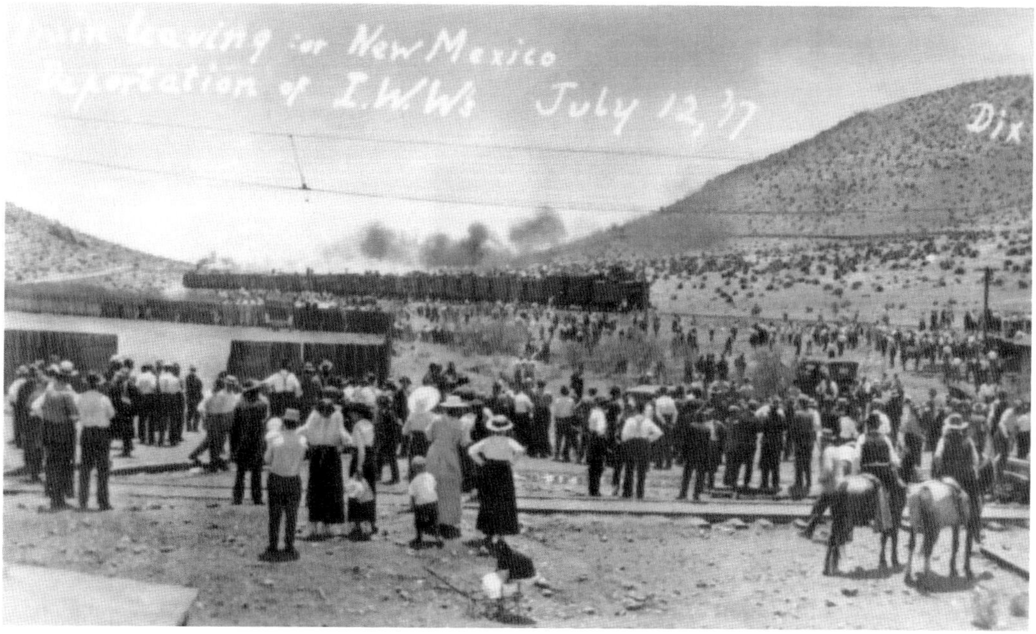

An estimated 1,182 strikers refused the offer to return to work and were prodded into the boxcars. The train then chugged out of town, heading east into New Mexico. When the Army refused to accept the train's cargo at Columbus, it backtracked to a siding at Hermanas, where the strikers were unloaded and warned never to return to Bisbee.

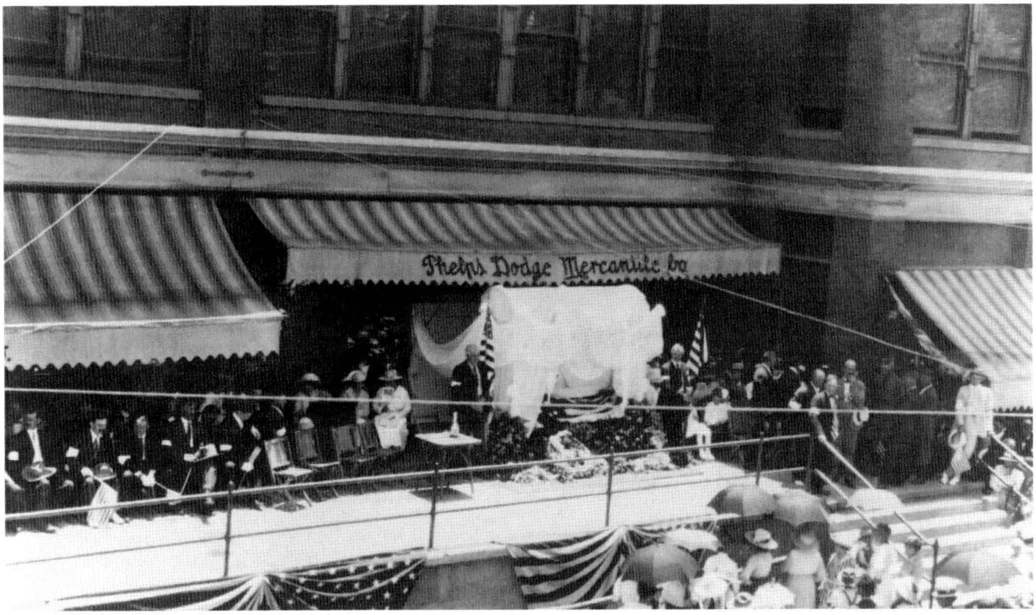

Back in Bisbee, the posse and its supporters buried their sole martyr, Orson McRae, the deputized shift boss who had been shot to death as he barged into the boardinghouse room of James Brew, an IWW member. Brew was killed moments later by other posse members and was hurriedly buried in the middle of the night by friends.

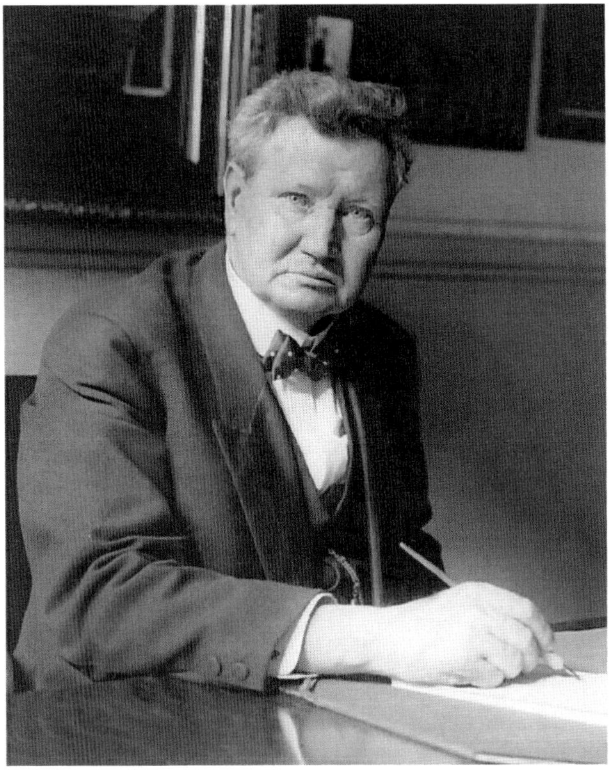

A presidential mediation commission led by secretary of labor William B. Wilson investigated the deportation and condemned the posse and its leaders for their actions. The commission characterized the deportation as unlawful and a violation of the strikers' constitutional rights. However, none of the planners or participants were convicted of crimes, and the war went on. Mining companies controlled Bisbee with little opposition from labor until the mid-1930s.

4

Baseball in a Minor Key

Organized baseball finally came to Warren Ballpark in 1928, with the creation of the Class D Arizona State League. Within three years, the league would expand to El Paso and be renamed the Arizona-Texas League.

Bisbee's minor league team, the Bees, was made up of entry-level players recruited locally or brought in from California. Managers were usually older players who could no longer compete on the big-league level but still played well enough to hold their own in the "bush leagues." They were expected to develop promising young players, who would then move up the professional baseball ladder. Of course, they were also expected to win ball games and pack the grandstands for the team ownership.

The Bees were usually a farm team for the Chicago Cubs and the California Angels of the Pacific Coast League, getting raw talent from those teams' pools of rookies and turning out players with improved skills for the parent clubs. Bisbee played a 130-game season against other teams from Phoenix, Tucson, El Paso, Globe, Miami, and for a few seasons, Nogales and Albuquerque.

In all, 13 Bees made it all the way up the ladder to successful careers in the major leagues. Several others made it just long enough for a so-called "cup of coffee." Two local boys made it to the major leagues, one who started with the Bees and another who played sandlot ball in Bisbee before signing a professional contract.

Most of the players never advanced to a higher level of baseball, but they played with as much enthusiasm as the big leaguers in front of crowds that supported their teams with as much passion as the fans in Brooklyn, Detroit, or Chicago.

Fields in the Arizona-Texas League ranged from manicured grass to bare dirt. Travel was usually by bus over two-lane paved and gravel roads. A road trip typically covered several hundred miles. There were no night games at Warren Ballpark until 1939, when the first lights were installed.

In 1932, the hard times of the Depression brought a temporary end to minor league ball in the southwest, but the Bees returned in 1937 to a new grandstand built by the WPA at Warren Ballpark and a new landlord: the Bisbee Unified School District. Play in the Arizona-Texas League was suspended during World War II but resumed in 1947.

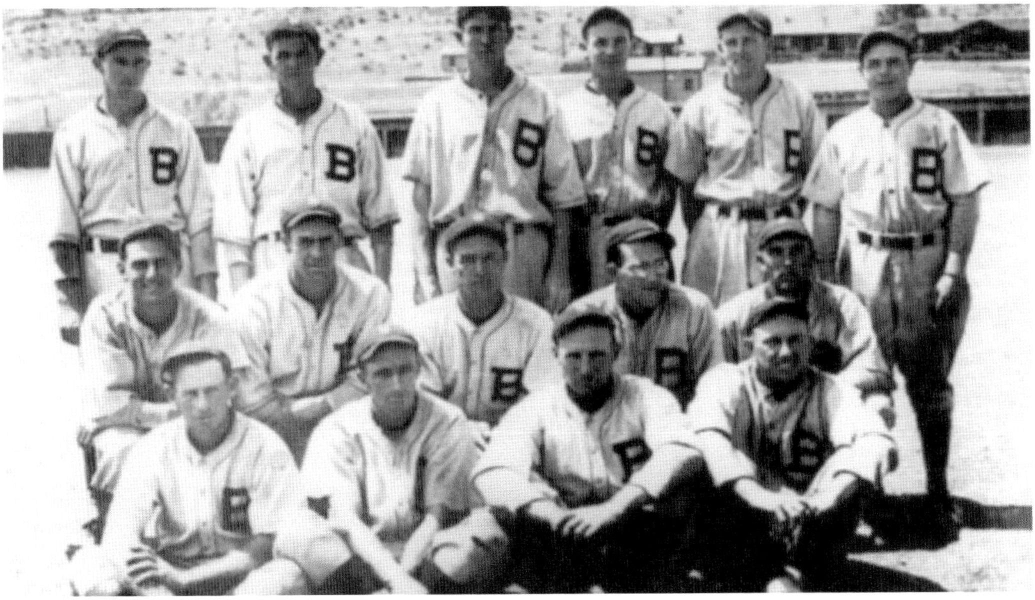

The Bisbee Bees minor league team commenced play in April 1928. Led by manager Roy "Hardrock" Johnson, the Bees provided a steady stream of players to higher-level leagues. This photograph of the 1930 Bees contains two future major leaguers: Roy Johnson (front row, third from left) and Syd Cohen (second row, far left). Tony Antista (third row, far right) would go on to set records for Bisbee.

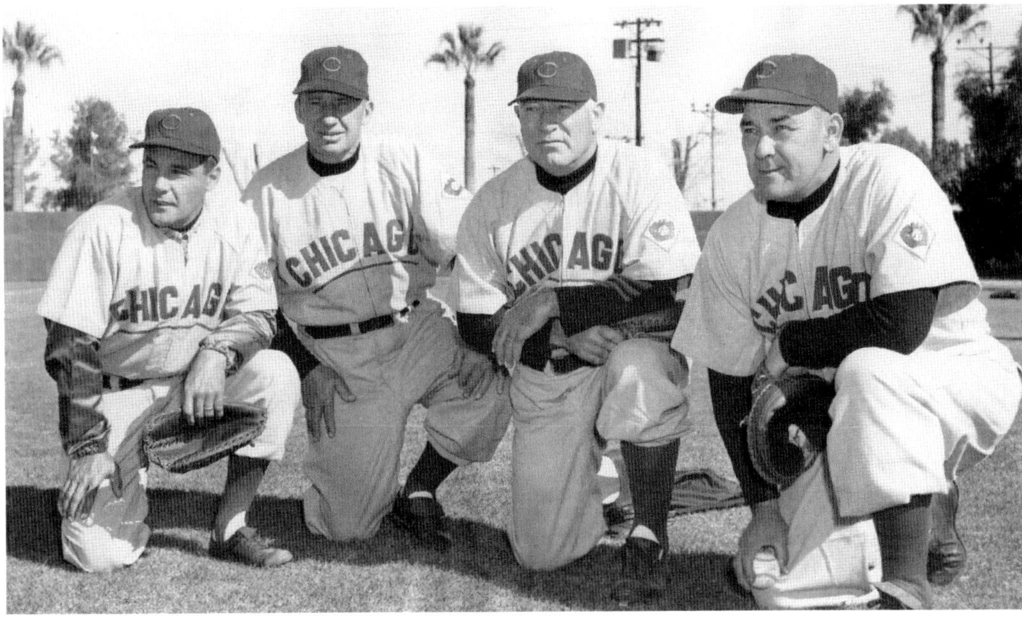

Roy Johnson would move from the Bees to a job with the Chicago Cubs. In 1935, he became a coach with the Cubs, and in 1944, he became the club's interim manager. This September 1945 photograph shows Johnson (second from left) with the Cubs field management. Manager Charlie Grimm is at far right. (Author's collection.)

Tony Antista was only five feet six inches and weighed 145 pounds, but he packed a powerful punch. Nicknamed the "Walloping Wop" by sportswriters, Antista set several league records for hitting during his three years at Bisbee. In 1930, he was the hottest hitter in all of professional baseball, ending the season with a .430 batting average and hitting safely in 45 consecutive games. (Courtesy Julie Harris.)

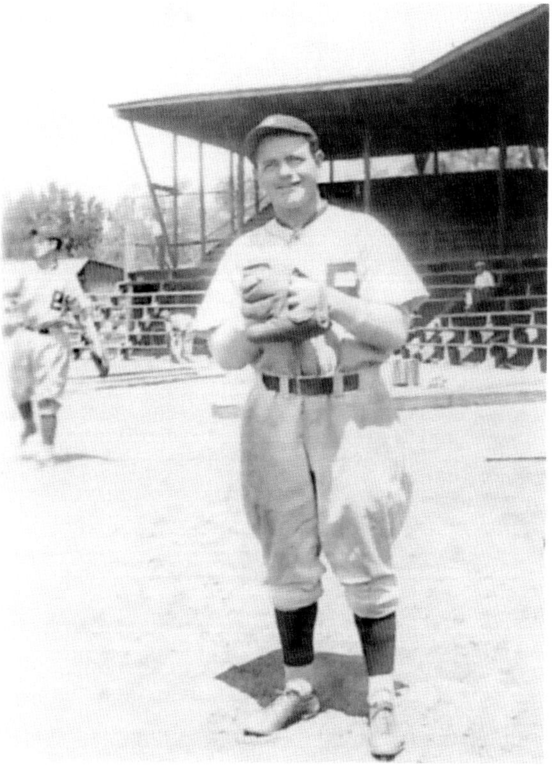

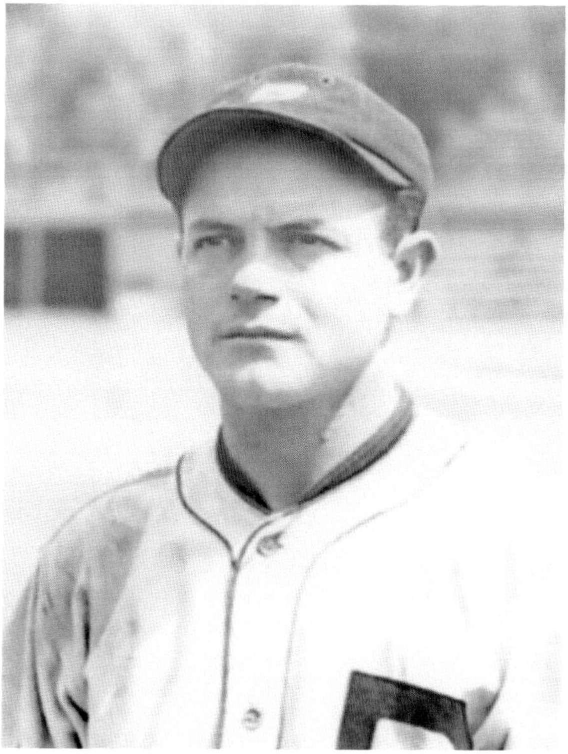

Considered by major league scouts to be too small to play major league baseball, Antista remained in minor league baseball through the 1932 season, then returned to Arcadia, California, where he became a professional musician and music teacher. He treasured the gold watch given to him by the citizens of Bisbee in 1930 for his achievements with the bat. (Author's collection.)

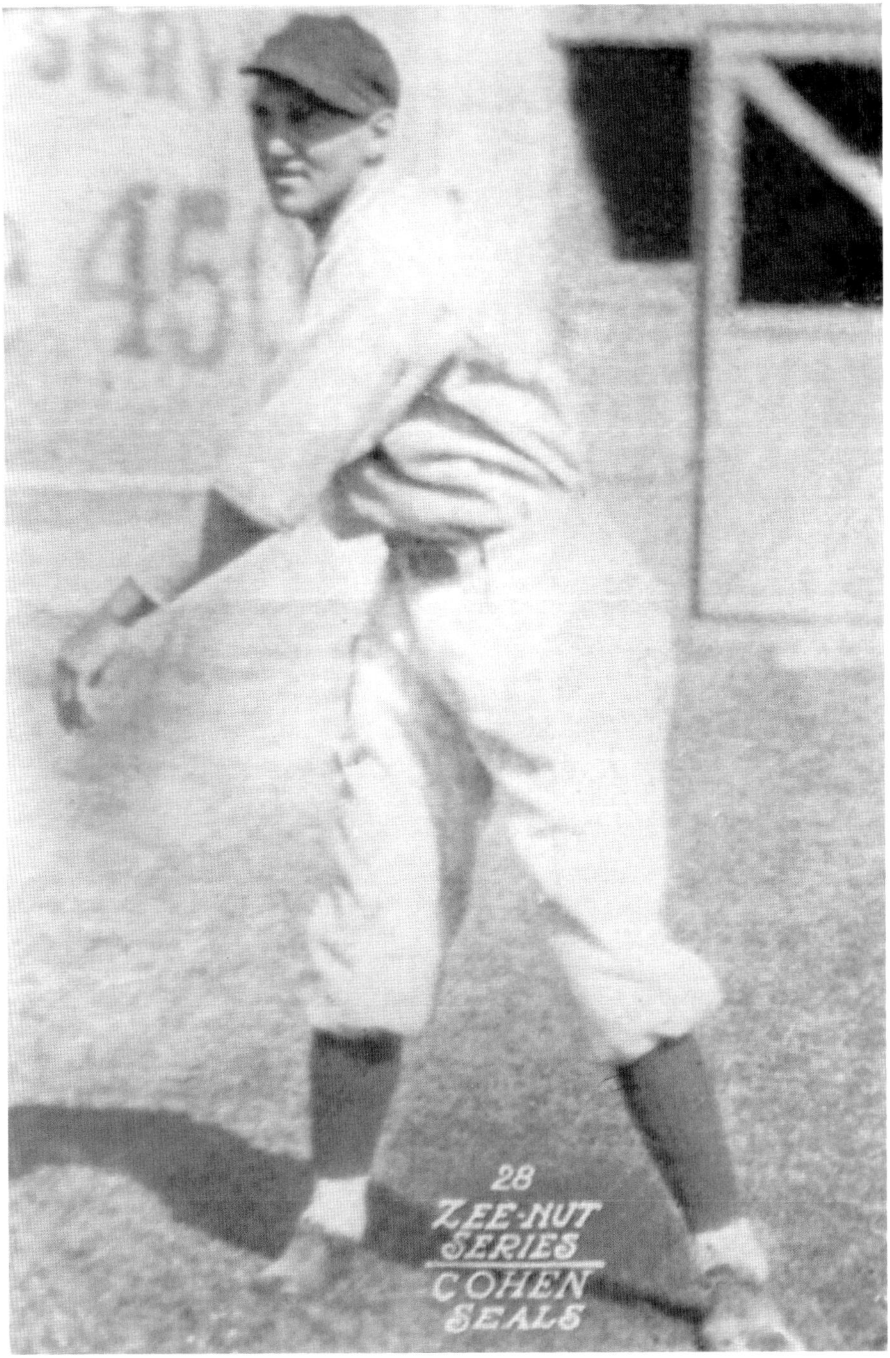

Syd Cohen is seen here in 1928 on a Zee-Nut trading card pitching for the San Francisco Seals of the Pacific Coast League. Cohen, who as a teenager played in the outlaw Frontier and Copper Leagues in New Mexico, was sold to the Bisbee Bees early in the 1928 season. He was popular with the fans at Warren Ballpark and would return to Bisbee in 1951 to manage the Bisbee-Douglas Copper Kings. (Photograph courtesy Ann Longmore.)

Syd Cohen, a left-handed pitcher from El Paso, energized the Bees from 1928 through 1930, on the mound and with his bat. Cohen spent several seasons with the Washington Senators and entered the record books in 1934 as the last man to strike out Babe Ruth as a Yankee and as the last man to give up a home run to Ruth as a Yankee—both in the same game. (Courtesy Hall of Fame.)

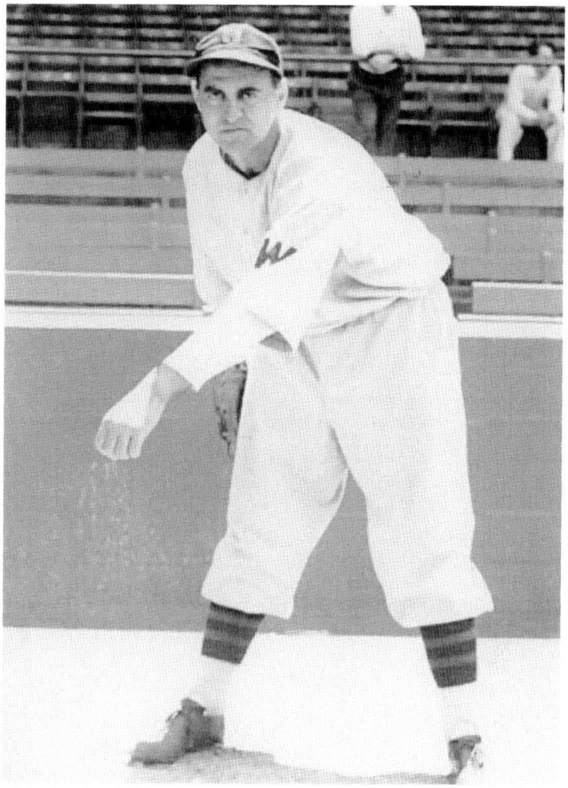

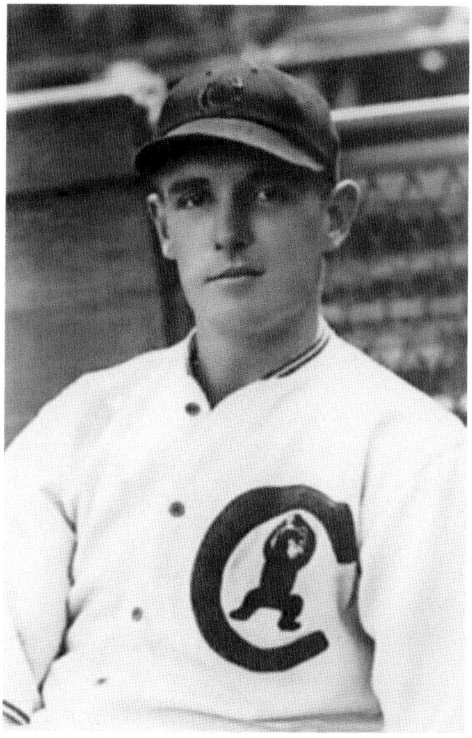

George "Tuck" Stainback started his baseball career in 1931 as an outfielder with the Bisbee Bees, hitting .315 for the season. He was promoted to the Chicago Cubs in 1934, hitting .306. Stainback remained in the majors for 13 years, playing for the Cubs, Cardinals, Phillies, Dodgers, Tigers, Yankees, and Athletics. (Courtesy Hall of Fame.)

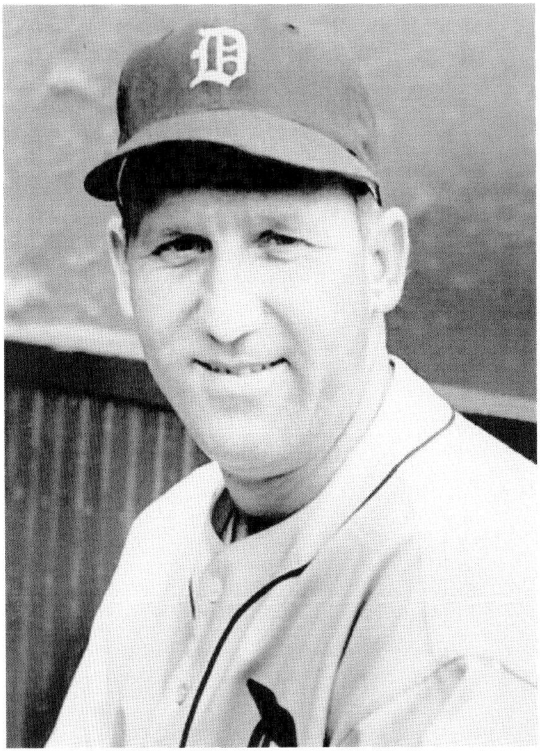

Right-handed pitcher Jim Tobin began his career with the Bisbee-Douglas Bees in 1932. In 1937, he was called up to the majors to play for the Pittsburgh Pirates. He remained in the big leagues through the 1945 season. Tobin threw two no-hitters in 1944, but was also known as a heavy hitter, belting three home runs in a single game in 1942. (Courtesy Hall of Fame.)

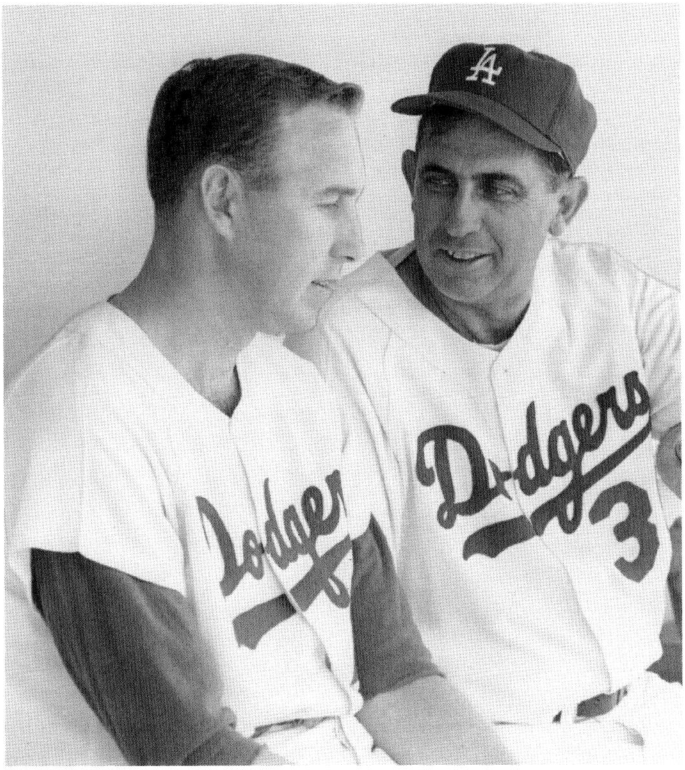

Los Angeles Dodger pitching coach Harold "Lefty" Phillips gives some pointers to Dodgers ace reliever Phil Regan in this 1966 photograph. Phillips began his professional baseball career in 1939 with the Bisbee Bees at Warren Ballpark, but was forced to give up pitching after suffering a crippling arm injury early in the season. As the Dodgers pitching coach, Phillips worked with Hall of Fame inductees Don Drysdale, Sandy Koufax, and Don Sutton. He later managed the California Angels. (Author's collection.)

Although he never played for a Bisbee minor league team at Warren Ballpark, Elvin "Buster" Adams was a local hero when he became the first boy from Bisbee to play in the major leagues. A 1935 graduate of Bisbee High School, Buster was signed by the St. Louis Cardinals organization, and by 1937, was playing outfield for the Sacramento Solons of the Pacific Coast League.

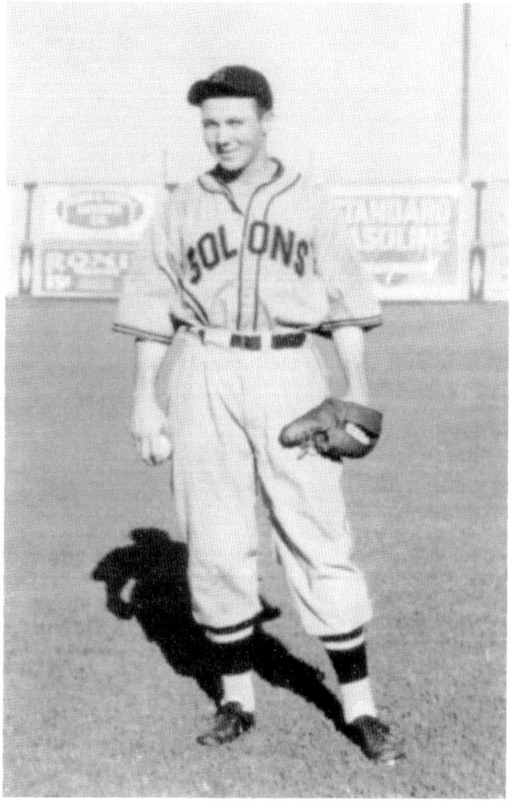

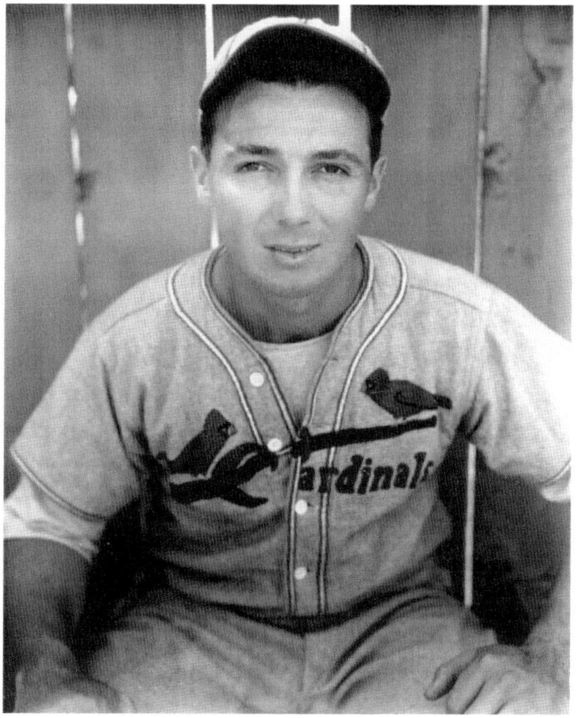

In 1939, Adams moved up to the St. Louis Cardinals at the end of the season for a "cup of coffee." He returned to the minor leagues for several years, but was called back to the majors in 1943, playing outfield with the Cardinals and Phillies through the 1947 season. Adams returned to play in the Pacific Coast League in 1948 and retired from professional baseball in 1951.

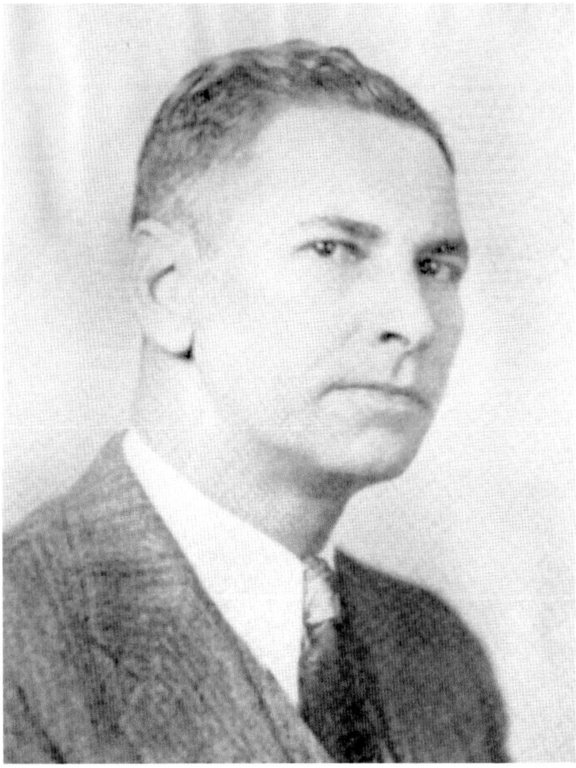

Warren Ballpark was in poor condition by 1936, when R.E. Souers, the Bisbee school superintendent and president of the Arizona-Texas League, finessed an agreement with the Phelps Dodge Corporation to sell the ballpark to the school district for $10. The sale allowed the Works Progress Administration to construct a new grandstand that was ready in early 1937. Minor league baseball returned to Bisbee in April 1937 when the Bees took the field for the first time since 1932.

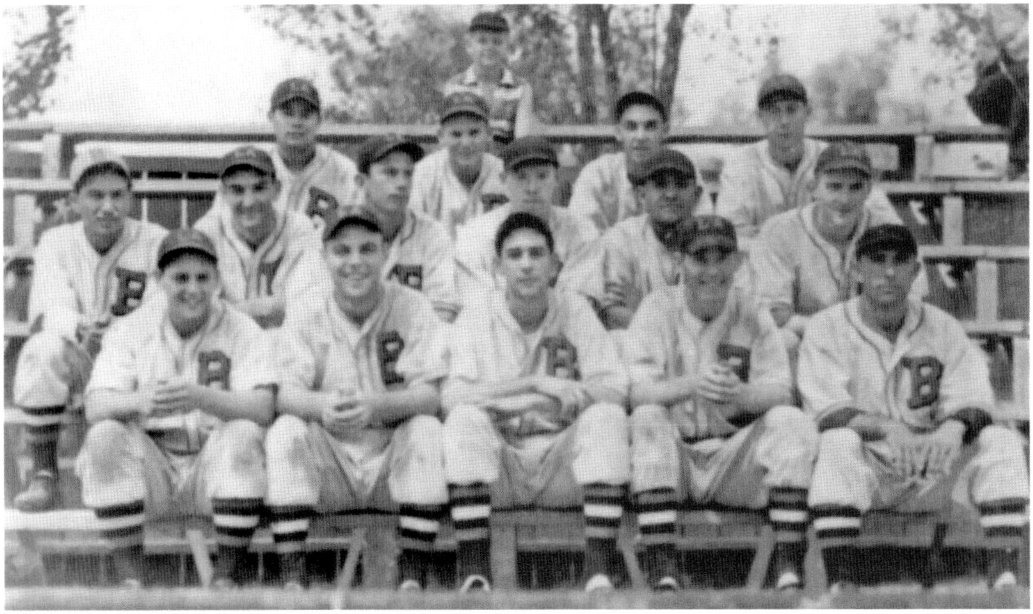

Two members of the league-leading 1938 Bisbee Bees made their way to the big leagues: Roy Partee (front row, far left) and Jesse Flores (middle row, third from left). The Bees, a farm team for the Los Angeles Angels of the Pacific Coast League, also had a working arrangement with the Chicago Cubs.

This unidentified member of the 1938 Bisbee Bees poses in his pinstriped uniform for a fan before a game. While British prime minister Neville Chamberlain and German chancellor Adolf Hitler negotiated the fate of Europe at Munich in September 1938, the Bees were playing a series with the El Paso Texans for the Arizona-Texas League pennant. El Paso won. (Bobby Holland collection)

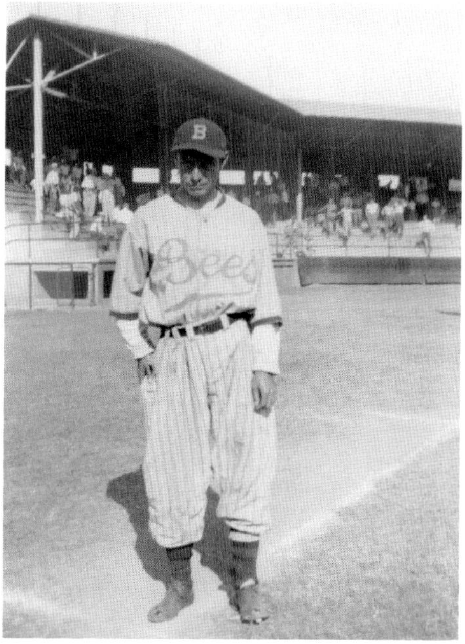

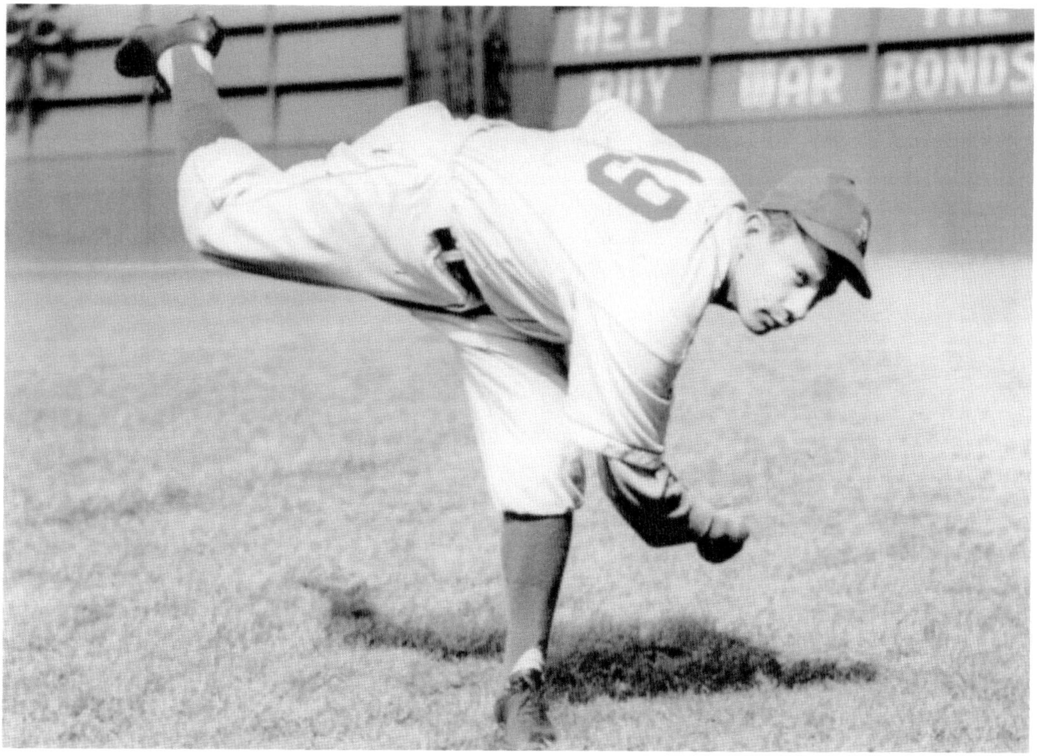

Jesse Flores, an ace screwball pitcher with the 1938 Bisbee Bees, was the first Mexican-born pitcher to make it to the major leagues, playing briefly for the Chicago Cubs in 1942. Flores also pitched for Connie Mack's Philadelphia Athletics and the Cleveland Indians before ending his career in the Pacific Coast League. (Courtesy Hall of Fame.)

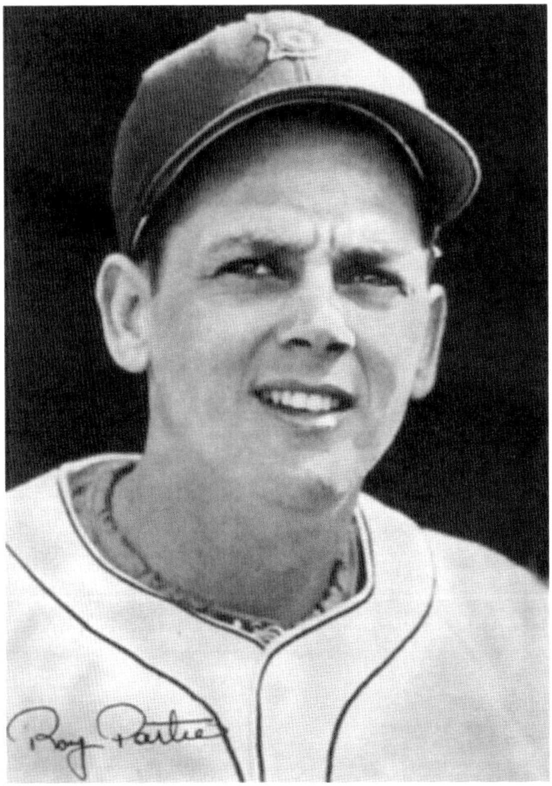

Roy Partee was Bisbee's hot-hitting catcher in 1938. By 1943, he was playing for the Boston Red Sox. In 1946, he caught several games for the Sox against the St. Louis Cardinals during the World Series. He was behind the plate when Enos Slaughter scored the series-winning run for the Cardinals from first base in the ninth inning of game seven. (Author's collection.)

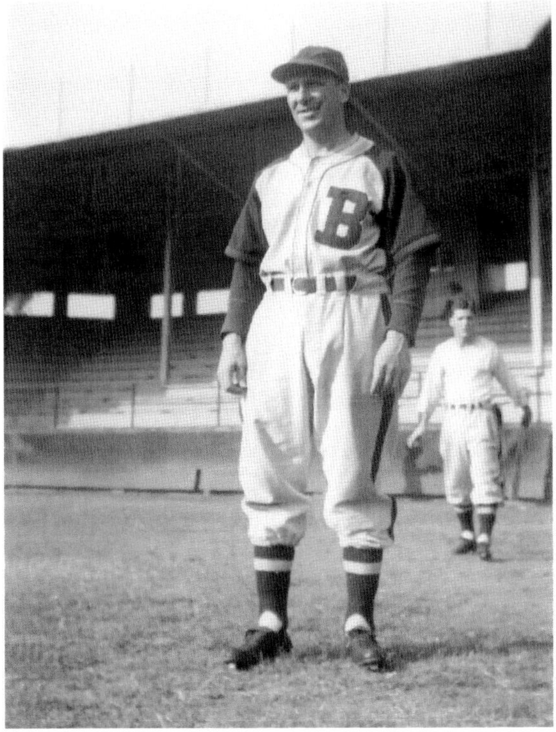

Carl Dittmar, the manager of the Bees from 1939 to 1941, had a long and distinguished career with the Los Angeles Angels of the Pacific Coast League before taking the job as Bisbee's skipper in 1939. Dittmar remained with Bisbee through the end of the 1941 season. (Courtesy Bobby Holland collection.)

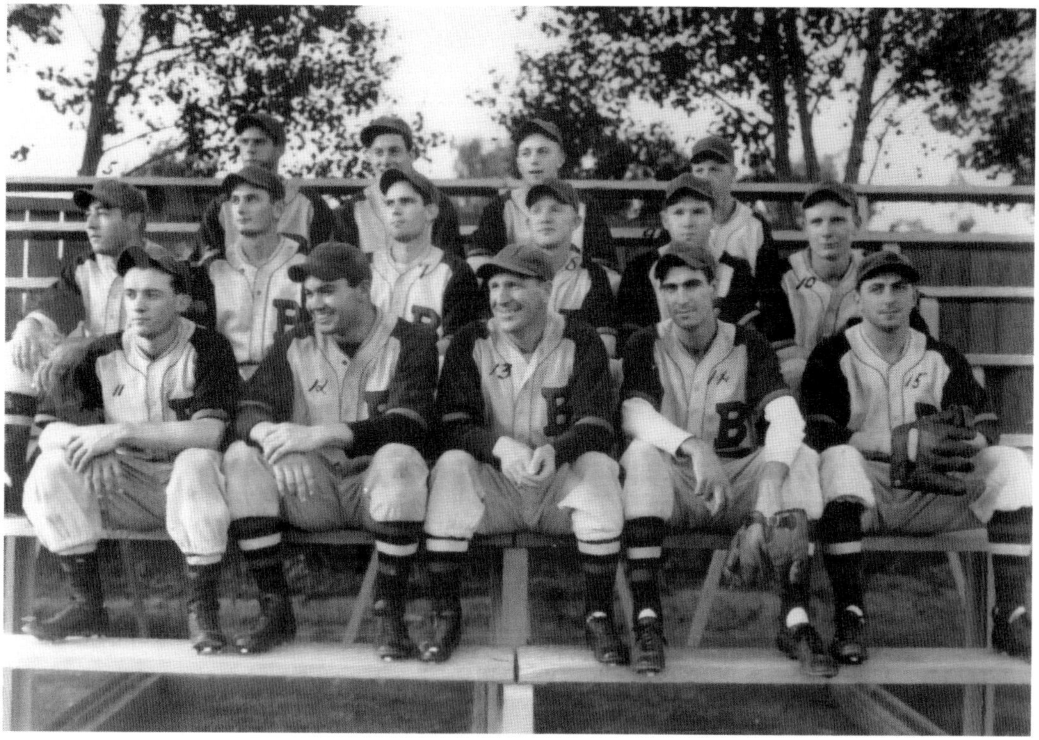

Four members of the 1940 Bees would make it to the major leagues: Dwight "Red" Adams, Clarence Maddern, Jim Devlin, and Len Gilmore. Adams and Maddern made careers out of baseball while Gilmore and Devlin had their "cups of coffee" during World War II.

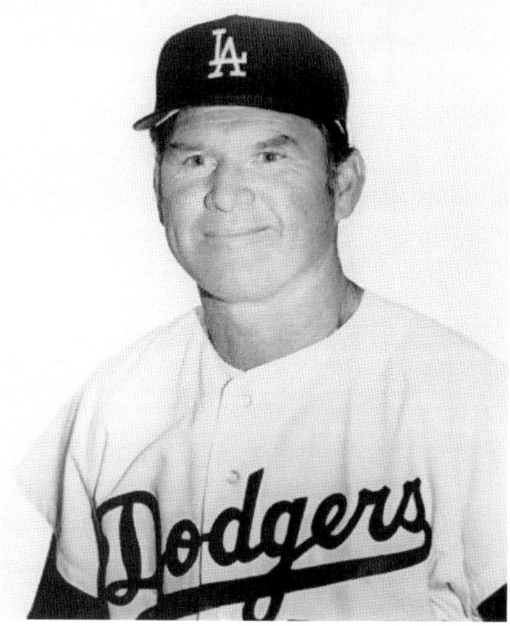

Dwight "Red" Adams broke into baseball in 1938 as a 17-year-old right-handed pitcher with the Bisbee Bees. Although not a success as a major league pitcher, he remained in the game, serving as a pitching coach for the Los Angeles Dodgers from 1969 through 1980. Hall of Fame inductee Don Sutton credited Red Adams with teaching him the pitching skills that made him a success. (Courtesy Hall of Fame.)

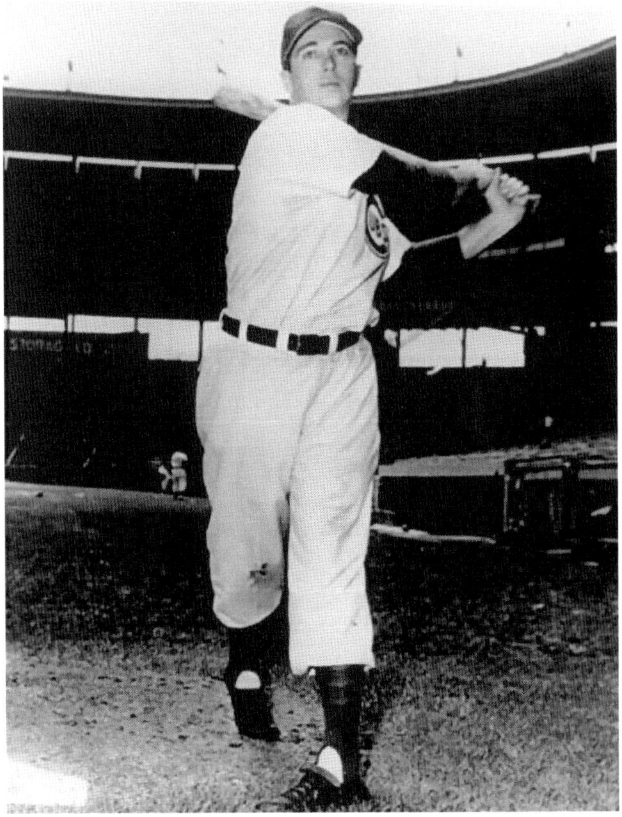

Clarence Maddern, Bisbee's first native-born big leaguer, started professional baseball as an outfielder with the Bees in 1940 and 1941. His career was interrupted by wartime military service, but by 1946, he was playing outfield for the Chicago Cubs. (Courtesy Hall of Fame.)

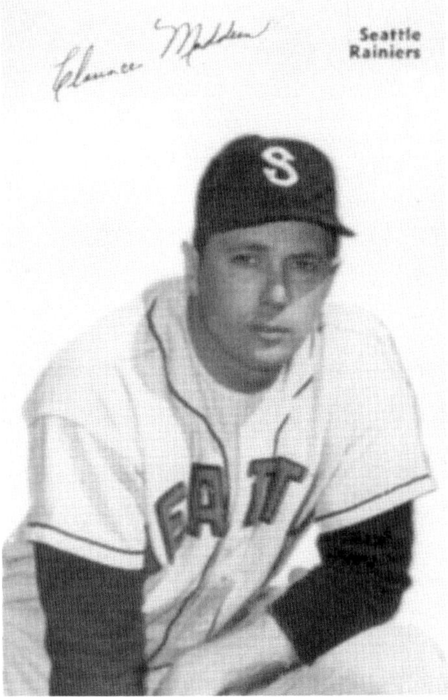

Maddern bounced between the Cubs and the Los Angles Angels through the 1950 season. In 1951, he was picked up by the Cleveland Indians, but he was back in the Pacific Coast League with the Seattle Rainiers in 1952. He retired from baseball in 1957, returning to Bisbee, where he worked as an insurance agent. (Author's collection.)

Infielder Eddie Bockman started with the Bees in 1939. His path to a promising major league career was interrupted by World War II, but he reached the majors in 1946, playing for the Yankees and later for the Cleveland Indians and Pittsburgh Pirates. (Courtesy Hall of Fame.)

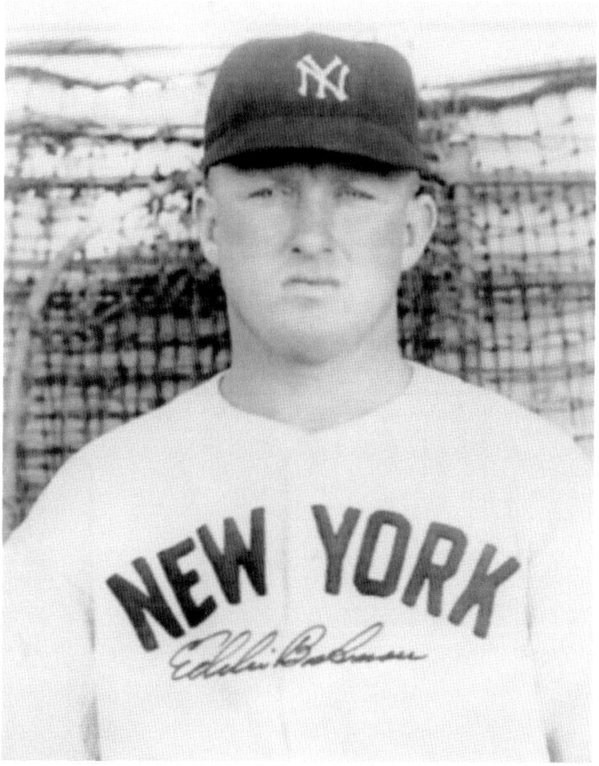

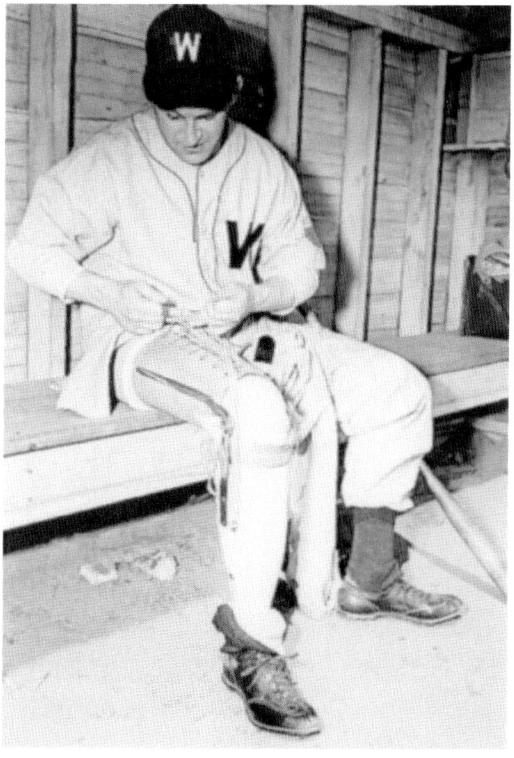

Bert Shepard was a left-handed pitcher for the 1941 Bisbee Bees. His professional career was put on hold in 1942 when he enlisted in the Army Air Force. In May 1944, Shepard's fighter plane was shot down over Germany and his shattered leg was amputated by a German doctor. Shepard was given a tryout with the Washington Nationals, and on August 4, 1945, he entered a game against the Boston Red Sox, making history as the only man to pitch in the major leagues on an artificial leg. (Author's collection.)

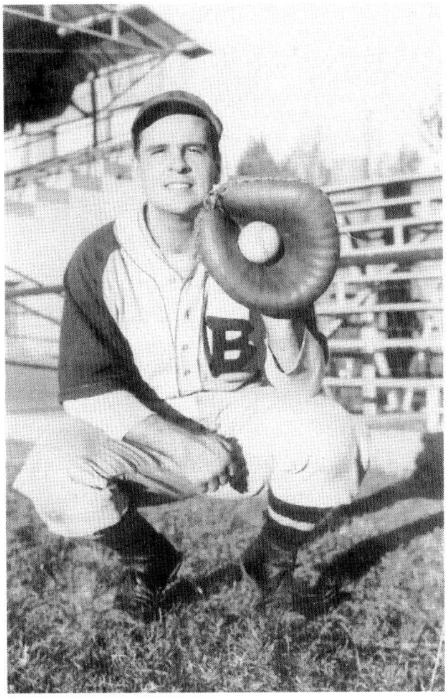

Winfred Alfred "Winn" Wittcke was the regular catcher for the 1941 Bees. His professional baseball career came to an end when he was inducted into wartime military service. In 2010, Wittcke's son, Darrell, brought his father's catcher's mitt back to Warren Ballpark, where he caught the first pitch thrown at that year's Copper City Classic Vintage Base Ball Tournament. (Courtesy Darrell Wittcke.)

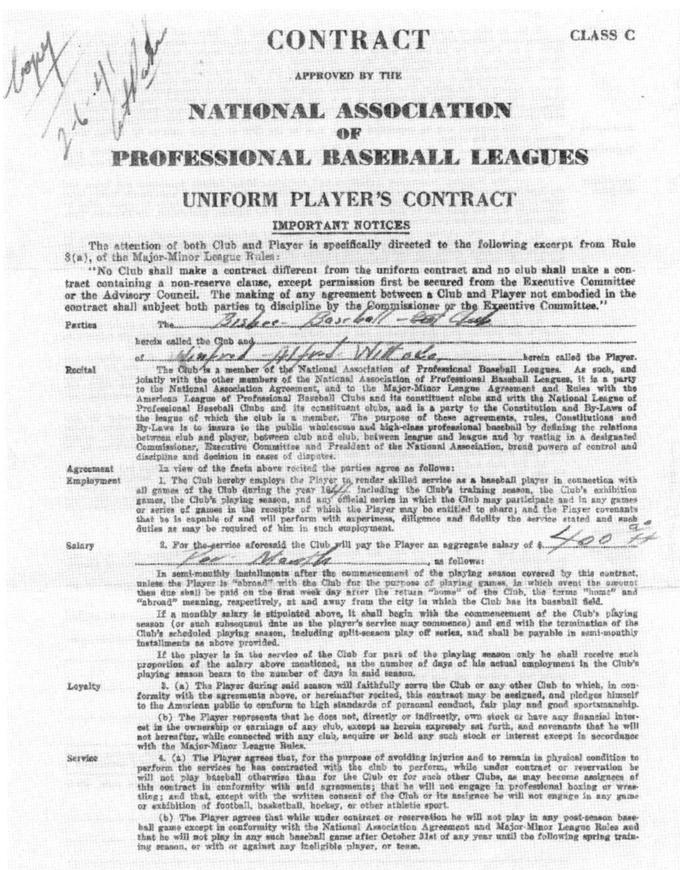

CONTRACT CLASS C

APPROVED BY THE

NATIONAL ASSOCIATION OF PROFESSIONAL BASEBALL LEAGUES

UNIFORM PLAYER'S CONTRACT

IMPORTANT NOTICES

The attention of both Club and Player is specifically directed to the following excerpt from Rule 8(a), of the Major-Minor League Rules:

"No Club shall make a contract different from the uniform contract and no club shall make a contract containing a non-reserve clause, except permission first be secured from the Executive Committee or the Advisory Council. The making of any agreement between a Club and Player not embodied in the contract shall subject both parties to discipline by the Commissioner or the Executive Committee."

Parties — The Bisbee Baseball Club herein called the Club and of Winfred Alfred Wittcke herein called the Player.

Recital — The Club is a member of the National Association of Professional Baseball Leagues. As such, and jointly with the other members of the National Association of Professional Baseball Leagues, it is a party to the National Association Agreement, and to the Major-Minor League Agreement and Rules with the American League of Professional Baseball Clubs and its constituent clubs and with the National League of Professional Baseball Clubs and its constituent clubs, and is a party to the Constitution and By-Laws of the league of which the club is a member. The purpose of these agreements, rules, Constitutions and By-Laws is to insure to the public wholesome and high-class professional baseball by defining the relations between club and player, between club and club, between league and league and by vesting in a designated Commissioner, Executive Committee and President of the National Association, broad powers of control and discipline and decision in cases of disputes.

Agreement — In view of the facts above recited the parties agree as follows:

Employment — 1. The Club hereby employs the Player to render skilled service as a baseball player in connection with all games of the Club during the year 1941 including the Club's training season, the Club's exhibition games, the Club's playing season, and any official series in which the Club may participate and in any games or series of games in the receipts of which the Player may be entitled to share; and the Player covenants that he is capable of and will perform with expertness, diligence and fidelity the service stated and such duties as may be required of him in such employment.

Salary — 2. For the service aforesaid the Club will pay the Player an aggregate salary of $400.00 Per Month, as follows:

In semi-monthly installments after the commencement of the playing season covered by this contract, unless the Player is "abroad" with the Club for the purpose of playing games, in which event the amount then due shall be paid on the first week day after the return "home" of the Club, the terms "home" and "abroad" meaning, respectively, at and away from the city in which the Club has its baseball field.

If a monthly salary is stipulated above, it shall begin with the commencement of the Club's playing season (or such subsequent date as the player's service may commence) and end with the termination of the Club's scheduled playing season, including split-season play off series, and shall be payable in semi-monthly installments as above provided.

If the player is in the service of the Club for part of the playing season only he shall receive such proportion of the salary above mentioned, as the number of days of his actual employment in the Club's playing season bears to the number of days in said season.

Loyalty — 3. (a) The Player during said season will faithfully serve the Club or any other Club to which, in conformity with the agreements above, or hereinafter recited, this contract may be assigned, and pledges himself to the American public to conform to high standards of personal conduct, fair play and good sportsmanship.

(b) The Player represents that he does not, directly or indirectly, own stock or have any financial interest in the ownership or earnings of any club, except as herein expressly set forth, and covenants that he will not hereafter, while connected with any club, acquire or hold any such stock or interest except in accordance with the Major-Minor League Rules.

Service — 4. (a) The Player agrees that, for the purpose of avoiding injuries and to remain in physical condition to perform the services he has contracted with the club to perform, while under contract or reservation he will not play baseball otherwise than for the Club or for such other Clubs, as may become assignees of this contract in conformity with said agreements; that he will not engage in professional boxing or wrestling; and that, except with the written consent of the Club or its assignee he will not engage in any game or exhibition of football, basketball, hockey, or other athletic sport.

(b) The Player agrees that while under contract or reservation he will not play in any post-season baseball game except in conformity with the National Association Agreement and Major-Minor League Rules and that he will not play in any such baseball game after October 31st of any year until the following spring training season, or with or against any ineligible player, or team.

The minor league contract offered to Winn Wittcke by the Bisbee Bees in 1941 provided a hefty salary of $400 per month as well as meals and lodging while "abroad" on road trips. The contract also contained the infamous reserve clause, which bound a player to the team unless the team owner traded or released him. (Courtesy Darrell Wittcke.)

5

GLORY DAYS

Professional baseball returned to Warren Ballpark in 1947 when the Class C Bisbee Yanks took the field to play in the resurrected Arizona-Texas League. A farm team for the New York Yankees, the Yanks lasted only one season but provided plenty of thrills for capacity crowds. Three of the Yanks would go on to successful careers in major league baseball. One of them, a young catcher named Clint Courtney, would begin a feud with the legendary player and manager Billy Martin that would spill over into the American League.

After the Yanks pulled up stakes, Bisbee shared a team with its sister city of Douglas from 1948 through 1955. Three teams, the Javelinas, the Miners, and the Copper Kings, would take the field at Warren Ballpark to play half their home games. None would post a winning season. As in past years, the Bisbee-Douglas teams were a mix of local boys and players sent to Bisbee from farm teams out of state.

Four years after Jackie Robinson integrated major league baseball, Clifford Prelow, a speedy infielder from Los Angeles, would break a similar barrier as the first black player to take the field for a home team at Warren Ballpark. The Copper Kings would blaze other trails in professional baseball as well. Syd Cohen, a Spanish-speaking manager from El Paso, stocked his Bisbee-Douglas club with players from Mexico, starting a trend of recruiting Latin American players that continues today.

Only three Copper Kings players would reach the major leagues from Warren Ballpark, but one of them, young black pitcher Earl Wilson, would work his way to the very top of his craft, while waging his own private struggle against racism.

Declining attendance and gate receipts prompted the Copper Kings management to pull out of Bisbee in 1955. Minor league baseball would not return to Warren Ballpark until 2003, when the Copper Kings took the field as a team in an independent minor league. Women also played at Warren Ballpark, on fast-pitch softball teams that took the field in conjunction with men's baseball or softball games.

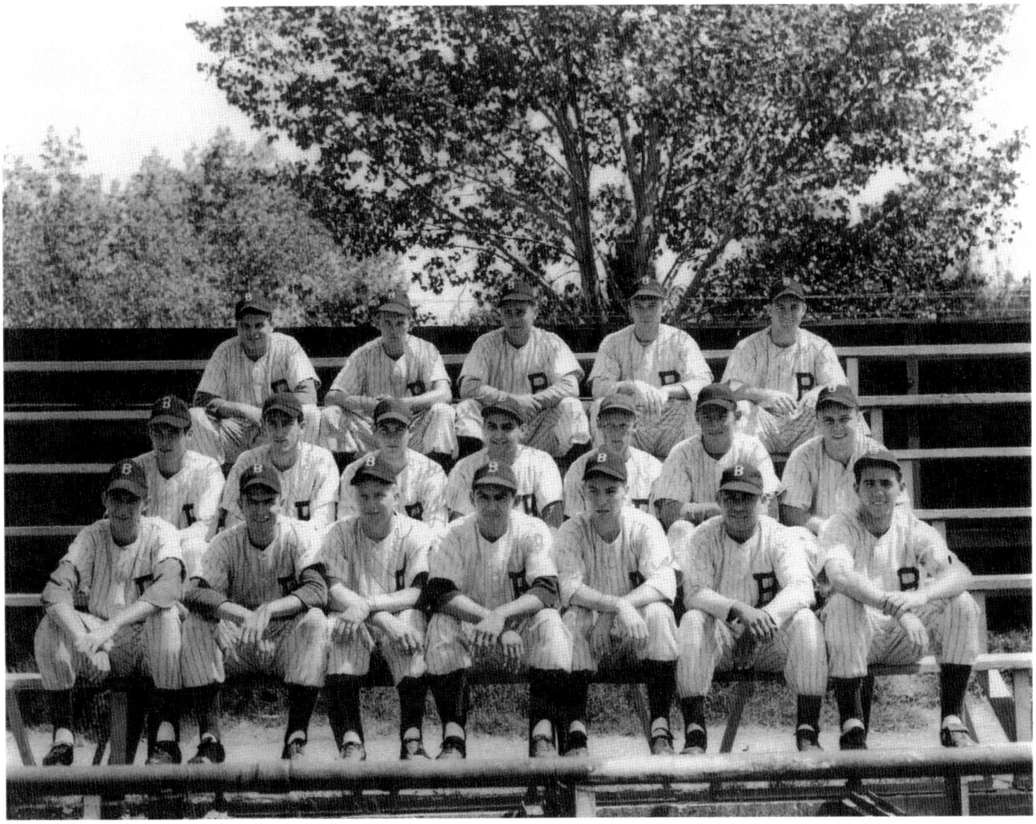

Professional baseball returned to Warren Ballpark in a big way in 1947, when the Bisbee Yanks, a Class C farm club of the New York Yankees, came to town. Skippered by Charlie Metro, the Yanks provided fans with top-quality, exciting baseball, playing teams that featured several of baseball's most talented and colorful future stars. (Courtesy Pete Vucurevich.)

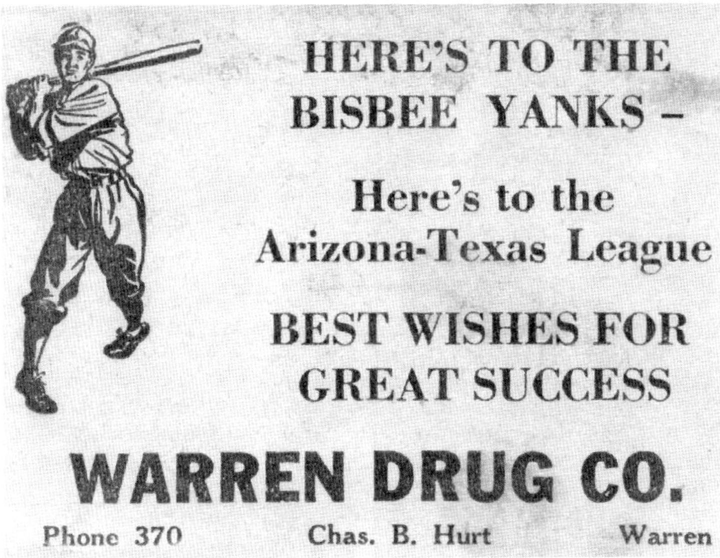

Community support for the new Bisbee team was strong. Fans filled the stands for each game and local businesses were eager to sponsor the Yanks. Umpires and star players on visiting team were often special objects of fans' wrath. (Courtesy Jim Propst.)

Charlie Metro had played for the Tigers and Athletics during the war years. In 1947, he was offered the manager's job in Bisbee. It was the first of many such jobs for him in the minor leagues. Metro had a knack for mentoring young players, including a teenager in Oakland named Billy Martin, who went on to play for and manage the New York Yankees. Metro and Martin became close, lifelong friends. (Author's collection.)

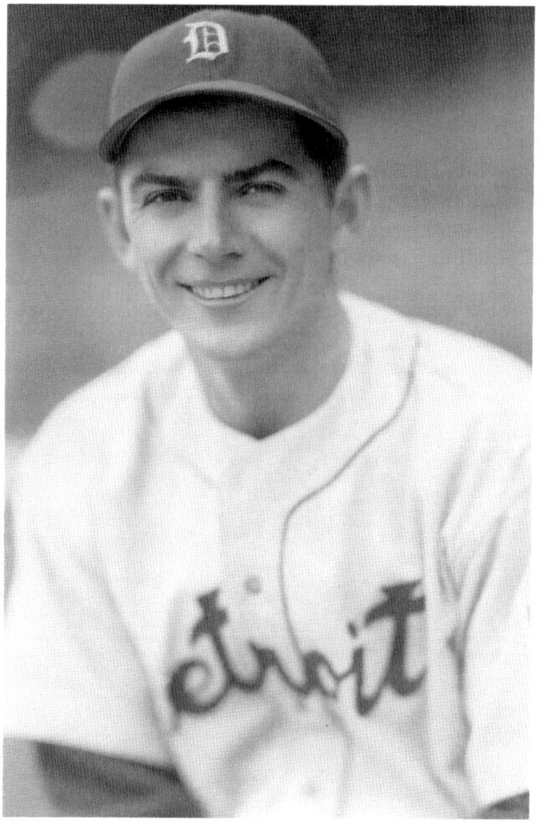

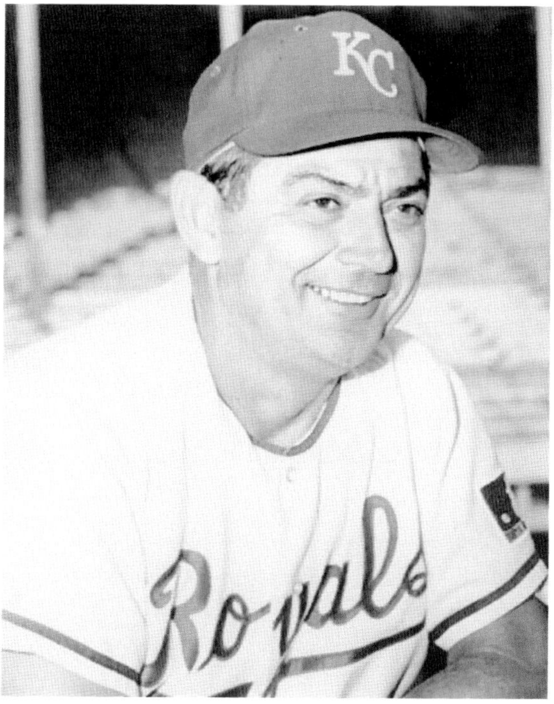

Metro would move up the professional managerial ladder, all the way from the low minors to AAA and then to the major leagues. His career included stints at the helm of the 1962 Chicago Cubs and the 1970 Kansas City Royals. He also worked as a major league coach, a director of player development, and scout over his long career. (Courtesy Hall of Fame.)

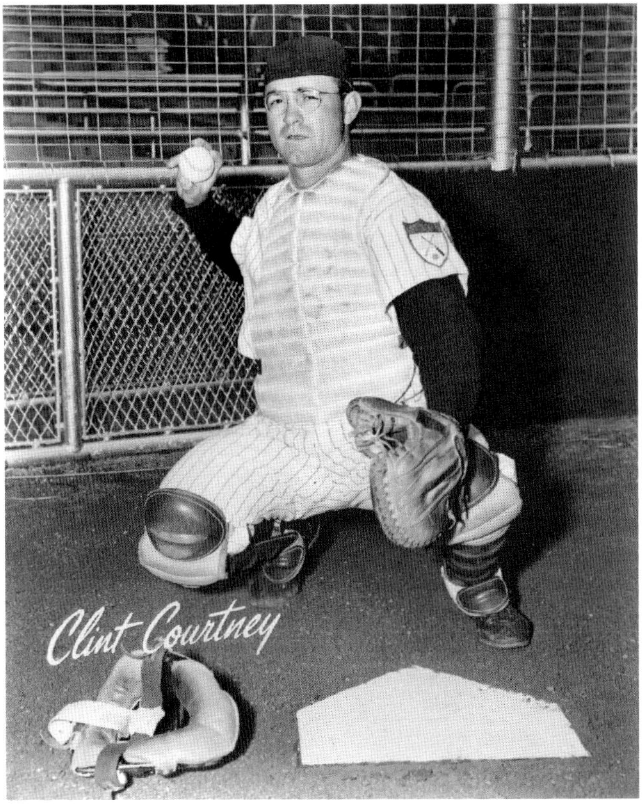

Clint "Scrap Iron" Courtney was a country boy from Louisiana who played aggressive baseball with skill and passion. As a catcher for the 1947 Bisbee Yanks, Courtney hit .319, ran the base paths with wild abandon, and developed a feud with Phoenix Senators infielder Billy Martin that brought fans in droves to the ballpark and carried over into the major leagues. (Author's collection.)

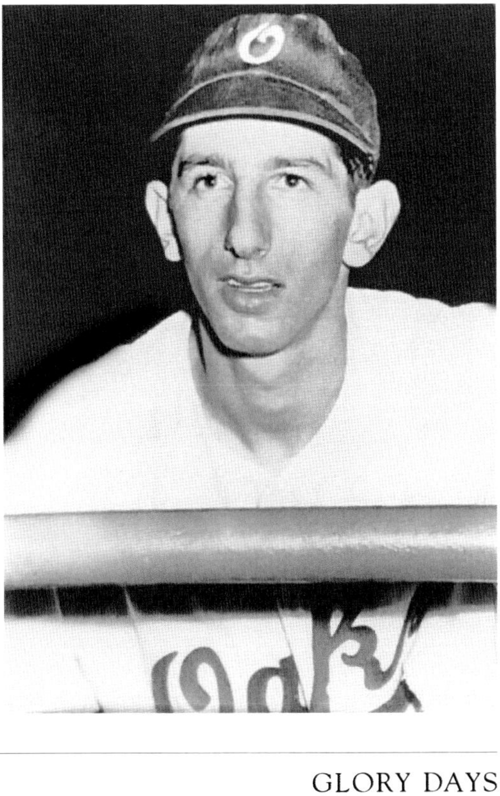

In 1947, Billy Martin was an emerging 19-year-old star infielder with the Phoenix Senators, batting .392 for the season and setting the base paths on fire. He could not help but collide with Bisbee catcher Clint Courtney at second base or home. Their feud continued in later years, when both were playing in the American League. (Photograph courtesy Hall of Fame.)

Frank Lucchesi went from playing infield for the Yanks in 1947 to managing the Medford Rogues at age 21 in 1951. During his 44-year career, Lucchesi successfully managed 17 minor league teams. His big league career included managing the Philadelphia Phillies, the Chicago Cubs, and the Texas Rangers. Like Metro, Lucchesi developed some of baseball's finest players. (Photograph courtesy Frank Lucchesi.)

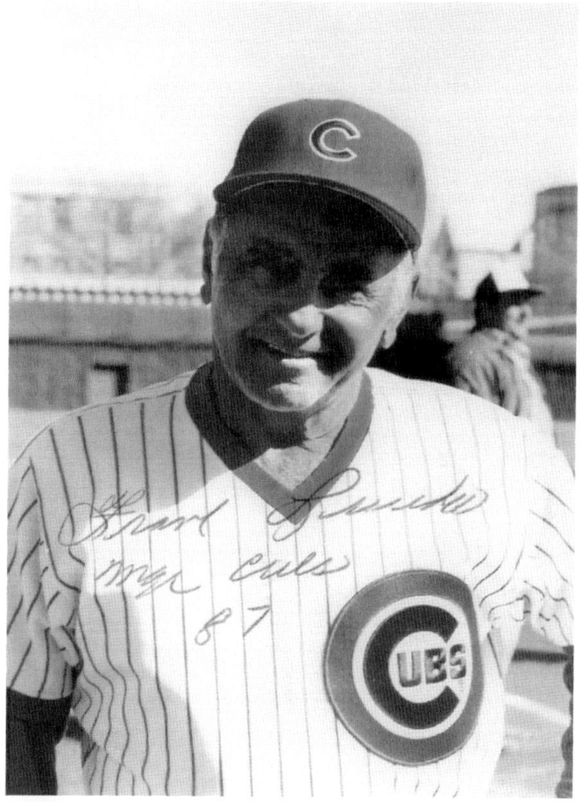

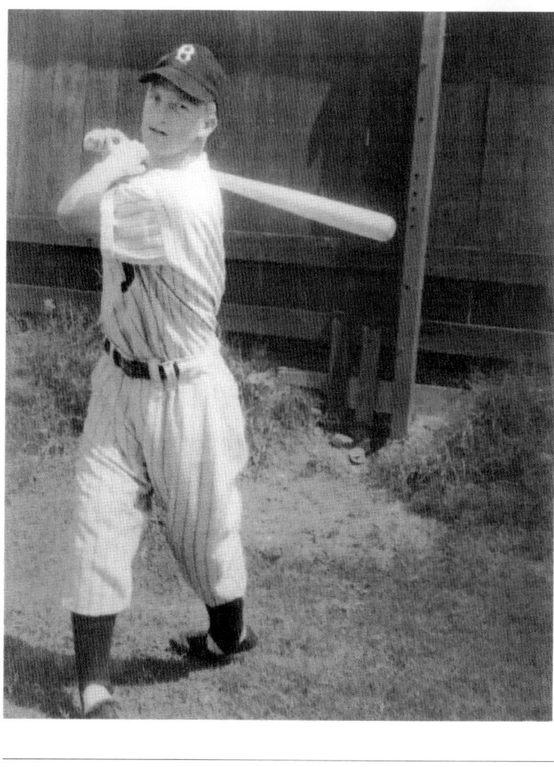

Warren "Bud" Howe's arthritis kept him from raising his arms over his head when he lived in colder climes, but the warm dry air of the southwest revived his health and his baseball career. Playing outfield for the 1947 Bisbee Yanks, Howe hit .335 and earned a reputation for playing the game for the sheer love of it. (Courtesy Cheryl Coffee.)

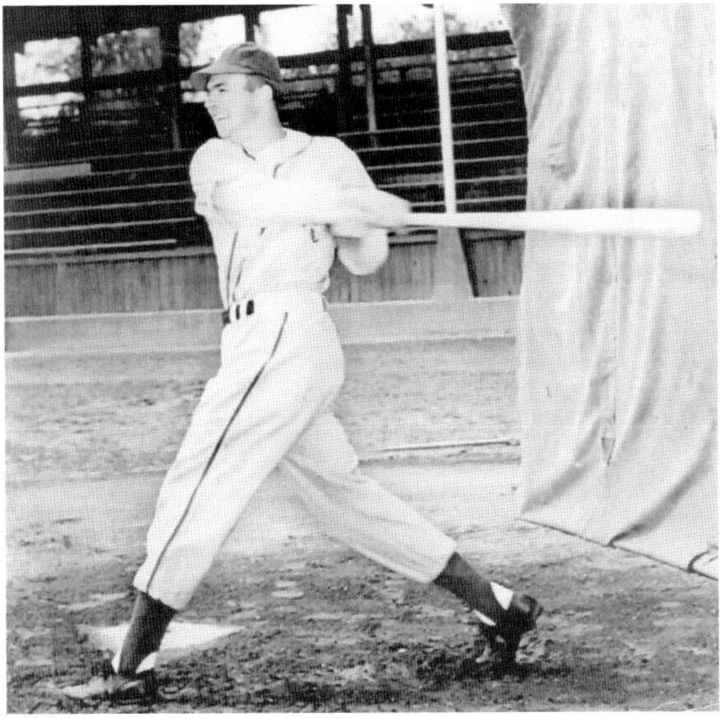

Bank bookkeeper turned ballplayer Jim "Boom-Boom" Bynon hit for power in 1947 (.325) with the Bisbee Yanks and again in 1948 (.295) with the Bisbee-Douglas Javelinas/Miners/Copper Kings. Bynon also hit safely in 34 consecutive games during both seasons. (Courtesy Edith Bynon.)

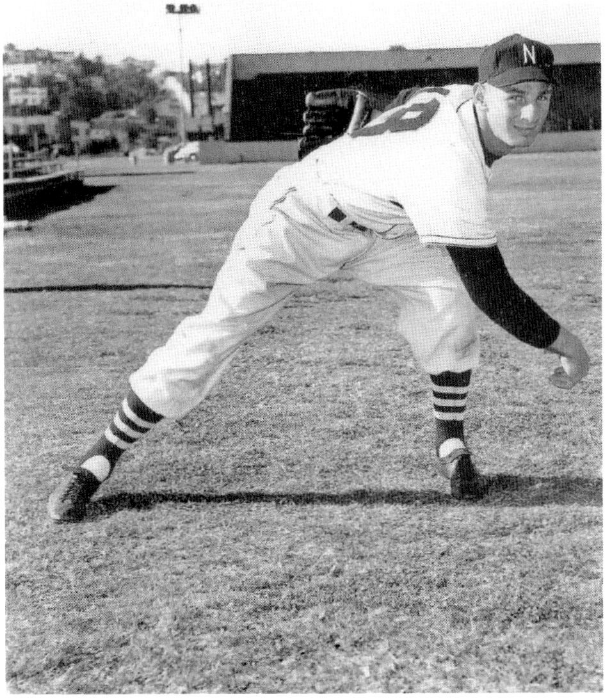

Pete Vucurevich went from pitching the Bisbee High School Pumas to their first state championship in 1947 to playing for the 1947 Bisbee Yanks. Vucurevich moved up through the Yankees' minor league system until the Korean War put a halt to his civilian career. He flourished as a pitcher for crack Navy teams, hurling a 7-0 shutout against Barksdale Air Force Base to win the Armed Forces All-Services Championship. (Courtesy Pete Vucurevich.)

Jim Propst was a heavily scouted high school star when his baseball career was interrupted by Marine Corps service. After his discharge, he returned to the game and was assigned to the Bisbee Yanks in 1947. The left-handed Propst was 15-6 on the mound for the Yanks in 1947. He pitched for several more years in the minor leagues. (Courtesy Jim Propst.)

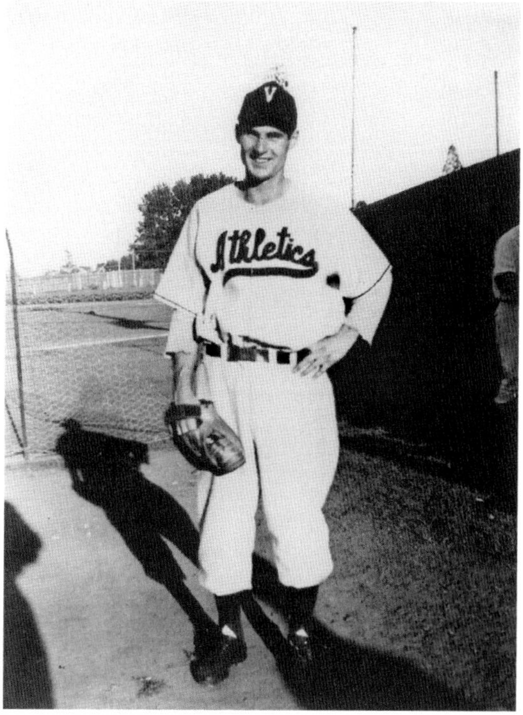

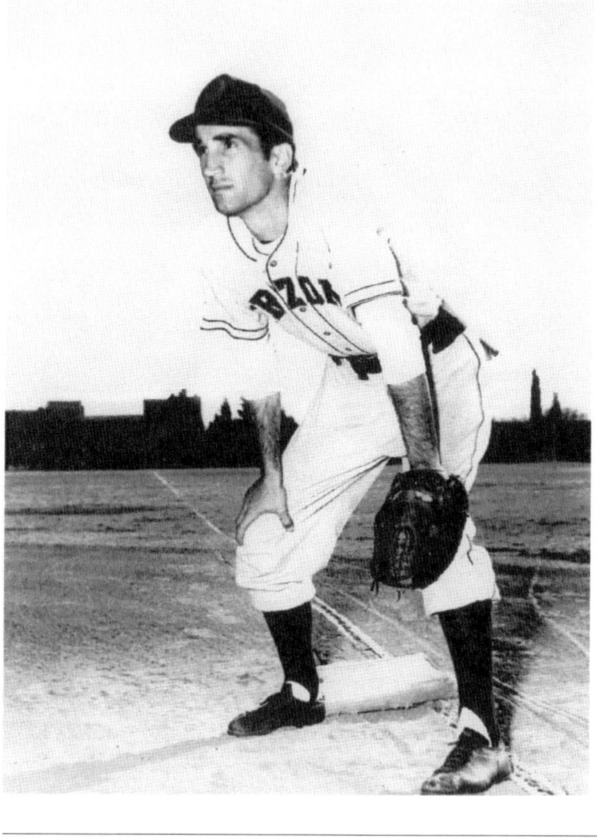

Robert "Bosco" Verbica was a member of the 1947 Bisbee High School state championship baseball team and then the 1947 Bisbee Yanks. He went on to play for the University of Arizona Wildcats varsity baseball team from 1949 through 1951, and then returned to Bisbee to play for the Bisbee-Douglas Copper Kings in the 1951 and 1952 seasons. (Courtesy Verbica family.)

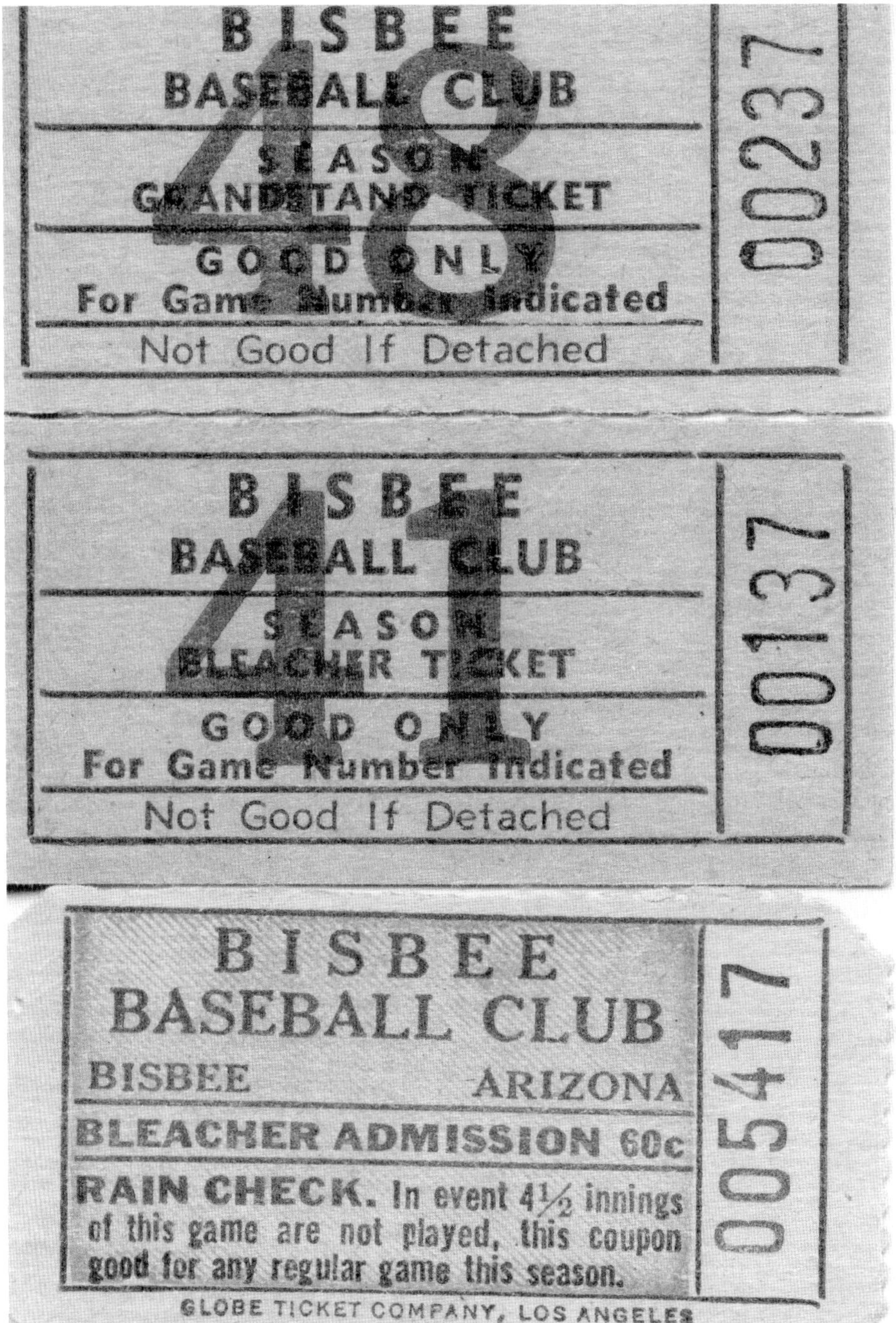

Ticket prices for Bisbee Yanks games at Warren Ballpark were affordable, with grandstand seats usually going for $1 and bleacher seats for 60¢. Season tickets were available at a discount price. Grateful fans rewarded good players by rolling up dollar bills and passing them through the chicken wire screening. (Courtesy Jim Propst.)

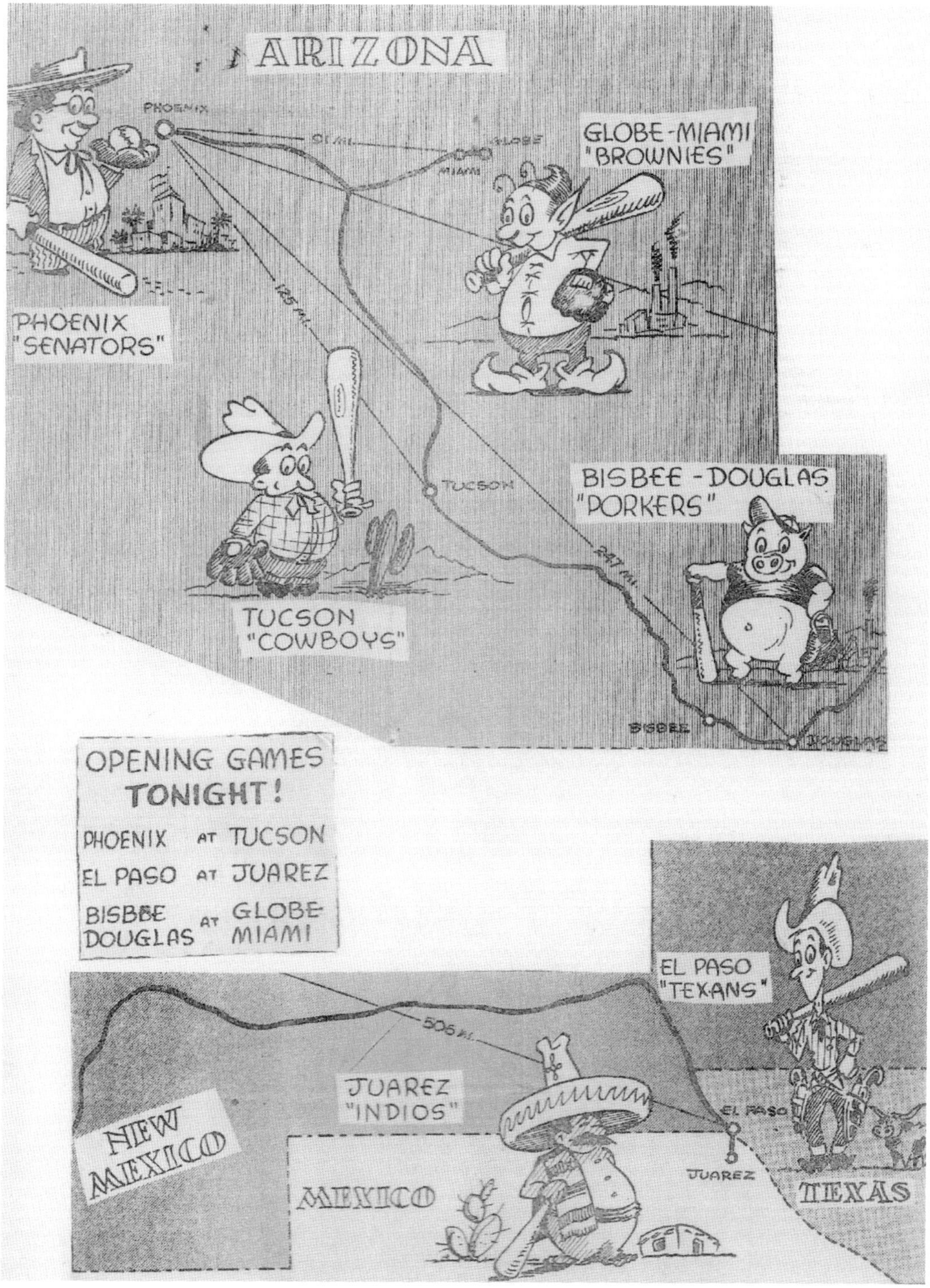

In the late 1940s, the Arizona-Texas League covered a lot of territory. Teams from larger cities such as Phoenix, Tucson, El Paso, and Juarez competed against those from smaller communities such as Globe-Miami and Bisbee-Douglas. (Courtesy Tim Kusmertz.)

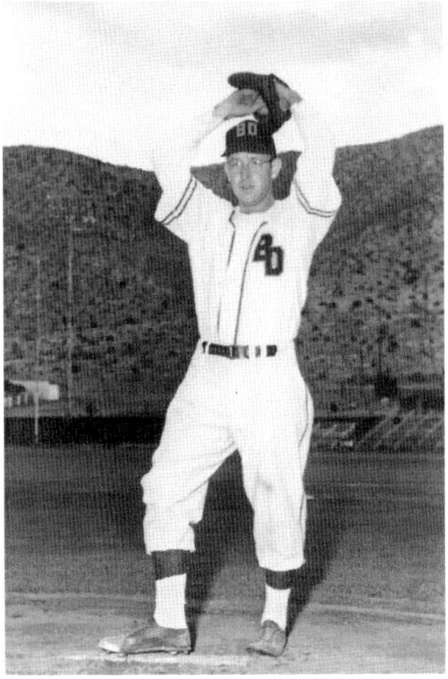

Russell "Russ" Kusmertz started with the Globe-Miami Browns in 1947 but moved to Bisbee in 1948 to pitch for the Bisbee-Douglas Javelinas/Miners/Copper Kings. Kusmertz took the mound again for the Copper Kings in 1949 and remained in Bisbee for the rest of his life, becoming one of the community's biggest supporters of high school sports. (Courtesy Tim Kusmertz.)

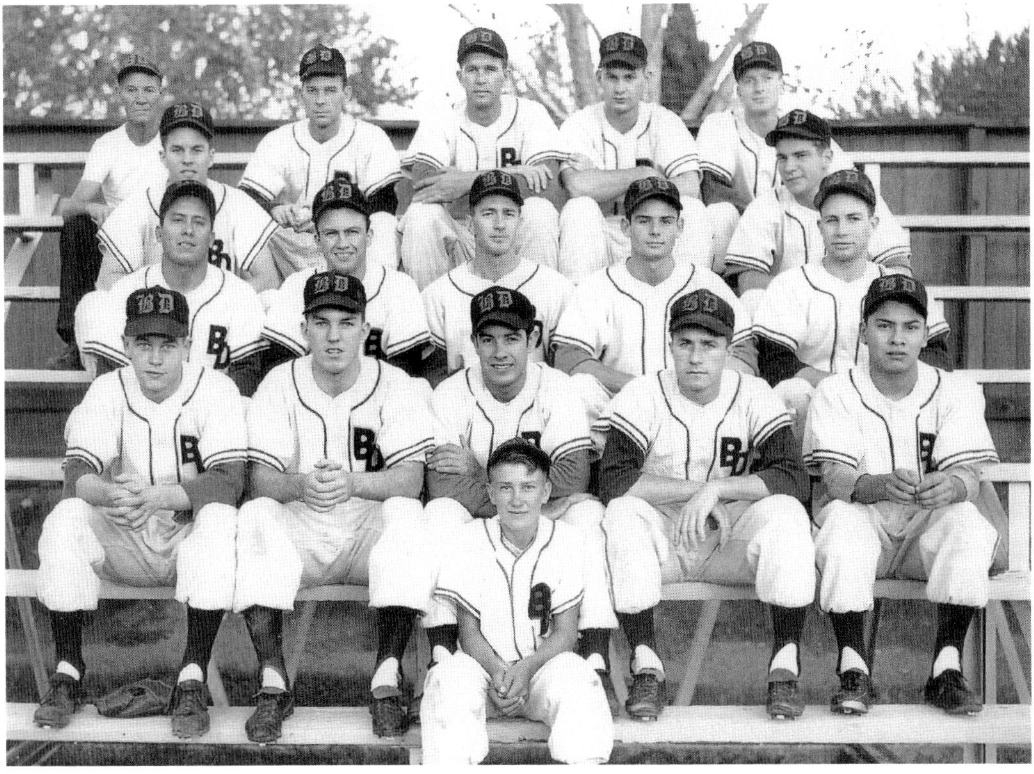

The 1949 Bisbee-Douglas Copper Kings included manager Arthur "Buck" Elliott (third row, second from left) and right-handed pitcher Manuel "Blackie" Morales (second row, far left). The Copper Kings' batboy was Clarence Dupnik (front center), who played varsity baseball for the Bisbee Pumas and has served more than three decades as the Pima County sheriff. (Courtesy Ann Henry.)

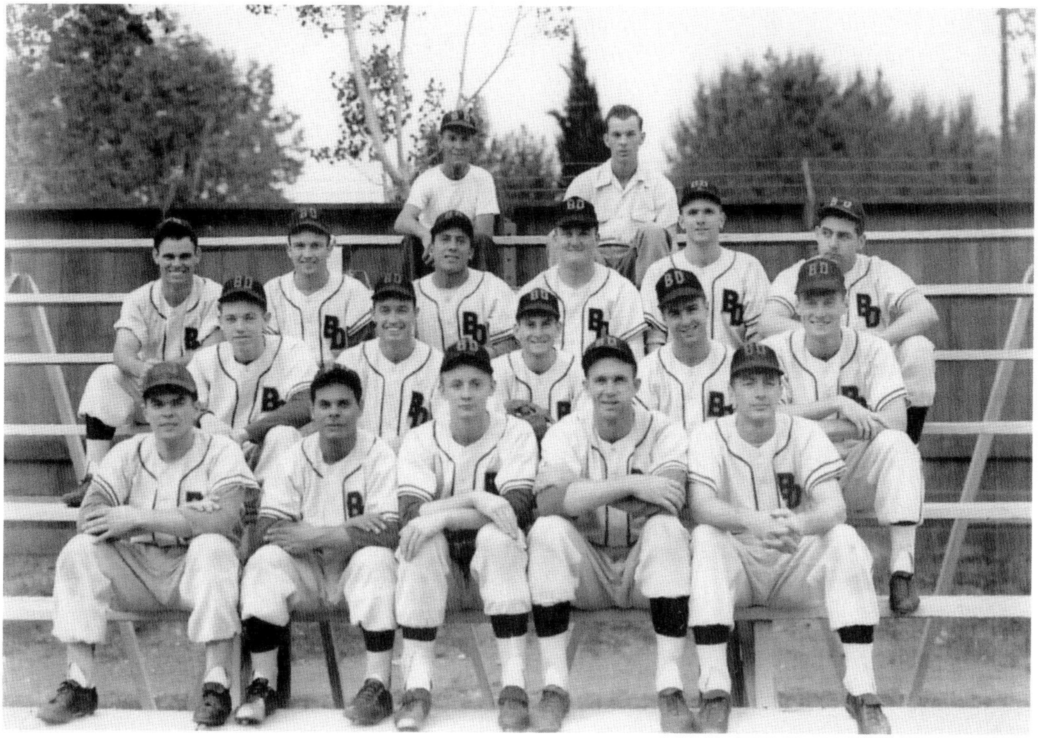

The 1950 Bisbee-Douglas Copper Kings improved their performance enough to qualify to play in the Governors' Cup postseason playoffs. They were the only Bisbee-Douglas minor league team to earn a postseason playoff berth. (Courtesy Ann Henry.)

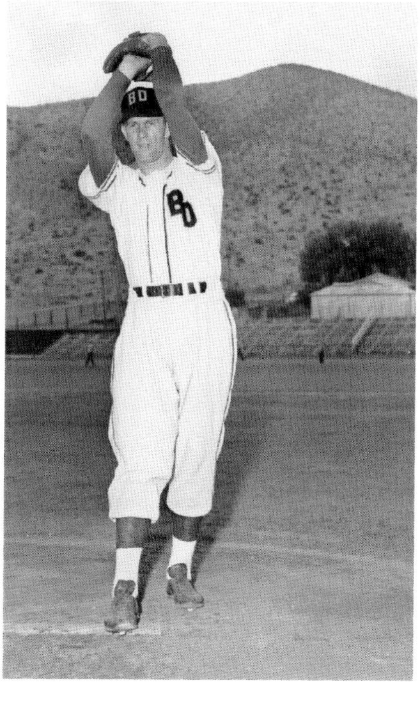

At six feet five inches, John Robert "Bob" Henry was an intimidating presence on the mound for the Copper Kings. Henry played three seasons for the Bisbee-Douglas team before hanging up his spikes to start a career with the Phelps Dodge Mining Corporation. Henry married Ann Mihelich, one of the best female ballplayers to come out of Bisbee. (Courtesy Ann Henry.)

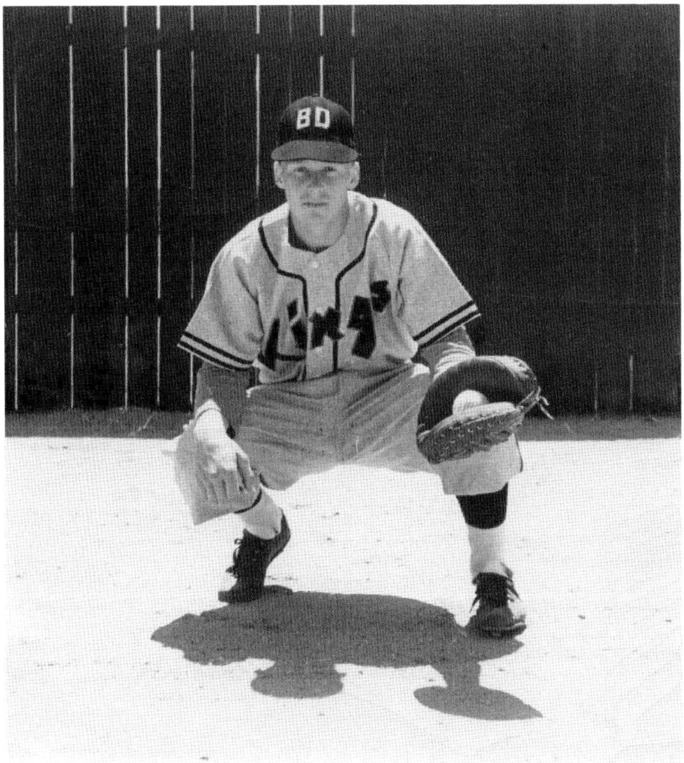

Robert "Bobby" Holland was a star high school baseball catcher before playing with the 1947 Bisbee Yanks and the 1949 Bisbee-Douglas Copper Kings. Holland was a strong supporter of Bisbee High School sports and kept the field lights at Warren Ballpark in good operating condition for many years. (Courtesy Bobby Holland collection.)

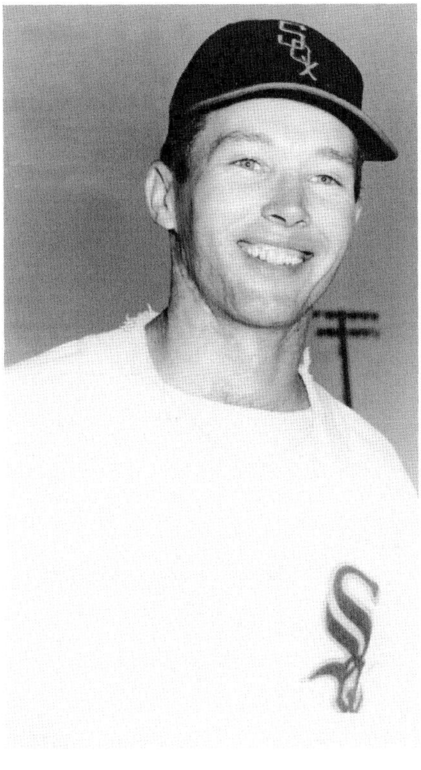

Don Maddern, the brother of Clarence Maddern, was a fine ballplayer in his own right, playing varsity baseball at Bisbee High School before moving up to the minor leagues. Maddern returned to play at Warren Ballpark in 1950 while with the Globe-Miami Browns. (Courtesy Maddern family.)

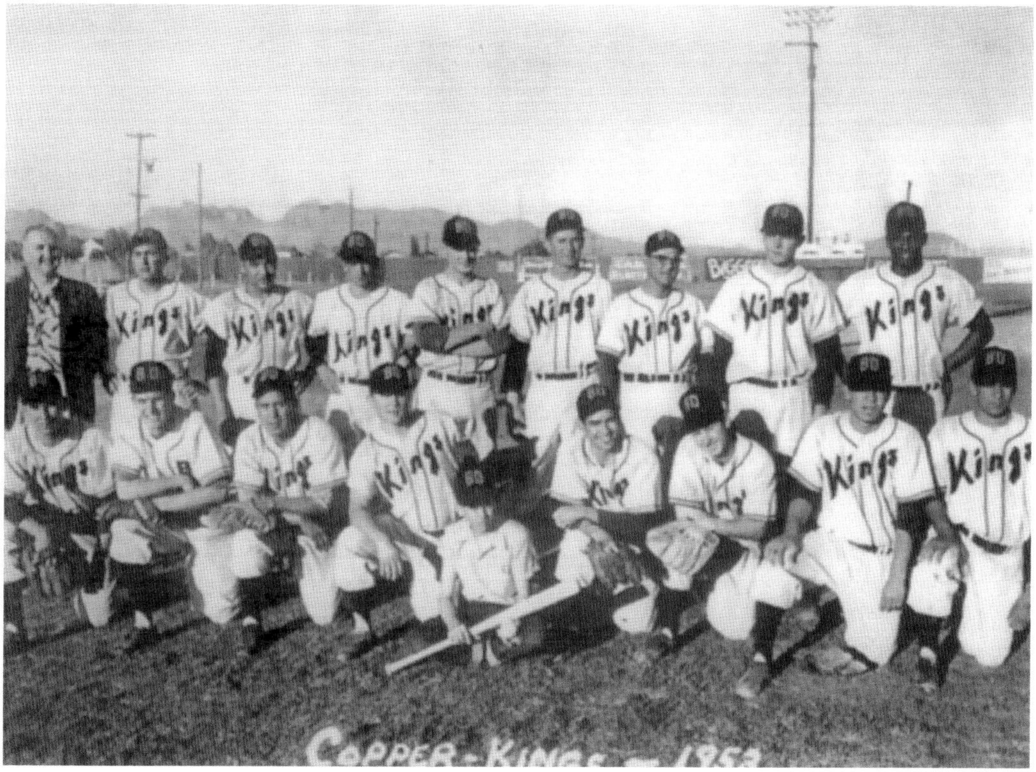

The 1953 Bisbee-Douglas Copper Kings were managed by southwestern baseball legend Syd Cohen (second row, far left), who was a star with the Bisbee Bees in the team's earliest years. Also on the team was pitcher Earl Wilson (second row, far right). (Author's collection.)

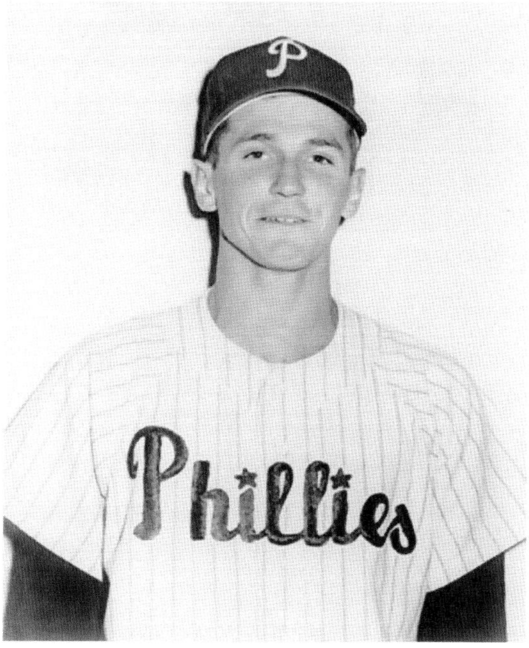

The Canadian-born Glen Gorbous played with the Bisbee-Douglas Copper Kings in 1950. He made the majors in 1955, playing for the Cincinnati Reds and Philadelphia Phillies. Gorbous holds the record for the longest throw of a baseball: 445 feet, 10 inches. (Courtesy Hall of Fame.)

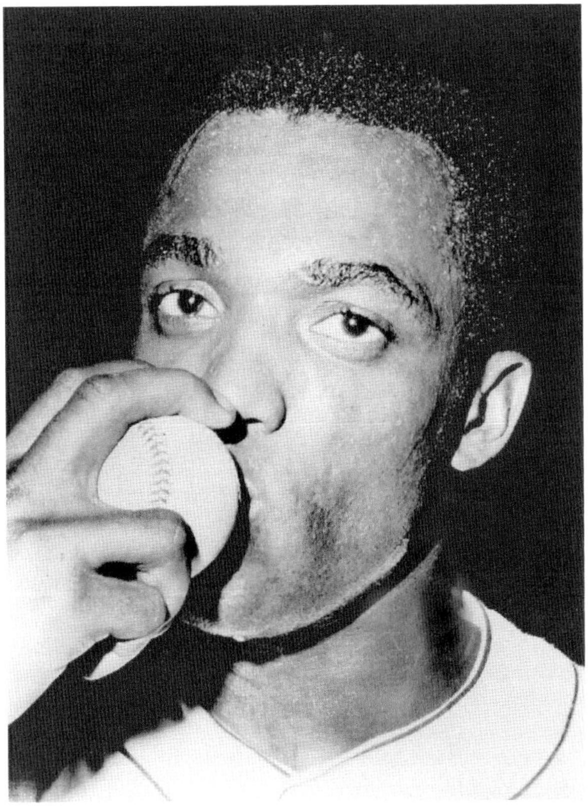

Robert Earl Wilson kisses the ball he used to finish a no-hit shutout against the Los Angeles Angels in June 1962. Wilson started with the 1953 Bisbee-Douglas Copper Kings as a catcher, but was converted to a right-handed pitcher by Syd Cohen. (Author's collection.)

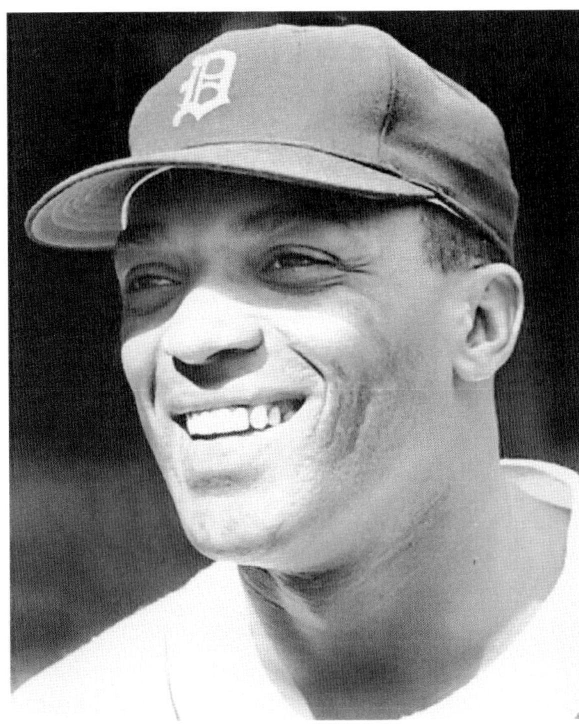

Traded by Boston to Detroit in 1966 after he complained about his treatment by a racist bartender during spring training in Florida, Wilson found a far more congenial home with the Tigers. In 1967, he was a 22-game winner for Detroit, and in 1968, he pitched for the Tigers in the World Series. (Courtesy Hall of Fame.)

Benjamin Beltran Valenzuela was known on both sides of the border as Papelero, or "paperboy." The native of Los Mochis, Sinaloa, Mexico, broke into professional baseball as a third baseman with the 1952 Bisbee-Douglas Copper Kings. He played for the 1958 St. Louis Cardinals and later became a successful manager in Mexican baseball. He was inducted into Mexico's Salon de Fama del Beisbol Profesional de Mexico. (Courtesy Hall of Fame.)

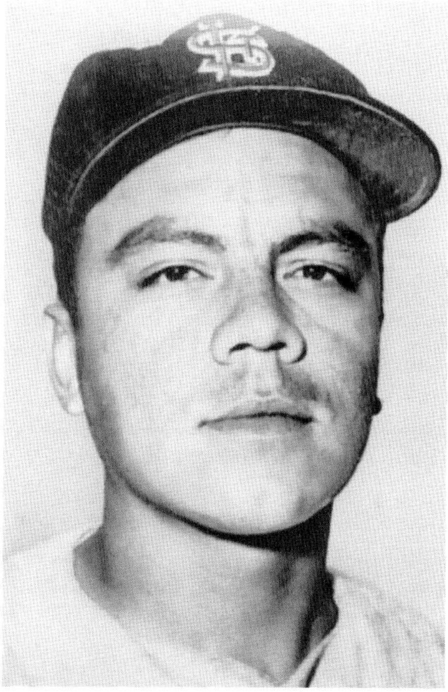

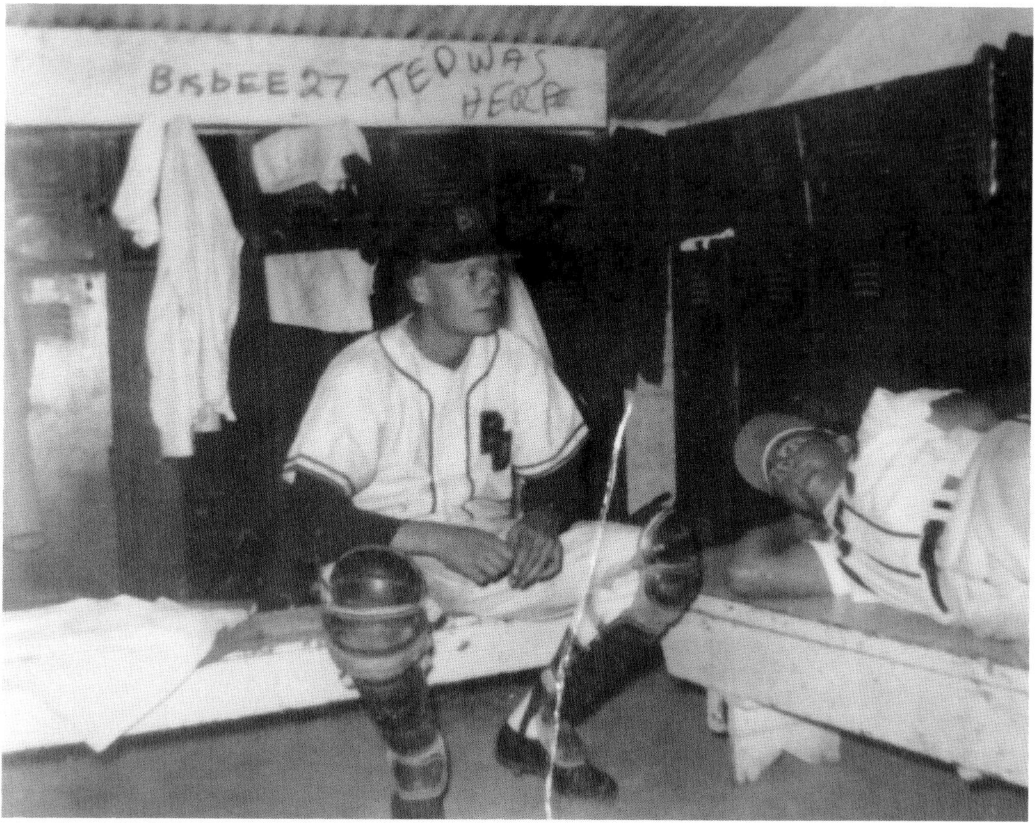

Copper Kings catcher Vern Highfield relaxes for a moment in the Warren Ballpark locker room. Highfield played for Bisbee-Douglas during the 1951, 1953, and 1954 seasons.

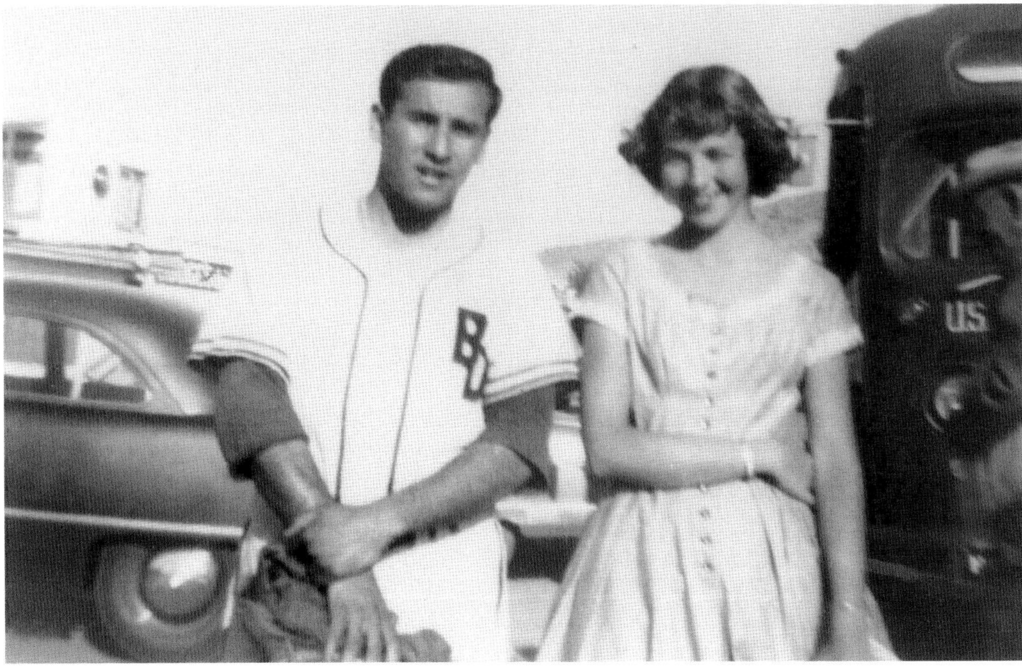

Manuel "Blackie" Morales had many fans during his six years as a right-handed pitcher with the Bisbee-Douglas Copper Kings. The Mexican-born Morales went 24-12 on the mound for the 1951 Copper Kings and finished the season with a 3.30 earned run average. His batting average with the young ladies was reportedly quite high as well.

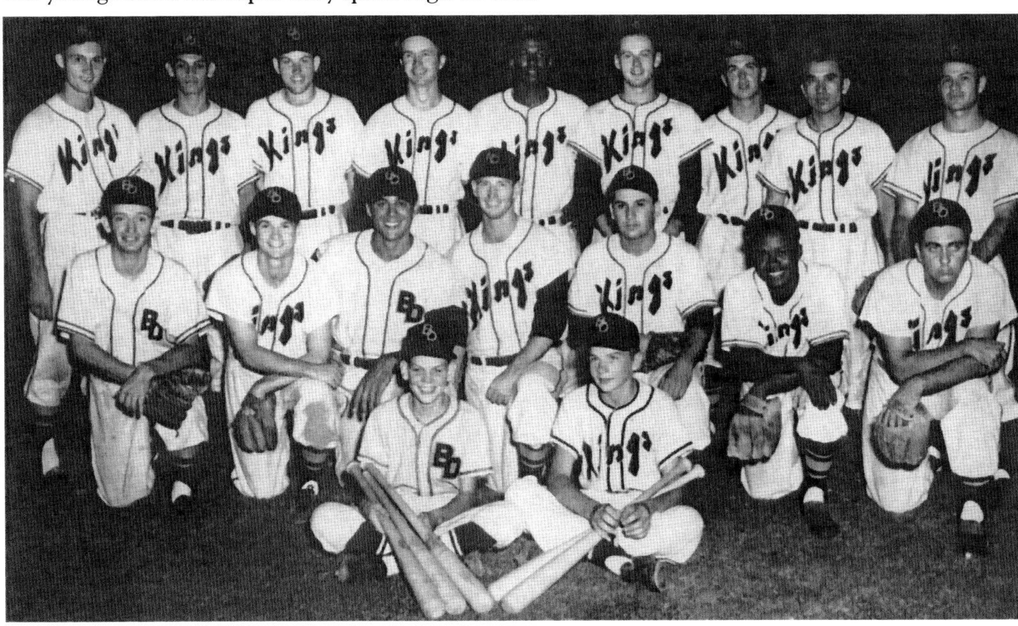

The 1955 Bisbee-Douglas Copper Kings were the last minor league team to play at Warren Ballpark until 2003. Declining attendance caused many minor league teams to fold or relocate in the 1950s. (Author's collection.)

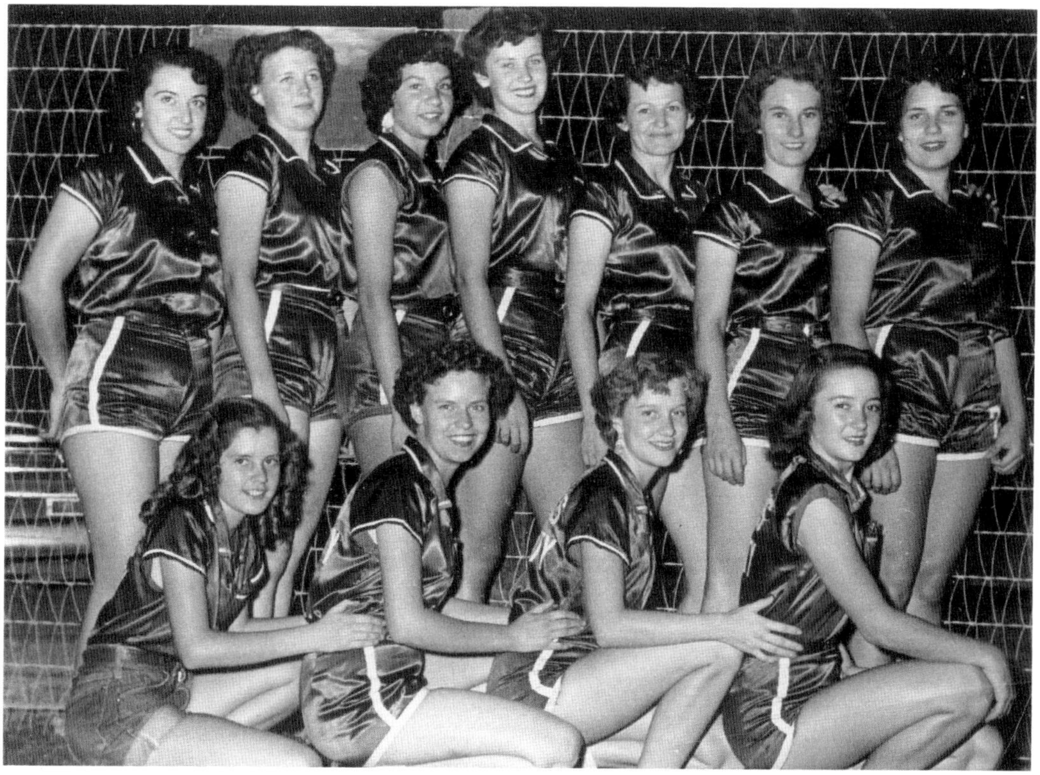

Women played fast-pitch softball with skill and verve at Warren Ballpark, usually in conjunction with a men's baseball event. The Bisbee Copper Queens, sponsored by Hargis Insurance, were one of several fine women's softball teams that played in Bisbee in the 1940s and 1950s. (Courtesy Snoody Borowiec.)

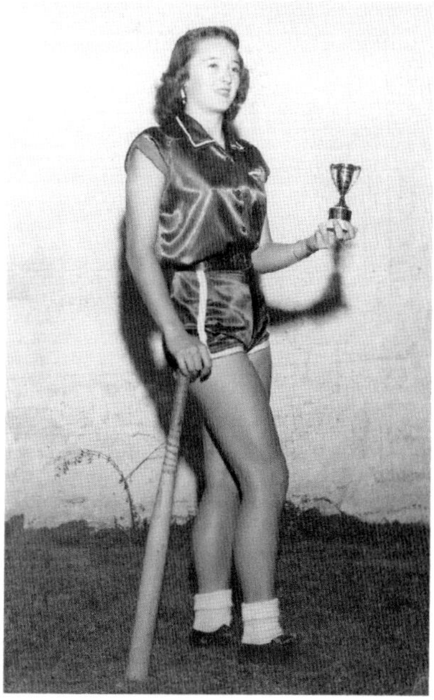

Copper Queen shortstop Charlene Pelot was the all-tournament shortstop at the 1954 Cochise County women's softball tournament. Better known to the people of Bisbee and the rest of Cochise County as Snoody Borowiec, she is very active in Bisbee Alumni Association activities and regularly assists at high school sporting events. (Courtesy Snoody Borowiec.)

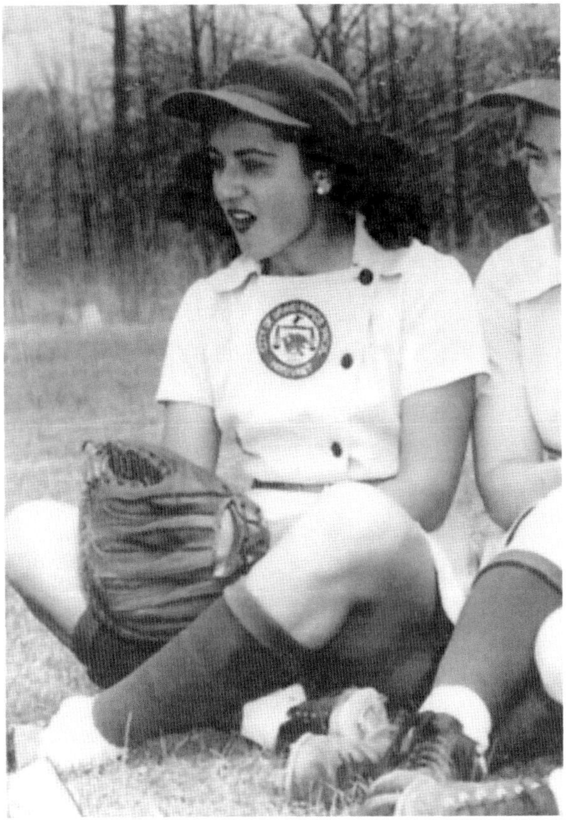

Betty Bays was good enough to play baseball with the boys. She was also signed by the legendary All-American Girls Professional Baseball League, playing catcher for the Grand Rapids Chicks, Springfield Sallies, and the Chicago Colleens in 1950 and 1951. Before leaving for the pros, Bays worked out at Warren Ballpark with her brother George, a pitcher with the Bisbee Pumas. (Courtesy Greg Shuller.)

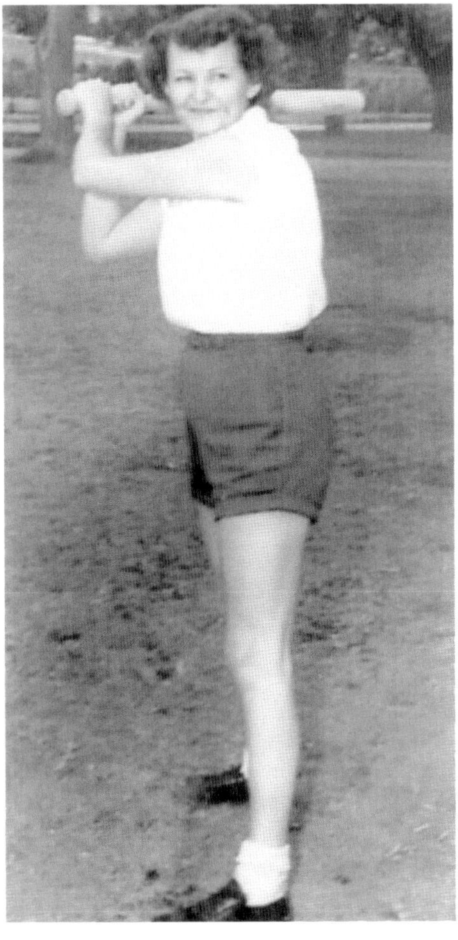

Ann Mihelich hit .620 in the 1946 fast-pitch softball season and made national news by hitting .760 in the first 20 games of the 1947 season. She was signed by the Rockford Peaches of the All-American Girls Professional Baseball League and played for the Bisbee Copper Queens traveling softball team. She later married Bisbee-Douglas Copper Queen pitcher Bob Henry, who she met at a softball game in Bisbee. (Courtesy Ann Henry.)

6

Puma Pride

Bisbee High school teams have played at Warren Ballpark since the facility was built in 1909. The Pumas' legendary football rivalry with Douglas High School began in 1906, when Bisbee defeated the Bulldogs 7-6. In 1909, Bisbee defeated Douglas 11-5 in the first Turkey Day game played at Warren Ballpark. Walter and John O'Malley scored touchdowns for the Pumas in that game, which was billed—with a bit of hyperbole—as the championship of the southwest.

The glory days for Bisbee football were the 1950s and 1960s, when the Pumas won three of their four unofficial state championships; all before the modern playoff system was developed. They had many stellar players over the decades, who set records for rushing, passing, scoring, and crowd thrilling at Bisbee High School.

Garner Barnett rushed for 240 yards and scored five touchdowns against Douglas during the Armistice Day rivalry game in 1940. All-American Hadley Hicks gained 480 yards, scored 44 touchdowns, and kicked 34 extra points during his four years on the varsity squad.

Quarterback Ted Sorich led the Pumas to back-to-back unofficial state championships in 1954 and 1955. Doug Knipp scored twice and threw a touchdown pass to lead Bisbee to a 21-19 win over the Bulldogs in the 1959 Turkey Day game.

The Puma baseball team has also proved to be a winner with the crowd every year, picking up five state championships along the way. Bisbee's first state title came in 1947 when the Pumas edged Tempe 2-1 for the Class B crown. Bisbee picked up its next state baseball title in 1966, when coach Dick Atkinson's Pumas downed Agua Fria 2-0.

Although Bisbee's athletic fortunes declined after the mines shut down in 1974, the Pumas have clawed their way back to competitiveness and, since the 1990s, to excellence. In 1993, Bisbee, under coach Mike Frosco and his staff, defeated Florence 8-5 to win the 2A state crown. The Pumas grabbed additional state baseball championships in 2002 and 2008. It is a rare year when Bisbee fails to qualify for the state playoffs in baseball.

Bisbee High School is now a much smaller school than Douglas, but the two teams continue to meet each year on the gridiron to battle for the Copper Pick. The Pumas last won the trophy in 2010, and each game, whether played in Bisbee or in Douglas, is a hotly contested and heavily attended event.

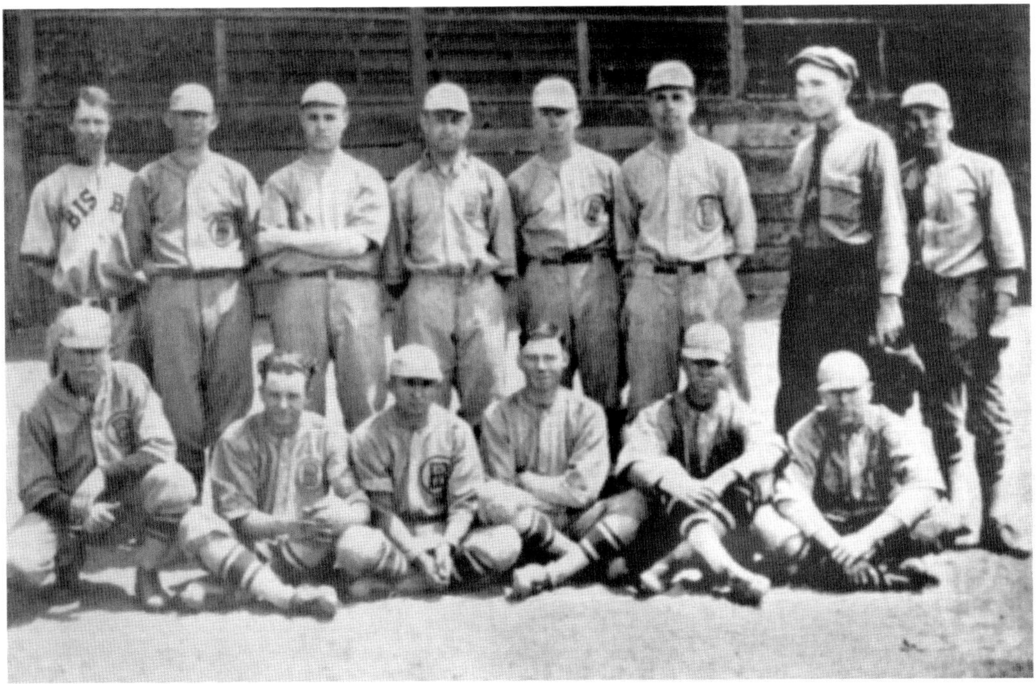

The 1921 Bisbee High School varsity baseball team included John B. "Button" Salmon (first row, second from left), a popular student and multisport star who became a legend at the University of Arizona (see page 104).

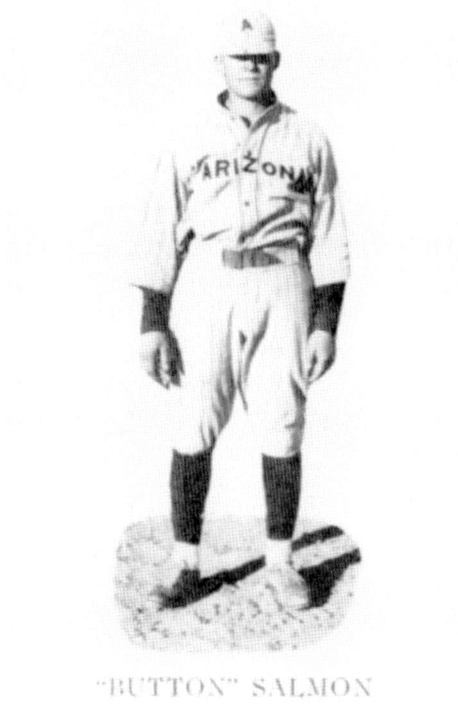

Salmon enrolled as a student at the University of Arizona in 1923, making the varsity baseball team as a catcher in 1924. He was considered by coaches and teammates to be a good prospect for professional baseball. (Courtesy Arizona Athletics photography.)

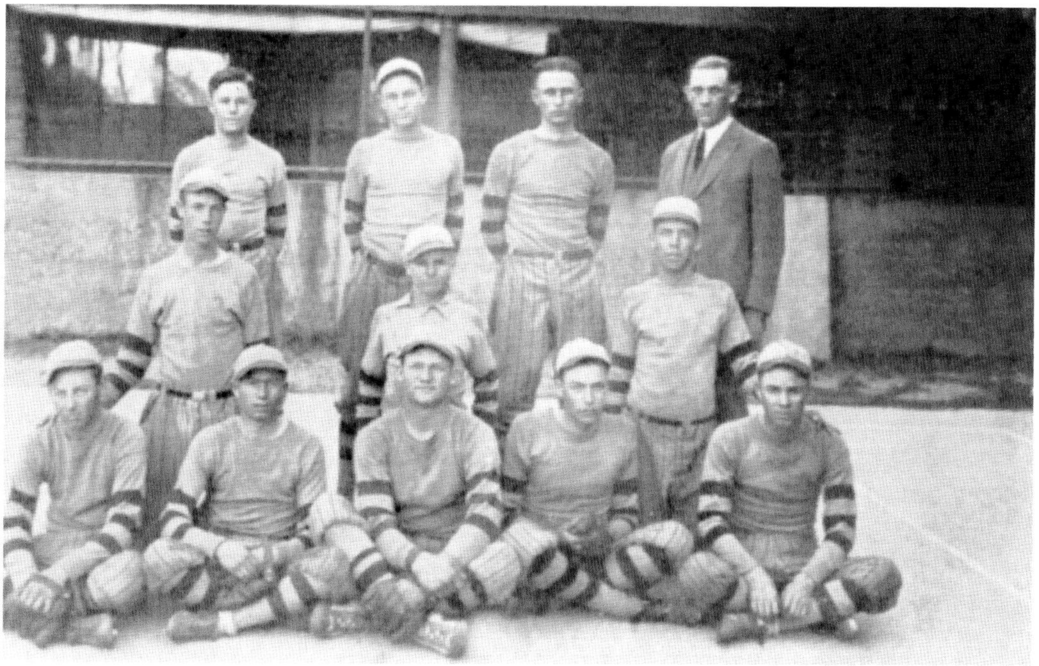

Bisbee High School's 1924 baseball team was light on numbers, but held their own in play against other teams in southern Arizona. High school baseball teams played half as many games in the 1920s as they do today.

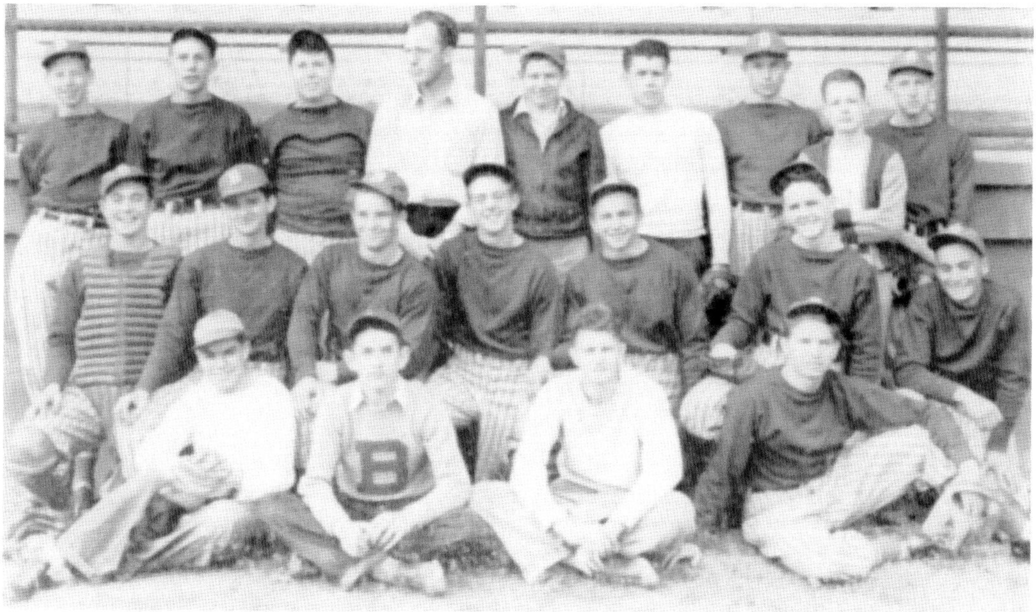

The 1939 varsity baseball team was the first Bisbee High School baseball team to take the field since 1934, when the program was put on hold because of hard economic times. The team went 8-1 during the season. The players had evidently kept up their skills playing sandlot ball and softball.

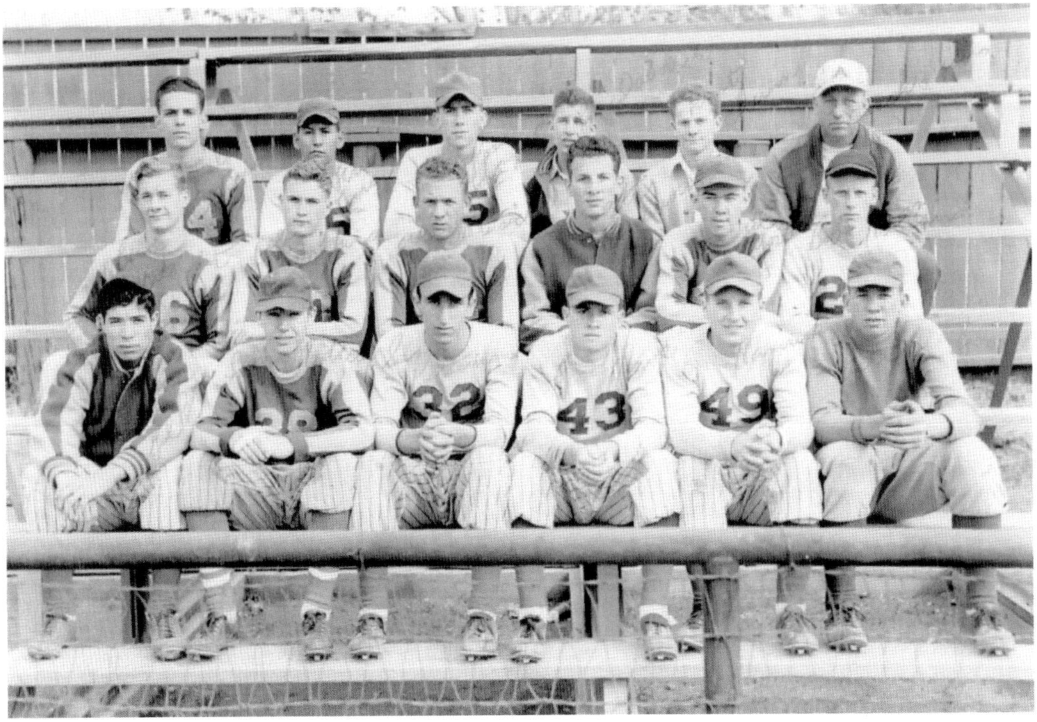

The 1947 Bisbee High School varsity baseball team was the first in the history of the school to win a state baseball championship. The Pumas, coached by Waldo Dicus, defeated Tempe High School 2-1 to capture the Class B crown. (Courtesy Pete Vucurevich.)

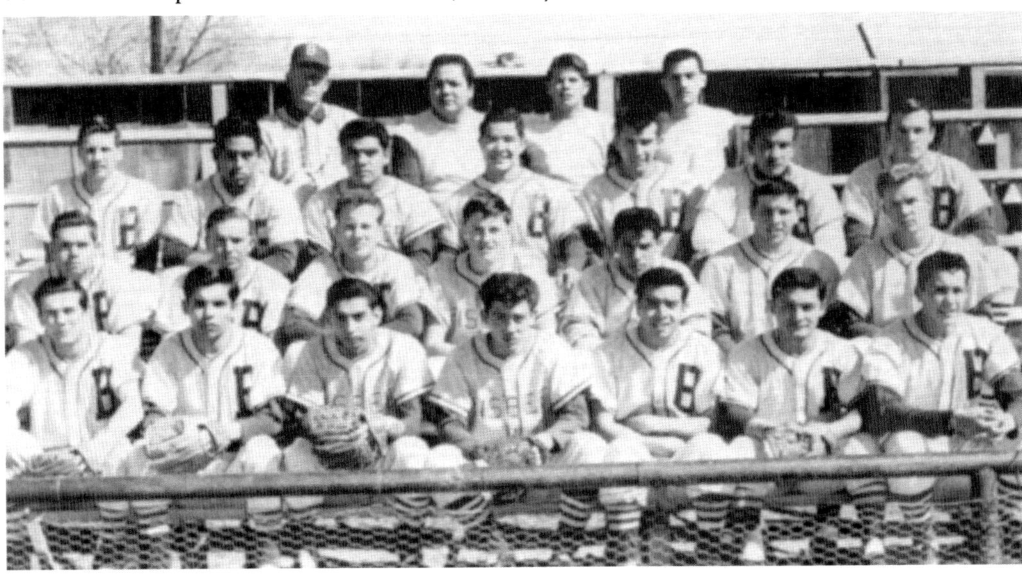

The 1966 Puma baseball team, under varsity coach Dick Atkinson, defeated Agua Fria 2-0 to capture Bisbee's second state title. The team went 20-3 on their way to the championship. It was Atkinson's first and only year as a Bisbee coach. He went on to coach baseball for Cochise College for 12 years. (Courtesy Mike Frosco.)

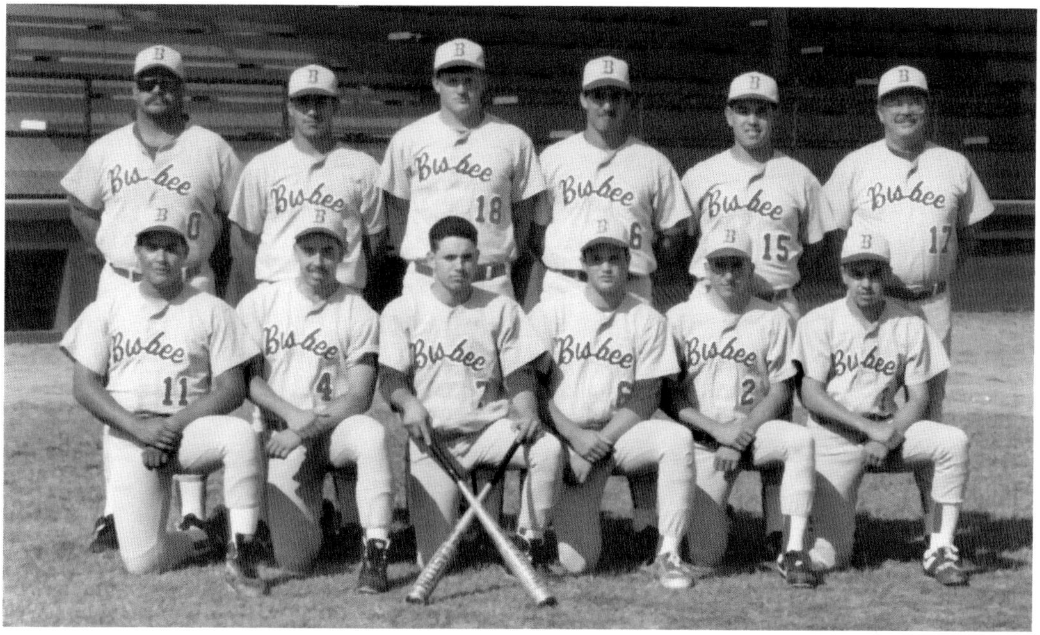

Although they did not win the 2A state baseball championship in 1992, the Pumas finished their season with a 20-4 record. It was an indication of better things to come in the immediate future. (Courtesy Mike Frosco.)

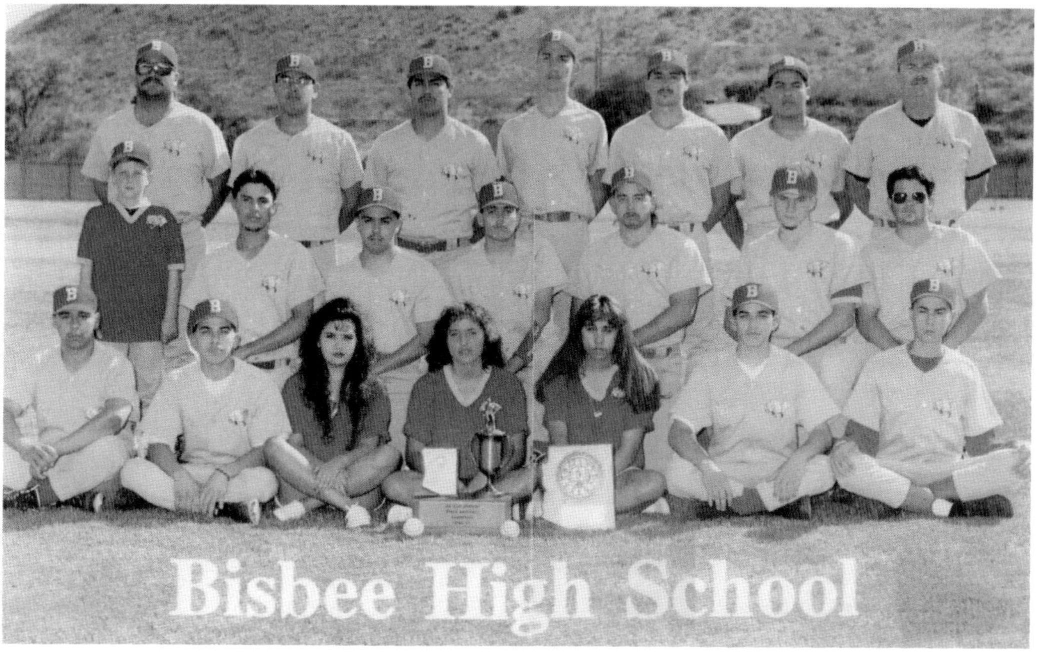

After years in the athletic wilderness following the 1974 shutdown of the copper mines, Bisbee High School's baseball team reached the top again in 1993. Varsity coach Mike Frosco and assistant coach Butch Hammett guided the Pumas to a 20-6 record and the state 2A baseball championship, with Bisbee downing Florence 8-5. (Courtesy Mike Frosco.)

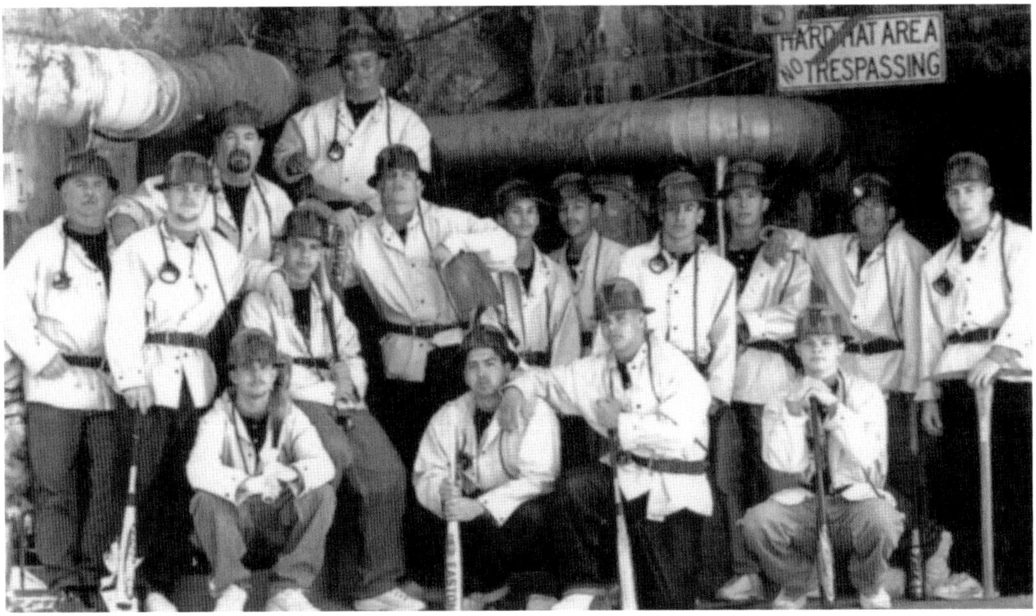

They may look like hard-rock miners, but these players are holding bats instead of drills and double jacks. The 2002 Pumas had this team photograph taken at Bisbee's Queen Mine Tour after they clinched their fourth state baseball championship when Mike Frosco came out of retirement to coach the Pumas to a 13-3 win over Thatcher in the 2A finals. (Courtesy Mike Frosco.)

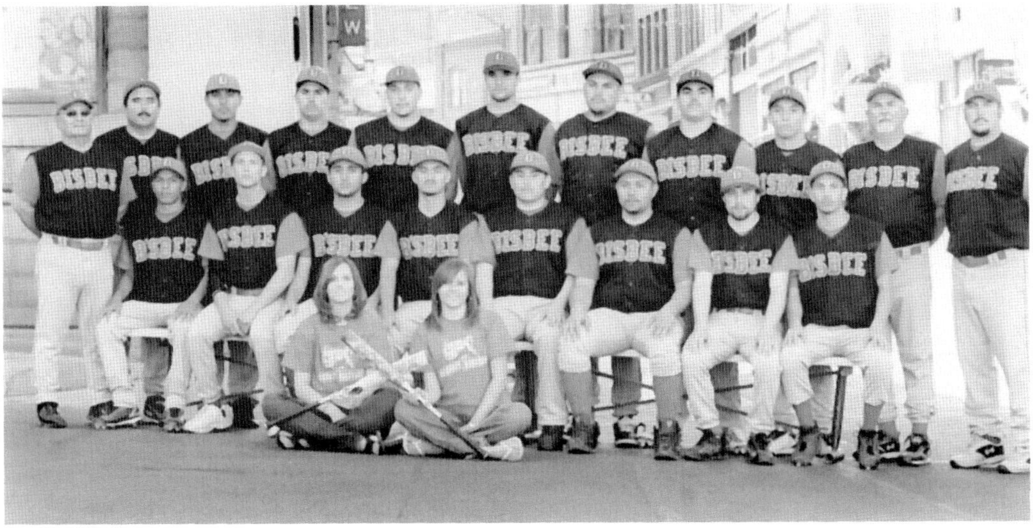

Bisbee earned its last state baseball crown to date in 2008 when the Frosco-led Pumas defeated Bourgade Catholic 9-8. Bisbee teams still qualify for the state playoffs on a frequent basis and baseball remains a very popular sport with Bisbee High School students and with fans in the community. (Courtesy Mike Frosco.)

Mike Frosco is approaching his 500th win as the varsity baseball head coach of the Pumas. A four-year letterman at Bisbee High School, he was named the coach of the year in 2008 by the Arizona Baseball Coaches Association. Frosco was inducted into the AZBCA Hall of Fame in 2005. (Author's collection.)

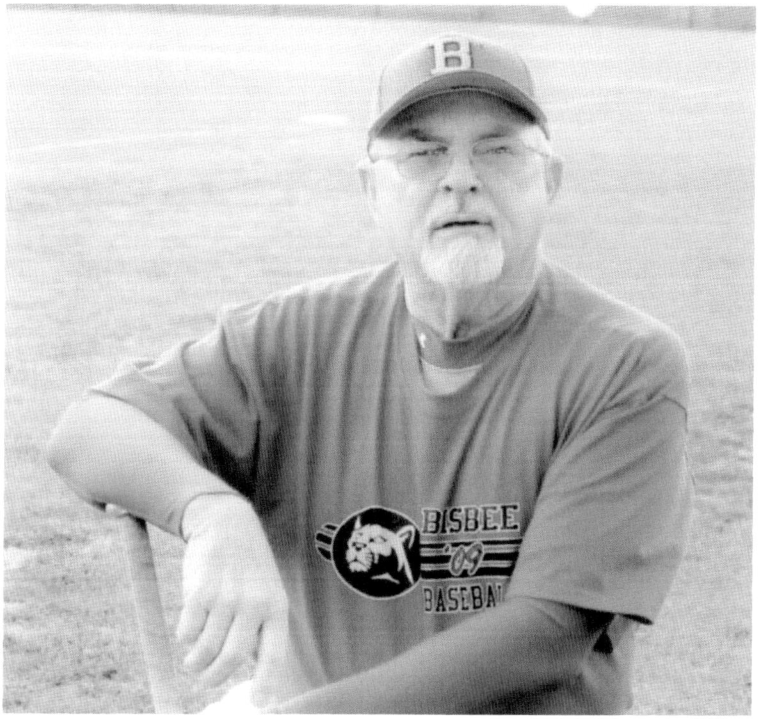

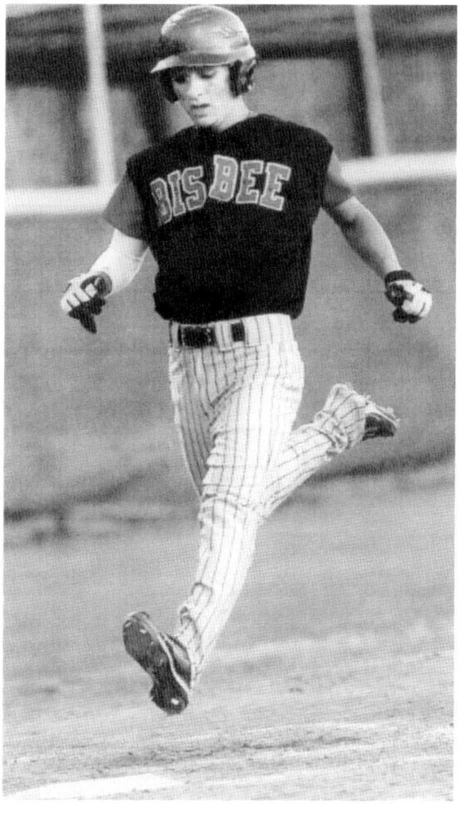

Center fielder Anthony Escalante plants his foot on home plate during a game at Warren Ballpark in 2012. As a Class 2A school, Bisbee plays southeastern Arizona schools such as Tombstone, Willcox, Thatcher, and Morenci. The Pumas have been playing against those teams and against their archrivals in Douglas for more than a century.

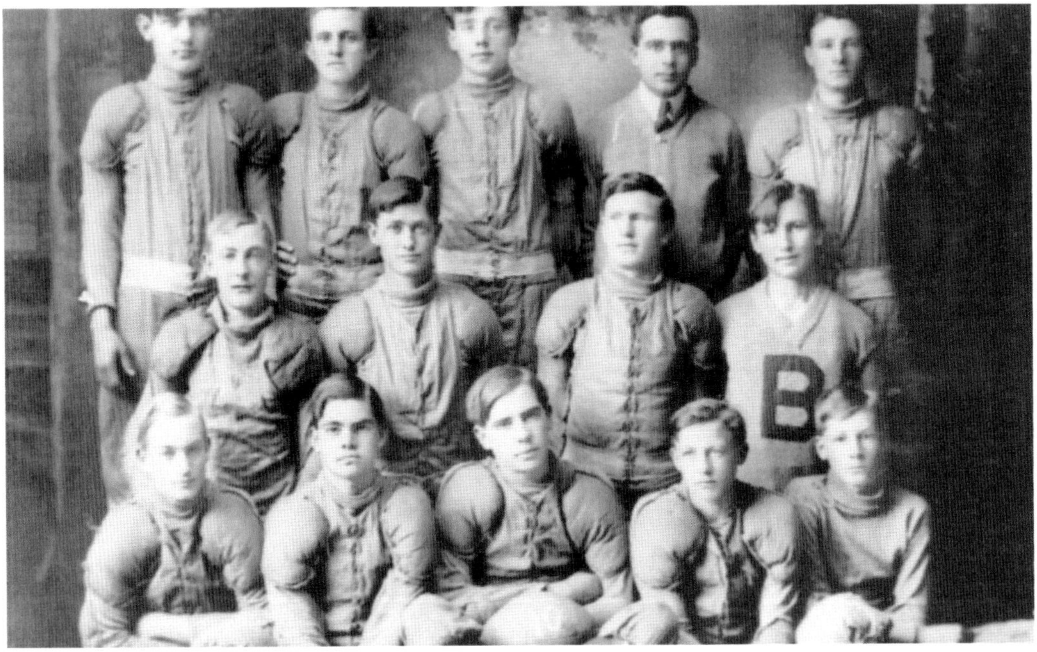

The 1910 Bisbee football team included Webb Hicks (second row, far left), Roswell Champion (second row, second from left), and Thomas Kriegbaum (first row, second from left). All three were star football players who also played baseball for Bisbee's high school and semiprofessional teams. The coach in this photograph is Pat "H.C." Henry (third row, second from right).

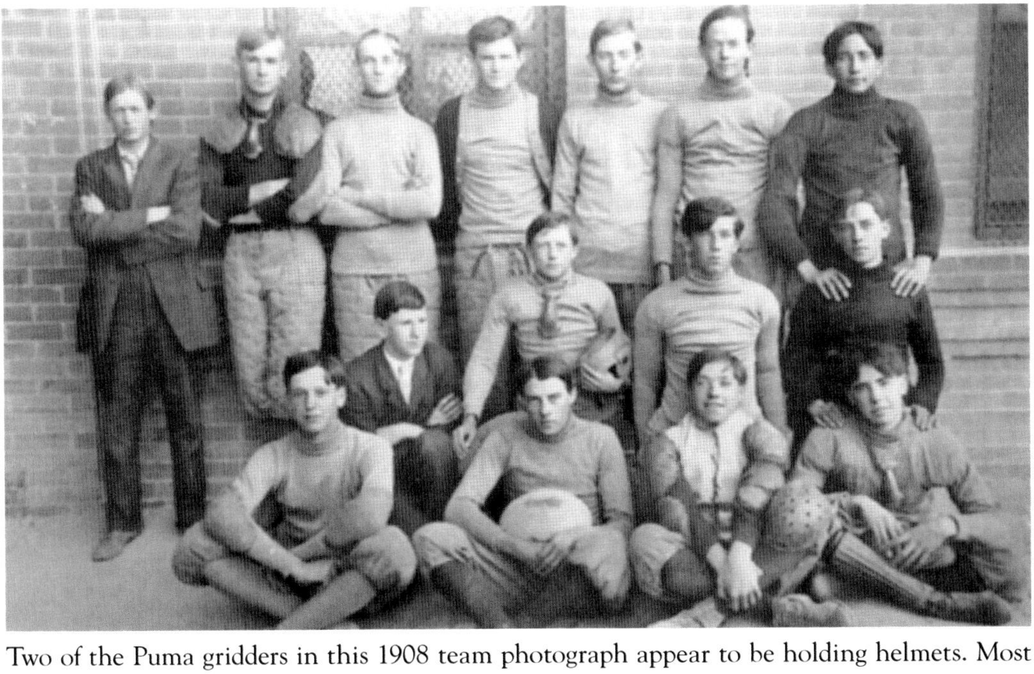

Two of the Puma gridders in this 1908 team photograph appear to be holding helmets. Most football players did not wear helmets at that time, and injuries were frequent and often severe. Helmet-less players often wore their hair long to cushion blows to their heads.

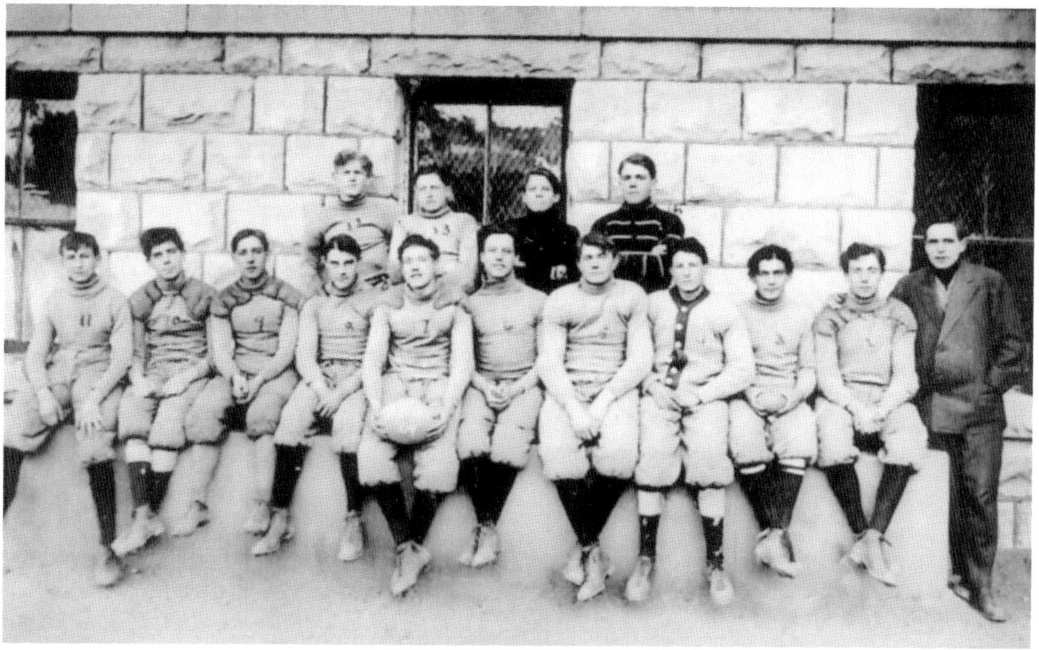

Football was played at Warren Ballpark within three months of the stadium's completion in 1909. The Puma varsity team defeated Douglas 11-5 on Thanksgiving Day, 1909, the first time the rivalry game was played on their new home field.

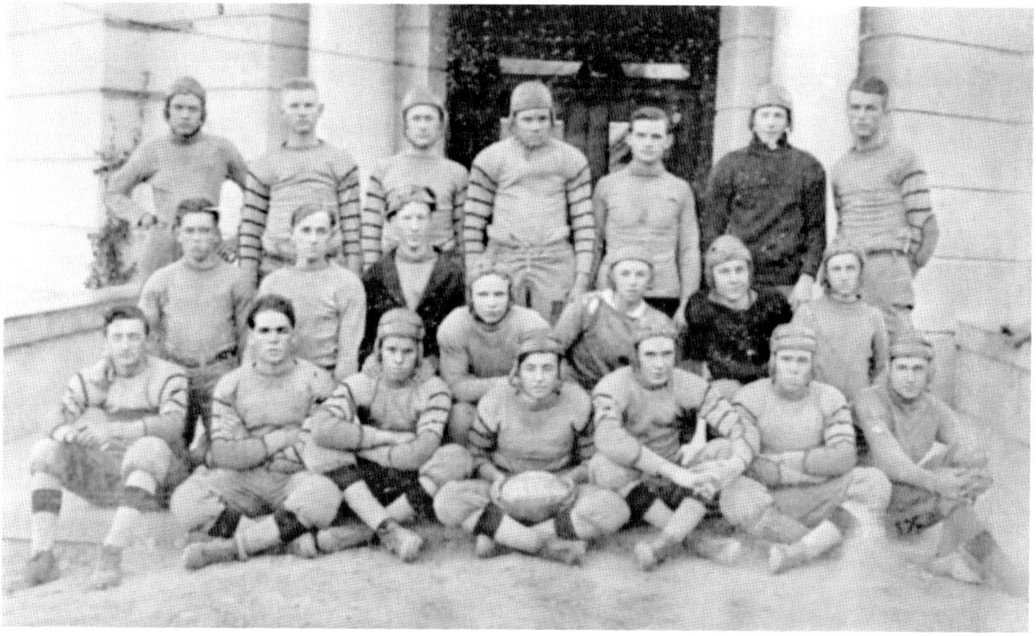

By 1917, all high school football players were wearing helmets. The 1917 Bisbee football team posed for its team photograph in front of the newly constructed high school. The 1917 varsity team took on archrival Douglas, Tucson High School, several Army teams, and a high school faculty team.

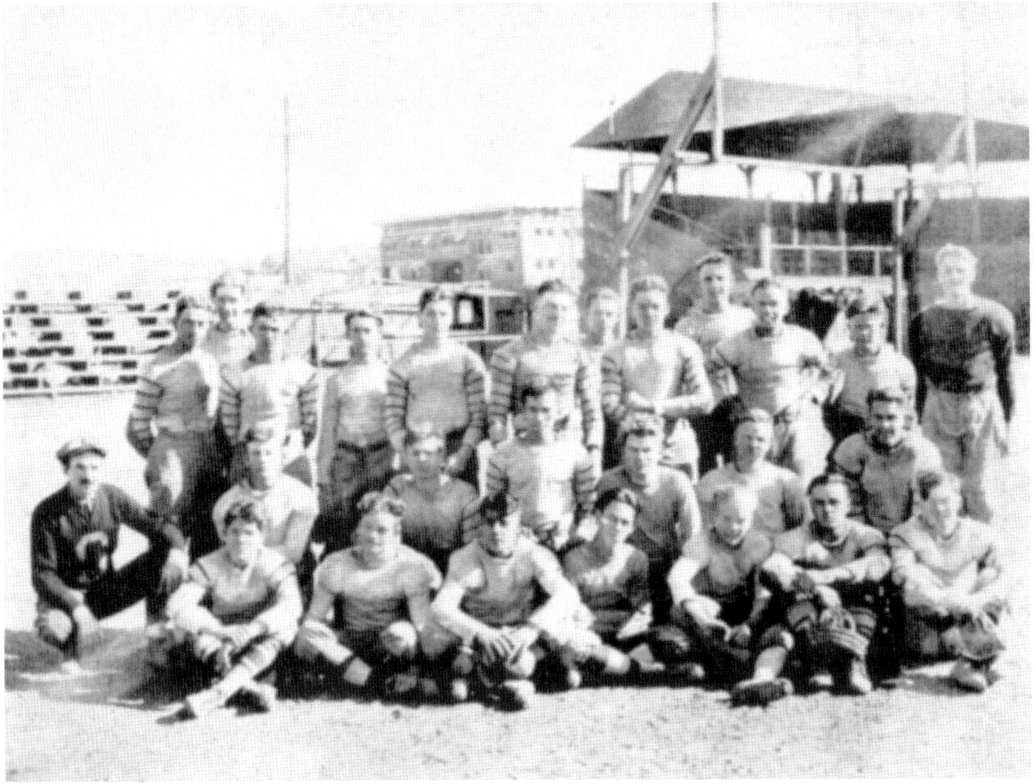

The 1920 Pumas had their team photograph taken in front of the old wooden baseball grandstands at Warren Ballpark. In the first row, second from left, is John Byrd "Button" Salmon, whose compact size, shock of unruly red hair, and wide grin belied his physical toughness and keen competitiveness.

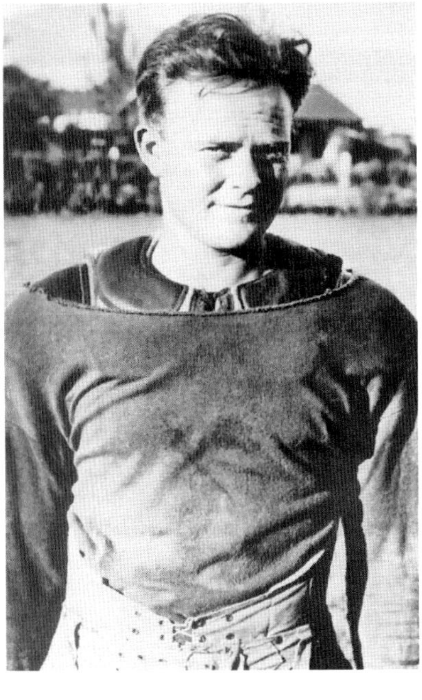

In 1926, "Button" Salmon was the student body president at the University of Arizona and the backup quarterback. While traveling back to Tucson from a practice game, the car Salmon and his friends were riding in overturned. Paralyzed from the neck down, Salmon lingered for two weeks before passing away. When asked if he had any message for his teammates, Salmon replied, "Tell the team to bear down." Salmon's deathbed message was the inspiration for the University of Arizona fight song and adorned Bear Down Gym. Salmon's bust stands outside the McKale Center on the campus. (Courtesy Arizona Athletics Photography.)

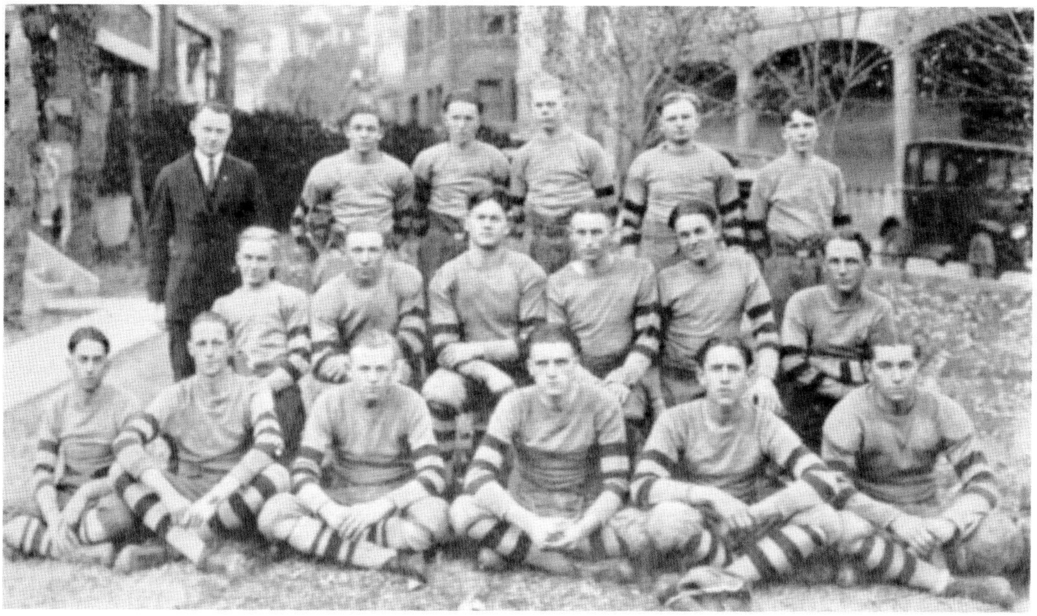

The boys on the 1924 Bisbee football team appear larger in size and more physically mature than the players on earlier teams. High school and college football increased in popularity in the 1920s, and it is likely that the pool of players was larger than in previous years, as boys from well-to-do families began taking up the game.

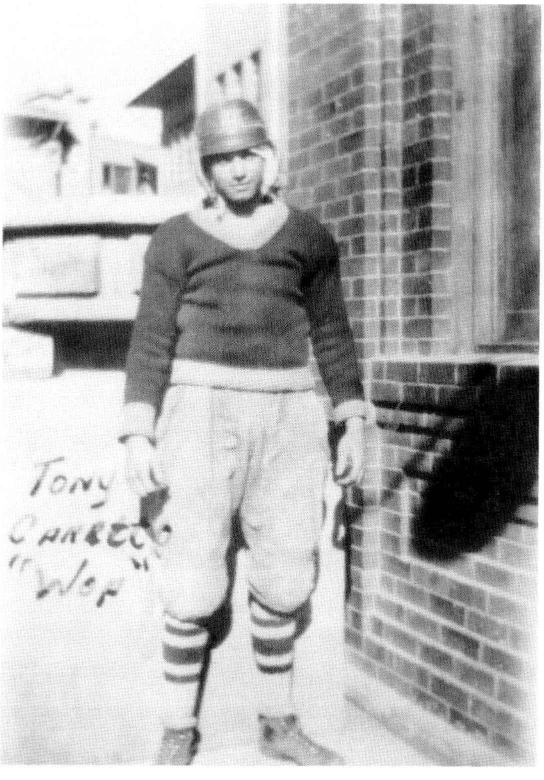

Tony Carretto, a member of the 1924 Puma team, was nicknamed "Wop" in the politically incorrect 1920s. He was the son of Baptisto Carretto, an Italian immigrant who rose to prominence in Bisbee as a businessman and community leader in the early 1900s.

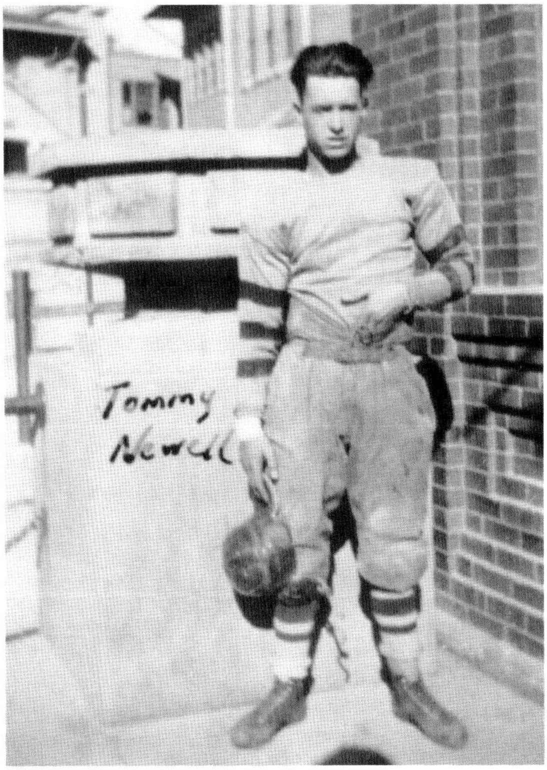

Tommy Newell, also on the 1924 Puma team, was the son of Johnny Newell, an Irish immigrant who homesteaded and ranched in the San Pedro Valley and became a prominent member of the community. Camp Naco, also known as Camp Newell, was an Army post constructed at the border town of Naco during the turmoil surrounding the Mexican revolution of 1910.

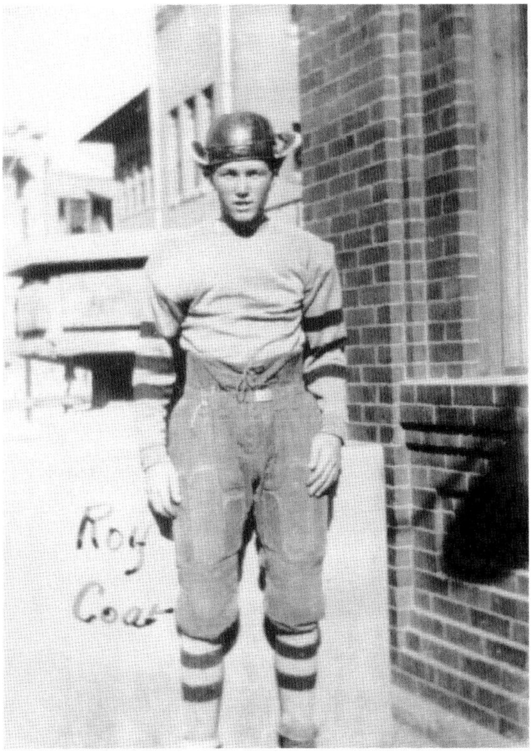

Roy Goar was also a member of the 1924 Bisbee football team. The Goar family was prominent in Bisbee during the 1920s, owning Goar Services & Supply, a business that had branches throughout the Southwest. Goar Park, at the entrance to Bisbee's Brewery Gulch, is on property where the Goars once owned and operated a garage.

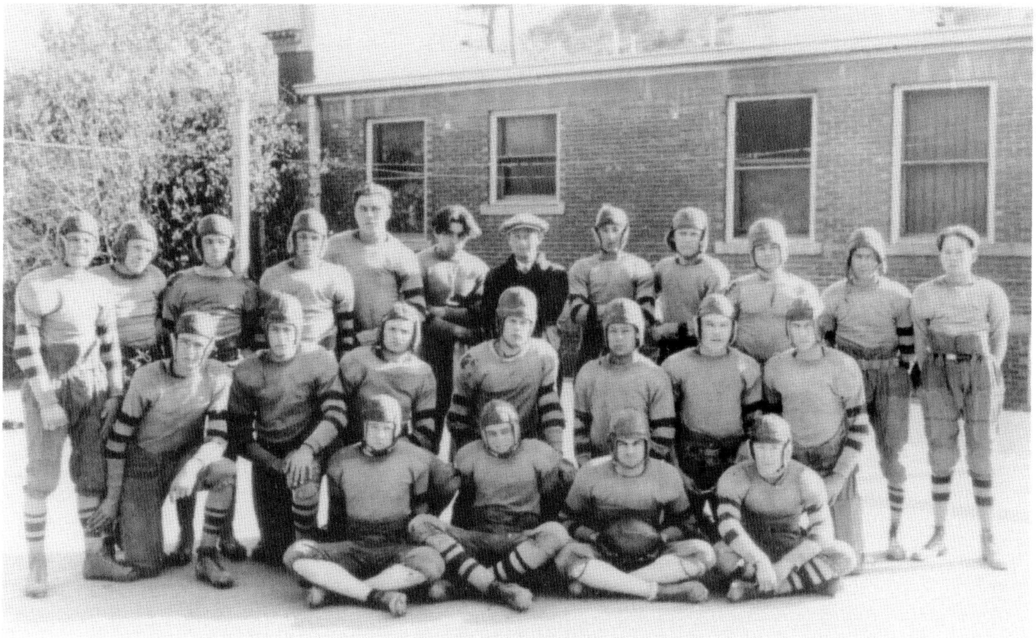

In 1926, the Pumas played teams from nearby communities such as Douglas and Tombstone. Bisbee also took on teams from other mining towns farther away, such as Clifton, Morenci, Globe, and Miami, and from bigger cities like El Paso, Tucson, and Phoenix.

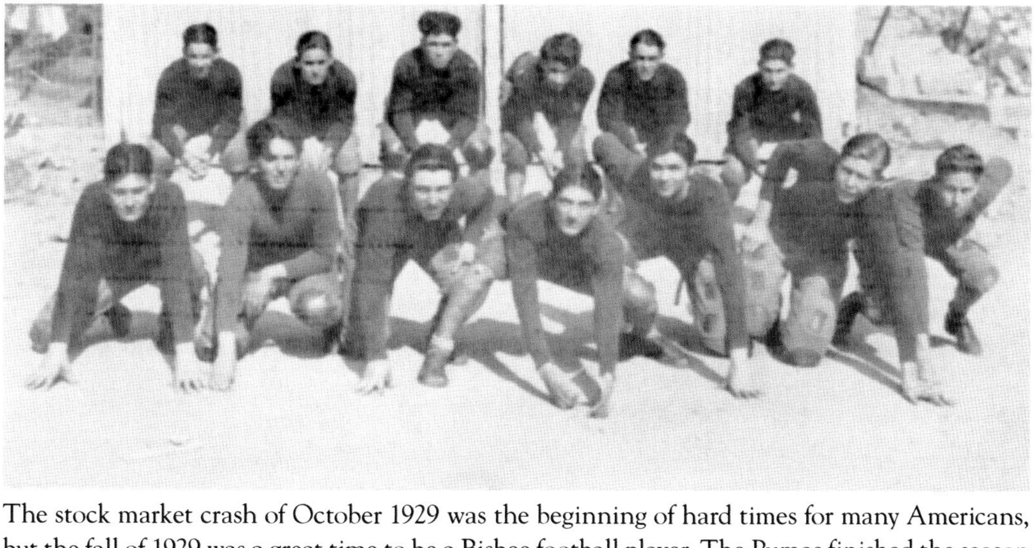

The stock market crash of October 1929 was the beginning of hard times for many Americans, but the fall of 1929 was a great time to be a Bisbee football player. The Pumas finished the season 7-1, with their only loss coming at the hands of Tucson High School. (Photograph courtesy Hall of Fame.)

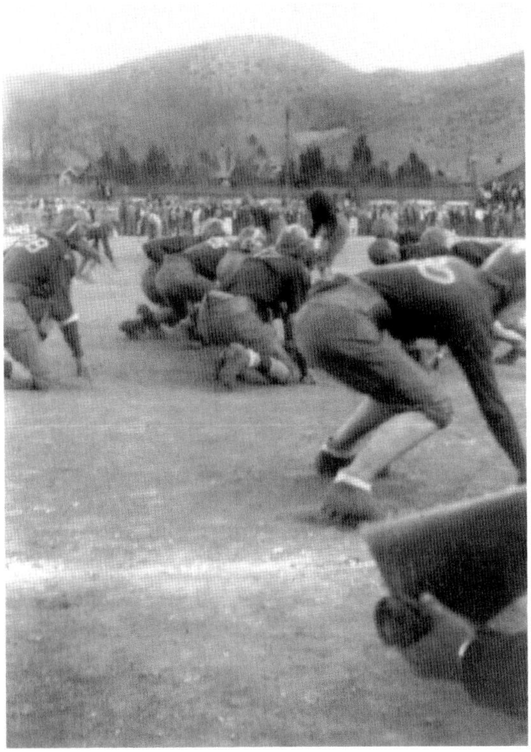

The crowd lined the field at Warren Ballpark as quarterback Johnny Hilton, sans helmet, called the signals for the 1929 Pumas. Bisbee's football team that year included star halfback Art Benko, who joined the Army Air Force in World War II and achieved national recognition as an ace aerial gunner on a B-24 bomber. Benko, who is credited with shooting down 16 Japanese aircraft, parachuted from his crippled bomber over China in November 1943 and was reported missing in action. His body was never recovered.

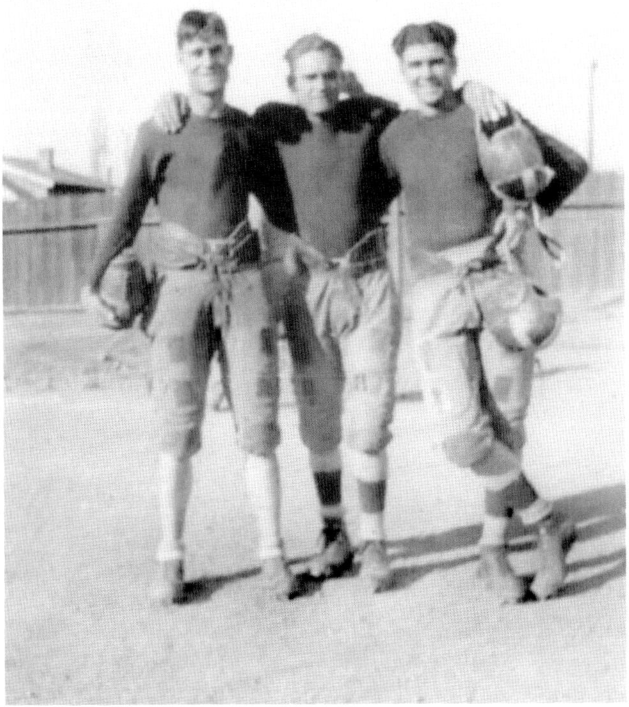

From left to right, Wes Rateree, Tom Murray, and Johnny Hilton were members of the 1929 Bisbee football team. Hilton was the team's starting quarterback. All three boys were the sons of English immigrants. Their fathers had played soccer at Warren Ballpark before World War I.

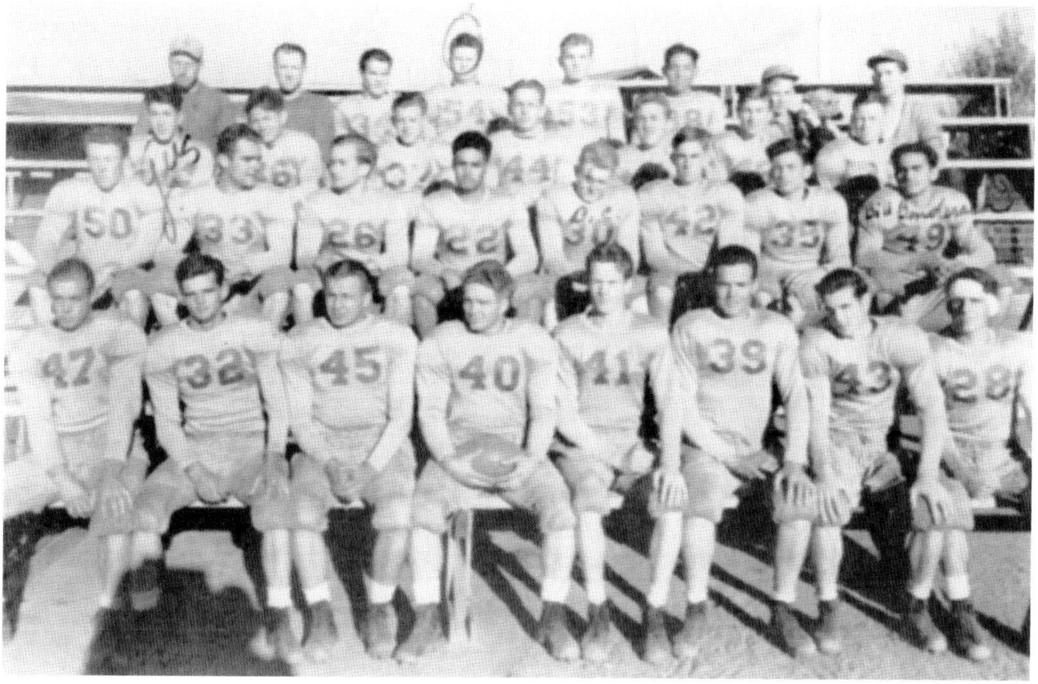

The 1940 Puma team included Garner Barnett, who scored seven touchdowns in the two games played against Douglas that year. Barnett, who later became a teacher and coach at Bisbee High School, was designated captain of the *Arizona Republic's* 1940 all-state high school football team.

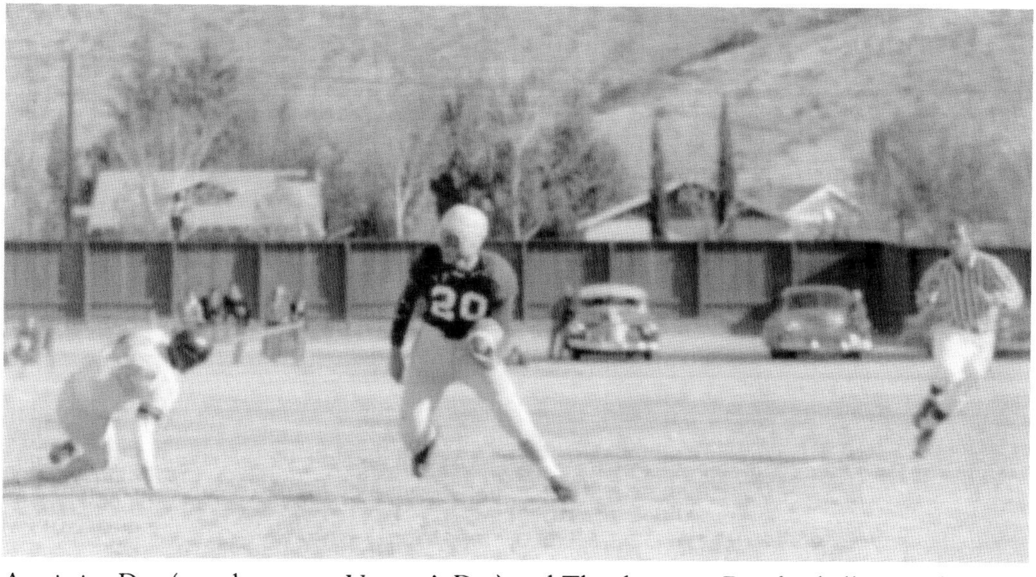

Armistice Day (now known as Veteran's Day) and Thanksgiving Day football games between Bisbee and Douglas at Warren Ballpark drew capacity crowds. A loss to Douglas put a pall over the entire community, while a win over the Bulldogs could salvage even a losing season. Fights before, during, and after the games were not uncommon. (Courtesy Hadley Hicks.)

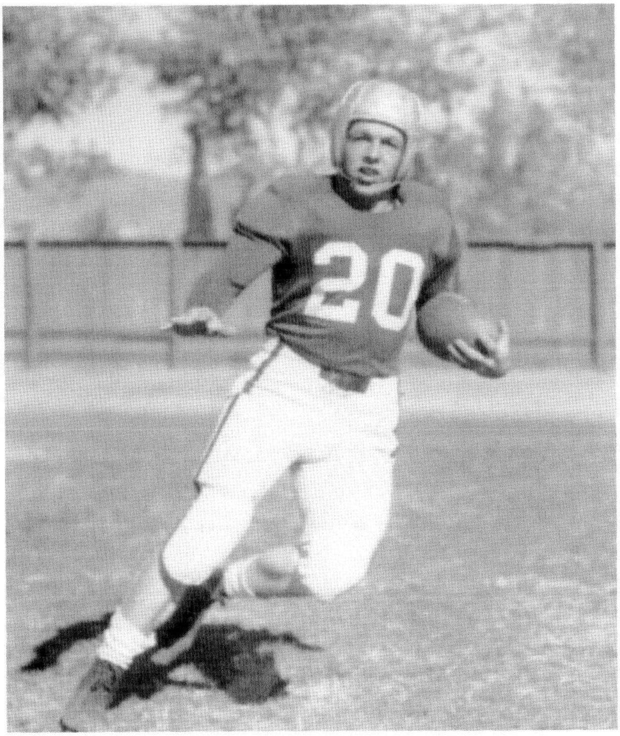

A high school All-American in football and track, Hadley Hicks was a power in the Puma backfield in the late 1940s and early 1950s. Hicks went on to become a high school teacher and coach. He is the author of *The B Shines Brighter: The Bisbee High School Legacy* and *So You Wanna Be a Legend. So Did I.: The Reflections of a Teacher-Coach, a Search for Significance.* (Courtesy Hadley Hicks.)

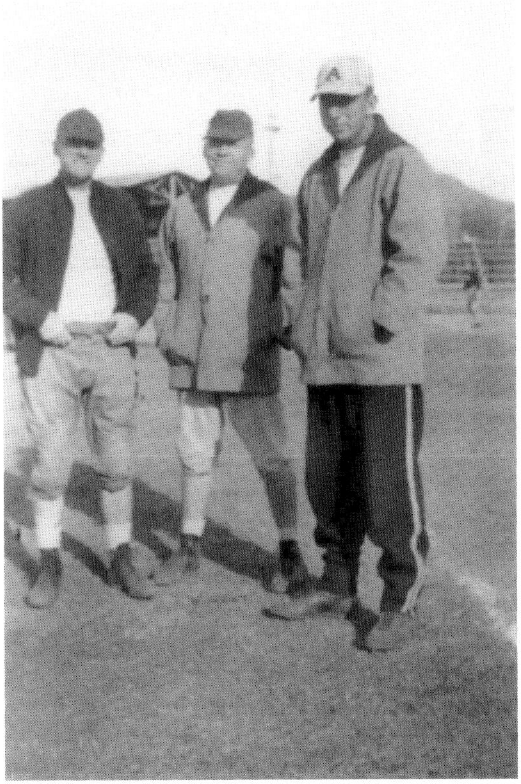

Bisbee High School was fortunate to have a series of good coaches running their football teams. In the 1940s and early 1950s, head coach Waldo Dicus (right), and his assistants Jack Miller (left), and "Fuzzy" Warren turned out tough and competitive teams for Bisbee year after year. (Courtesy Hadley Hicks.)

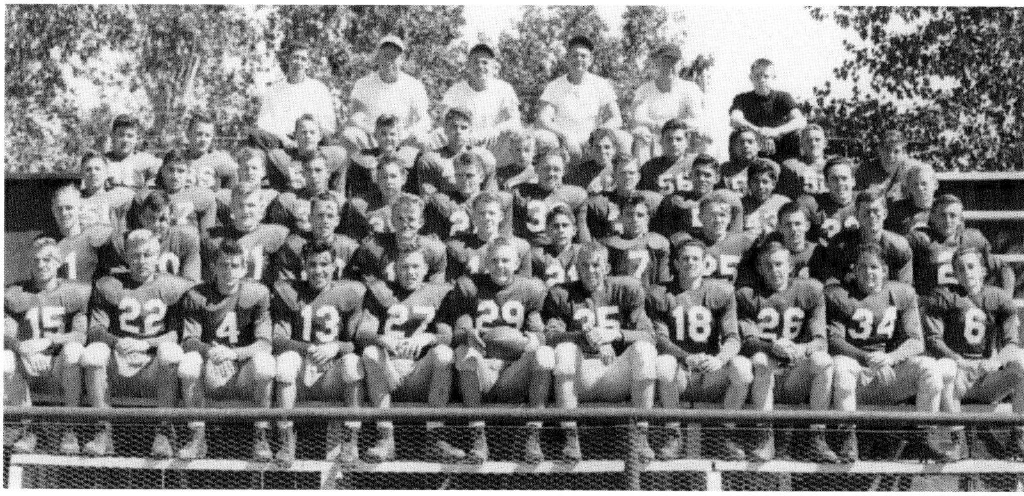

The Pumas surprised everyone but themselves in 1948 when they upset a powerful Douglas team led by the legendary future college All-American Gip Dawson. After the 25-0 win, the Copper Pick, the trophy awarded to the rivalry winners since 1944, was back in Puma hands. (Courtesy Hadley Hicks.)

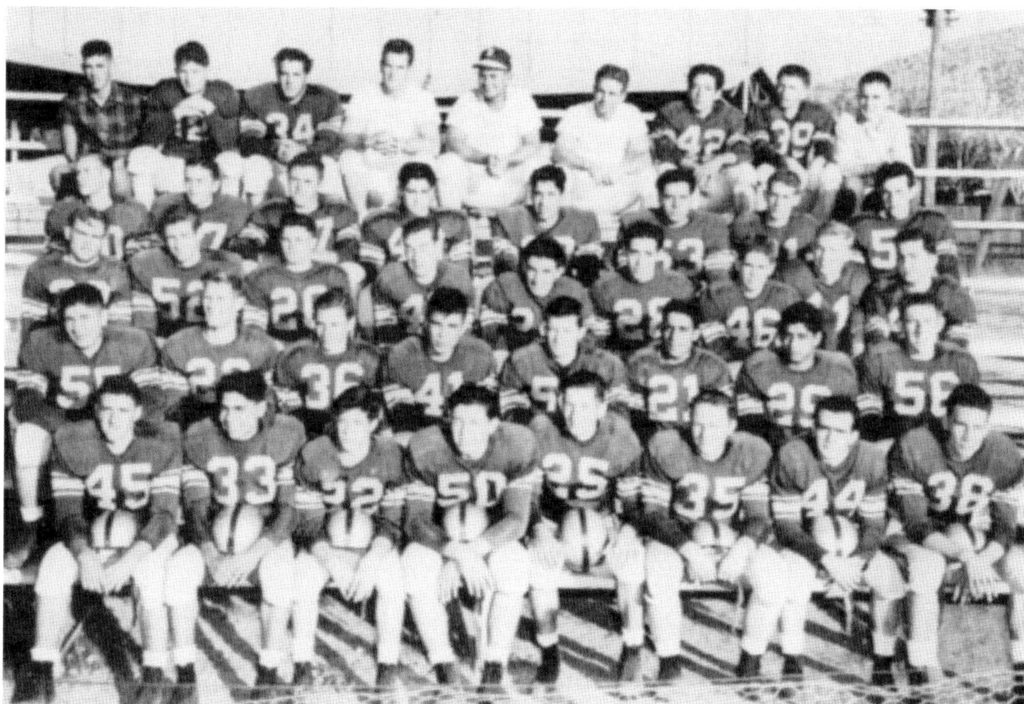

Max Spilsbury (fifth row, fourth from left) took over as varsity head coach for Waldo Dicus in 1952 and led the Pumas to new heights. A tough Marine combat veteran, Spilsbury demanded maximum effort from his players, and he got it. Spilsbury moved on to the University of Arizona and then to Arizona State College (now Northern Arizona University), where in 1958 he coached the undefeated Lumberjacks to the National Small College championship game.

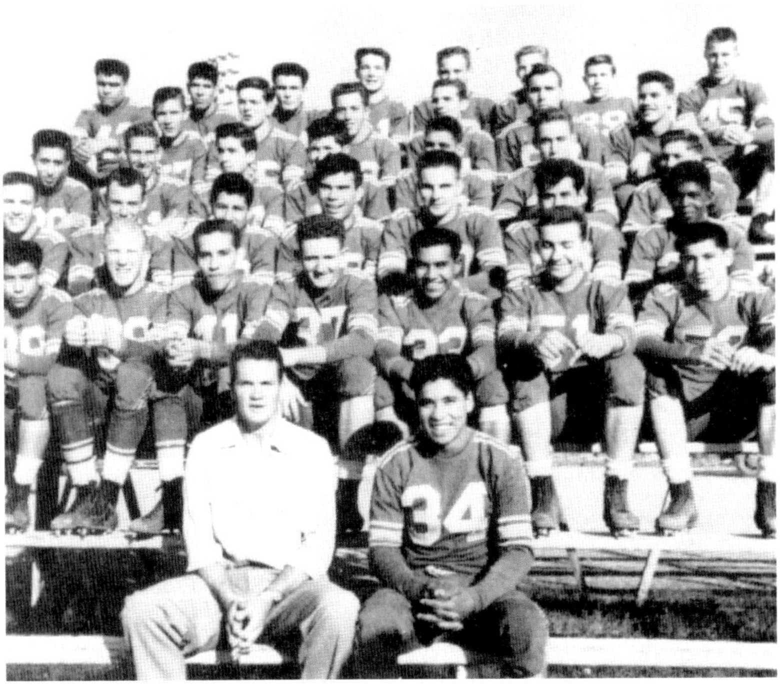

Spilsbury's 1954 Pumas were a juggernaut. They finished the year undefeated, with nine wins and a scoreless tie against Amphitheater, of Tucson. Bisbee outscored their opponents 314 to 46. Only one team, Ajo, scored more than one touchdown against the Pumas, who finished the season as unofficial Class A state champs.

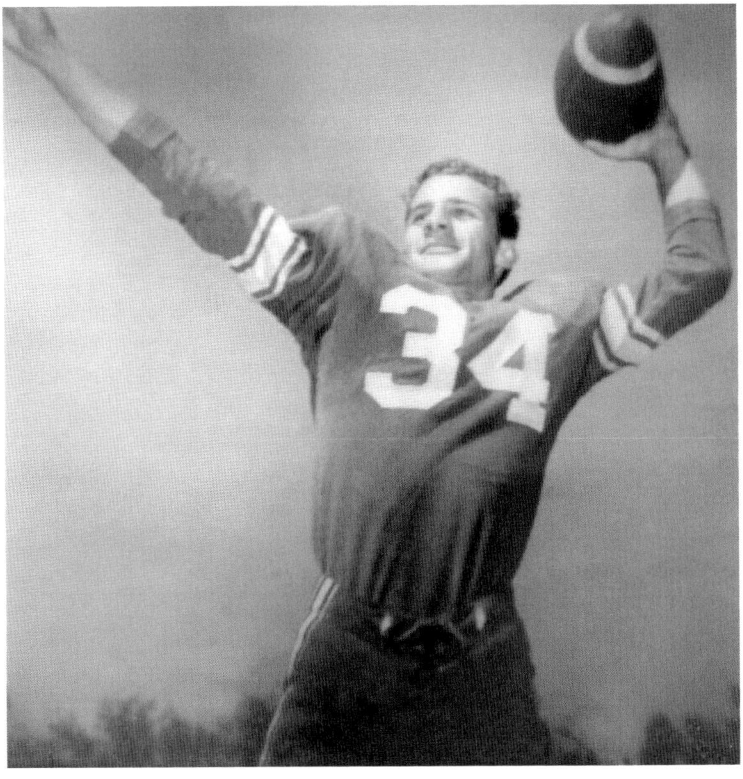

Quarterback Ted Sorich led the Pumas to a pair of conference championships and unofficial state championships in 1954 and 1955. Sorich later starred as a quarterback at Northern Arizona University under former Bisbee coach Max Spilsbury and became the athletic director at Flowing Wells High School in Tucson. (Courtesy Ted Sorich.)

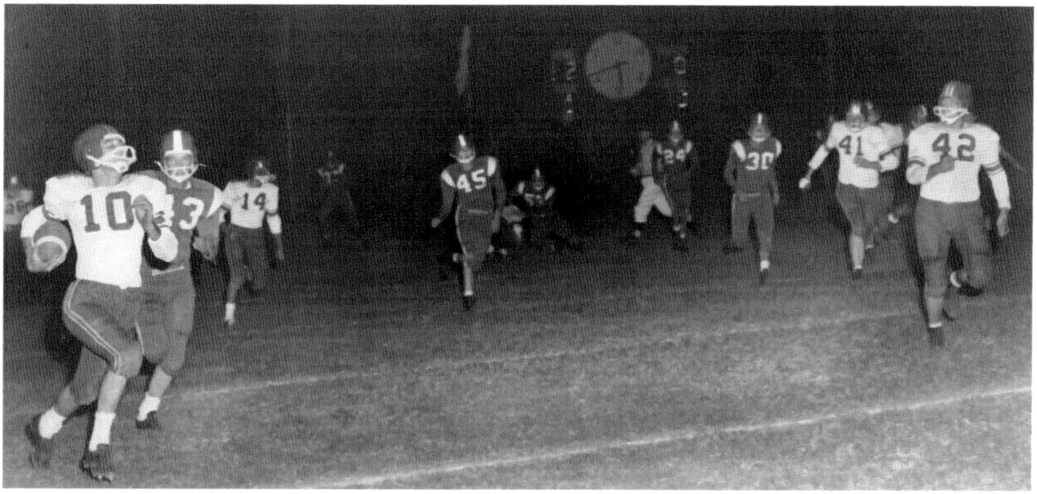

Doug Knipp, the quarterback for the Pumas in 1960, rockets downfield to a touchdown—unfortunately it was called back—in a game against the Safford Bulldogs. Bisbee crushed the Bulldogs that season, 27-0. The Pumas finished the year with seven wins, one loss, and one tie. Knipp later served as a Bisbee police officer and retired as the city's chief of police. (Courtesy Doug Knipp.)

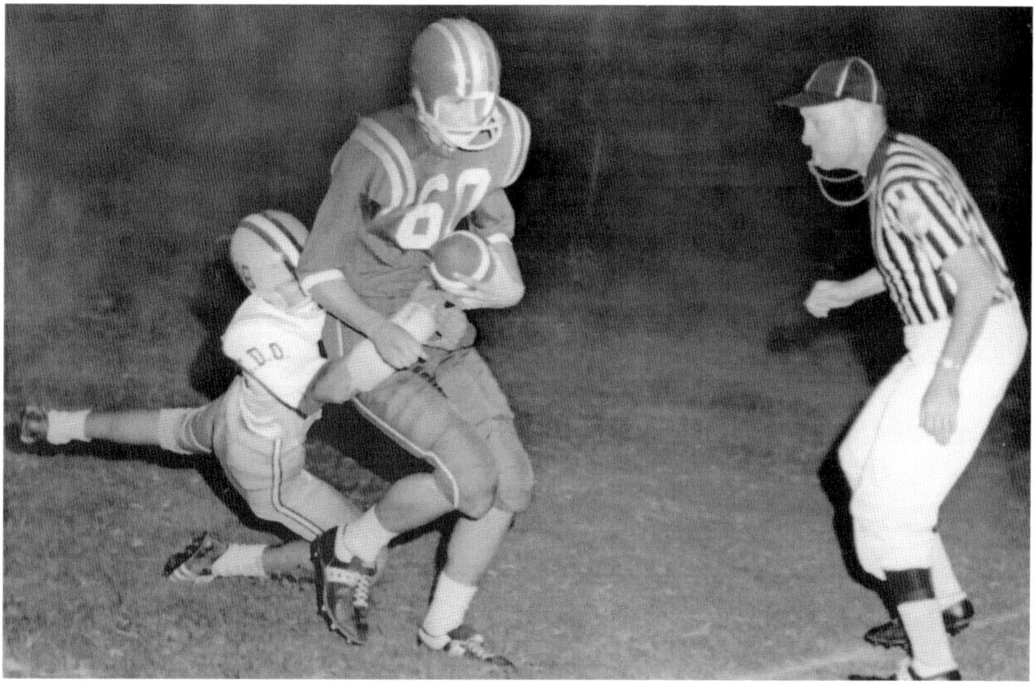

Senior quarterback Fred Giacoletti ground out yardage the hard way during a game against Canyon Del Oro in 1966. Giacoletti, the starting quarterback for the Pumas in 1964, 1965, and 1966, threw a 33-yard touchdown pass in the third quarter of this game, which ended in a 13-13 tie. Through the years, Giacoletti was a teacher, the football coach, the athletic director, the dean of students, and a school board member. (Courtesy Fred Giacoletti.)

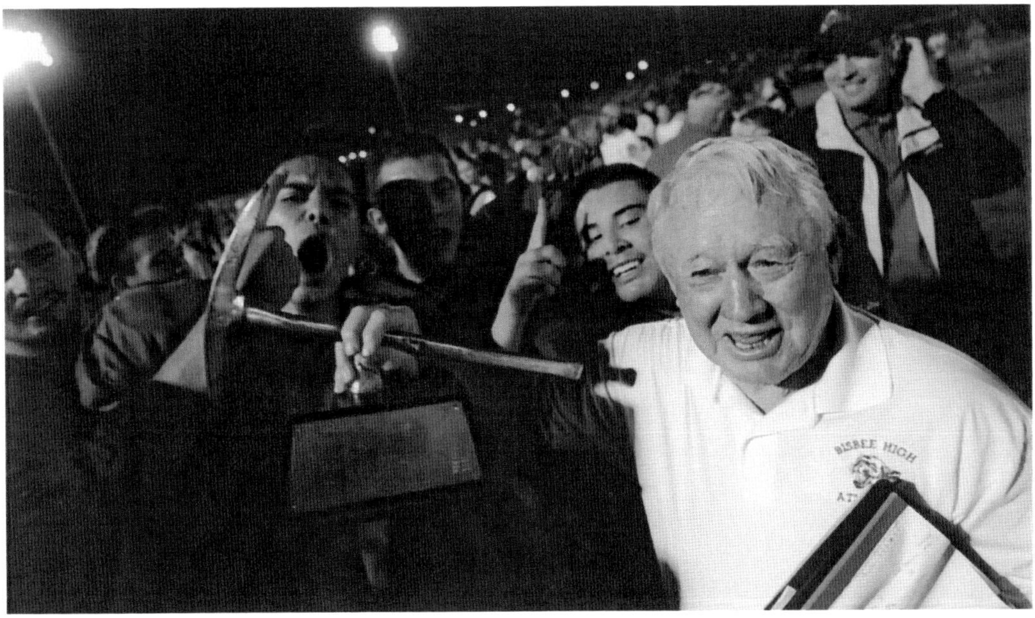

Bisbee head coach Truman Williamson proudly displays the Pick, the copper trophy awarded to the winner of the Bisbee-Douglas game, after the Pumas defeated the Bulldogs 20-19 in August 2006. The 2006 season was the first time Bisbee reached the state high school playoffs since 1963. Williamson, a beloved coach for the Pumas, died in 2010. (Courtesy *Sierra Vista Herald–Bisbee Daily Review.*)

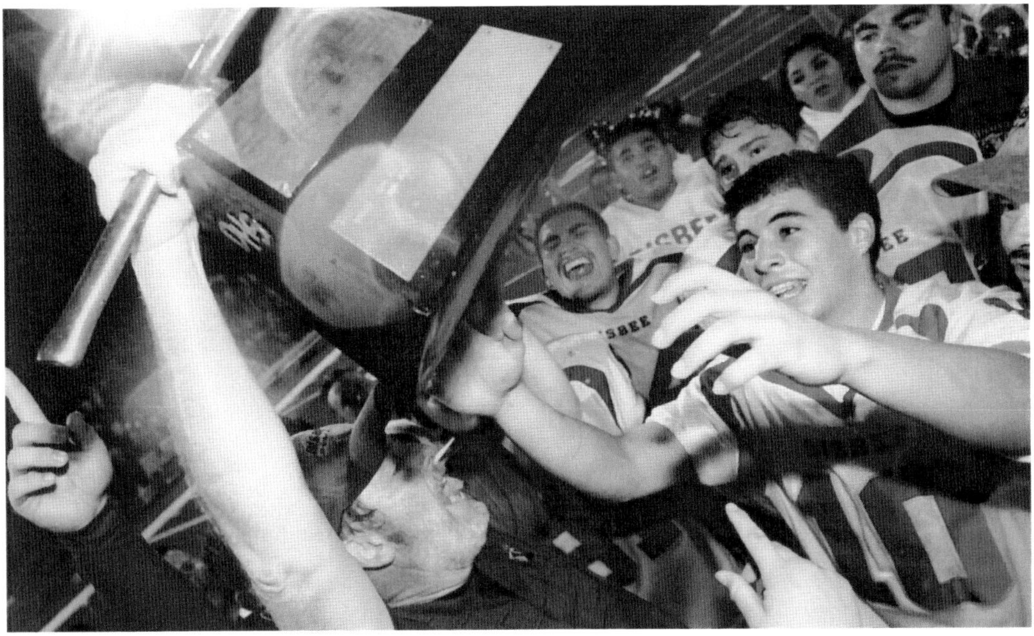

Assistant coach Chris Vertrees replaced Truman Williamson as Bisbee's head football coach in 2010. His goal was to win the Copper Pick back for Williamson, and his Pumas did just that, defeating the Bulldogs 14-8. (Courtesy *Sierra Vista Herald–Bisbee Daily Review.*)

7

THE GAME CONTINUES

The 1970s brought tremendous upheaval to Bisbee. Copper mining came to an end in 1974, resulting in the relocation of a substantial part of the population to Morenci, Silver City, and Ajo, where jobs in the industry were still available. The population exodus hit Bisbee High School sports hard. The school dropped to a lower classification, with many of its best athletes leaving with their parents for greener pastures in other mining towns.

High school football and baseball games continued to be played at Warren Ballpark, but the crowds were usually smaller, the enthusiasm lower, and the results unsatisfying, as a fractured community tried to hang on to its identity and traditions. The low point came in 1991, when Bisbee's consistent lopsided losses to Douglas led the two schools to cancel their annual rivalry game.

As the years passed, Bisbee redefined itself as a tourist community and the high school athletic programs began to rebuild. Puma athletic prowess, which never completely went away, began to show itself again at Warren Ballpark. A state high school baseball championship in 1993 was followed by the resumption of the Bisbee-Douglas annual rivalry game. Although Douglas usually won, the Pumas were motivated to win and occasionally did upset their much larger rivals.

In 2006, when Bisbee High School celebrated its 100th birthday, its faculty and students had reason to believe that good times had arrived and better days were yet to come. The Puma football team reached the state playoffs for the first time since 1963, when the Bisbee boys claimed the conference title and were crowned unofficial state champs. The baseball team also earned yet another state title in 2002.

Adult baseball was also back at Warren Ballpark. Minor league ball returned in the form of a new version of the Bisbee-Douglas Copper Kings, who made a brief appearance amid much hoopla and fanfare in 2003. Although the team was a hit with hometown fans, the league teetered and collapsed within three weeks. Undeterred by the demise of the minor league team, local businessmen and baseball enthusiasts tried again in 2006 with a semiprofessional team. The experiment was a success and Bisbee has enjoyed high-quality baseball each summer since.

Warren Ballpark's upcoming centennial in 2009 prompted community members to organize and plan the event, forming an organization called Friends of Warren Ballpark. After the centennial festivities, the Friends turned their focus to raising money to renovate and maintain the aging facility. Several projects have been completed and more are planned. Now 104 years old, Warren Ballpark continues to serve the Bisbee community in a variety of ways. Expectations are high that it will remain as a valued community resource and a historical treasure for many years to come.

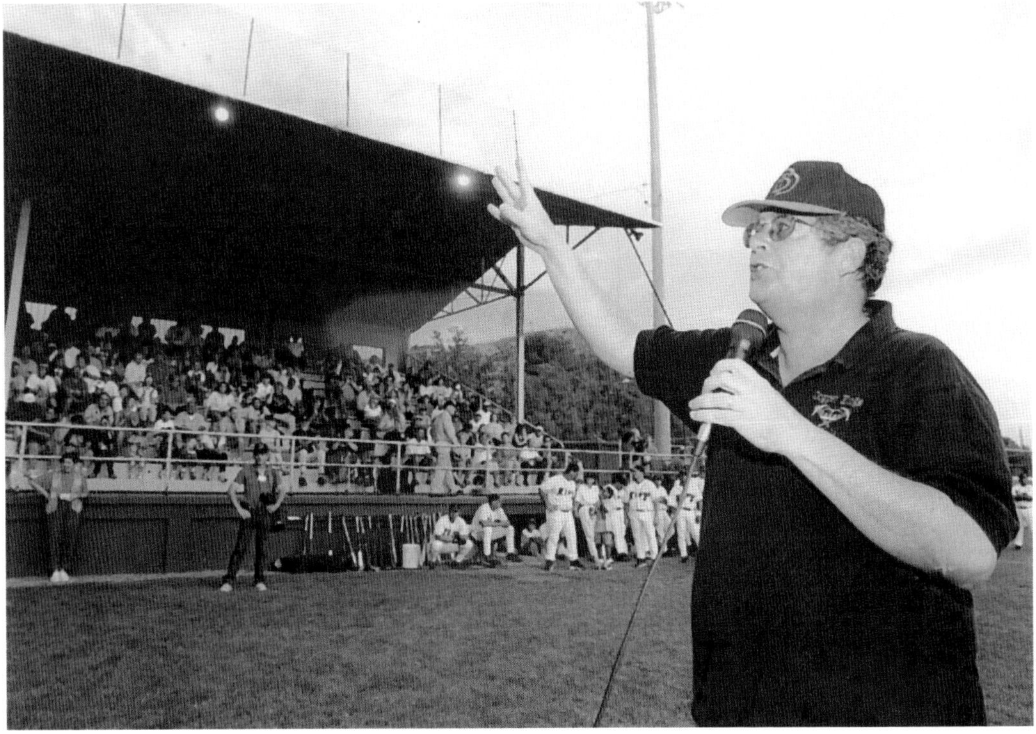

Bisbee-Douglas Copper Kings co-owner John Guy spoke to a capacity crowd on opening day for Bisbee's newest sports team. Minor league baseball returned to Bisbee with a flourish after a 48-year absence on May 30, 2003, when the Bisbee-Douglas Copper Kings took the field at Warren Ballpark. (Courtesy *Sierra Vista Herald–Bisbee Daily Review.*)

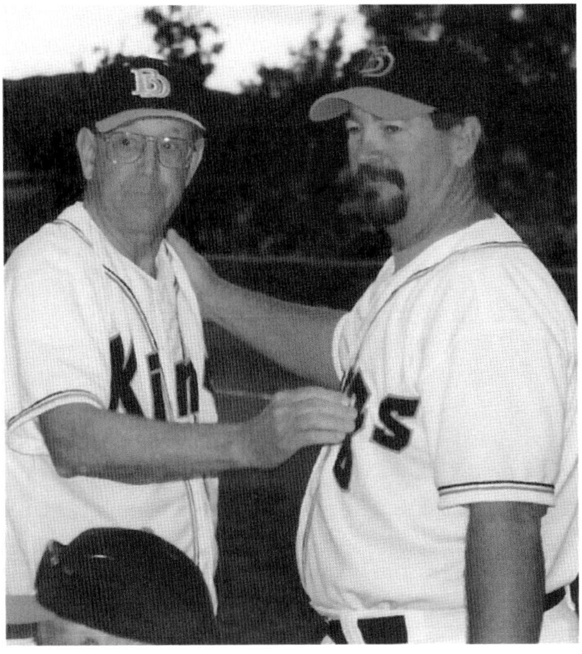

Bisbee-Douglas Copper Kings manager Butch Hammett (right) congratulates former Copper Kings pitcher Russ Kusmertz after the old right-hander threw out the ceremonial first pitch at Warren Ballpark during the opening day ceremony on May 30, 2003. Hammett, the last minor league manager to lead a team at Warren Ballpark, was a star athlete at Bisbee High School and later served as the assistant coach for two Puma state baseball championship teams. He also managed the semiprofessional Bisbee Kings and Copper Kings to three winning seasons from 2006 through 2008. (Photograph courtesy Russ Kusmertz.)

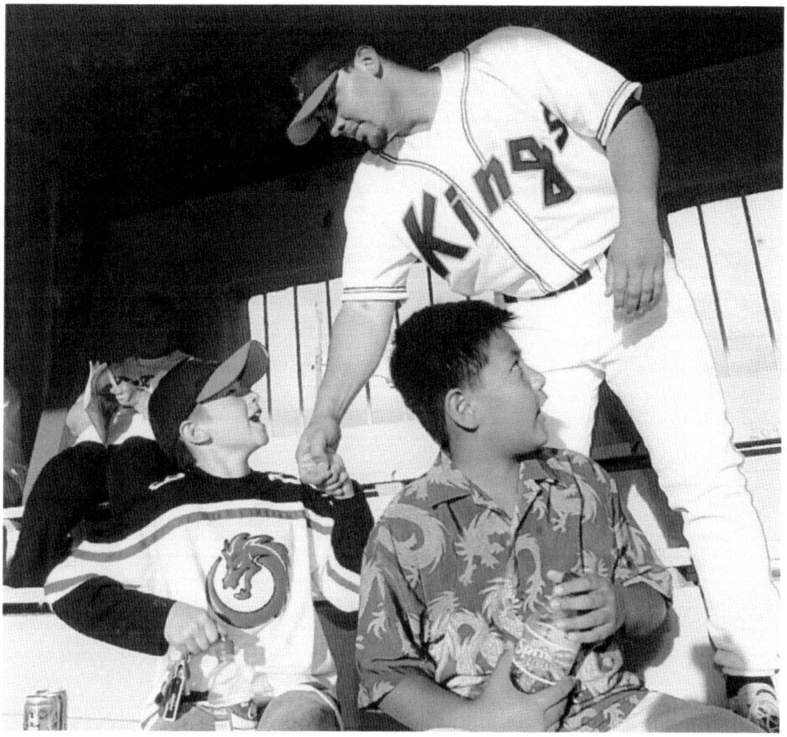

Efren Canchola greeted young fans in the grandstands prior to a home game at Warren Ballpark. An extensive publicity campaign conducted by the baseball club and by Arizona-Mexico League leadership preceded the Copper Kings' arrival in Bisbee. (Courtesy *Sierra Vista Herald–Bisbee Daily Review.*)

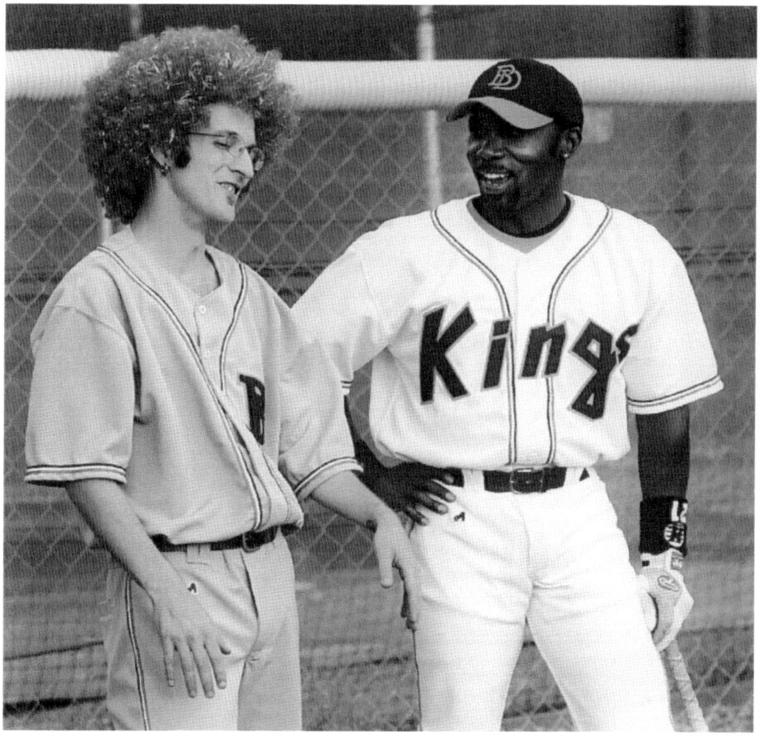

Player-coach Chuck Carr jokes with one of the fire-eating performers hired to entertain the crowd at Warren Ballpark. Promotions were a major part of the public relations plan carried out by the team ownership. Carr had played eight seasons in the major leagues and was attempting a comeback with the 2003 Copper Kings. (Courtesy *Sierra Vista Herald–Bisbee Daily Review.*)

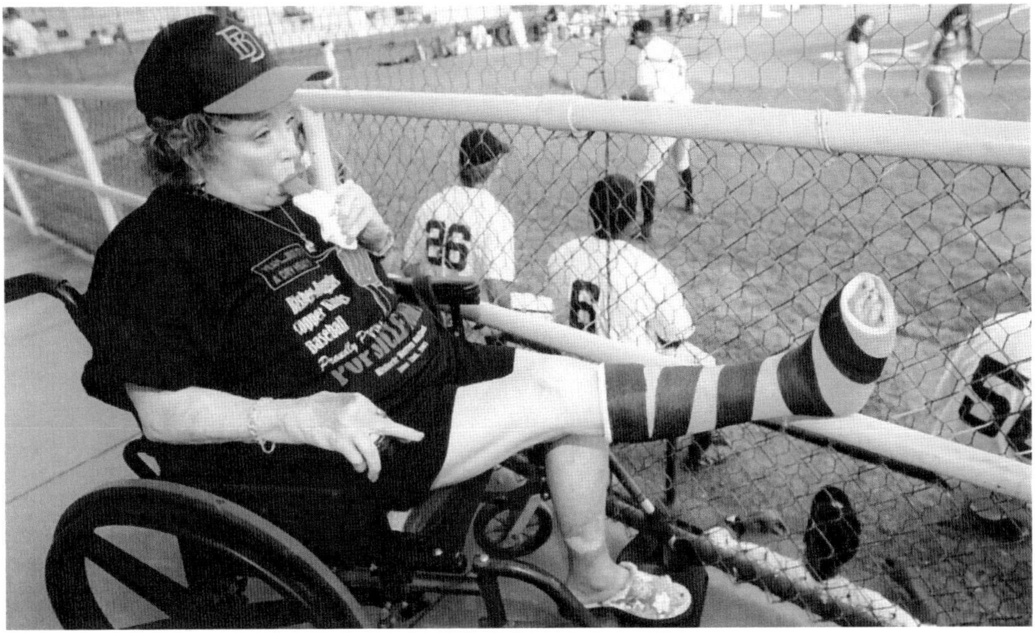

Ted Williams Night was the most talked-about and controversial promotional event of the 2003 Copper Kings season. The first 500 fans to enter the ballpark that night received a free popsicle in honor of Williams, the famous Boston Red Sox hitter who was cryogenically frozen in Arizona after his death. (Courtesy *Sierra Vista Herald–Bisbee Daily Review*.)

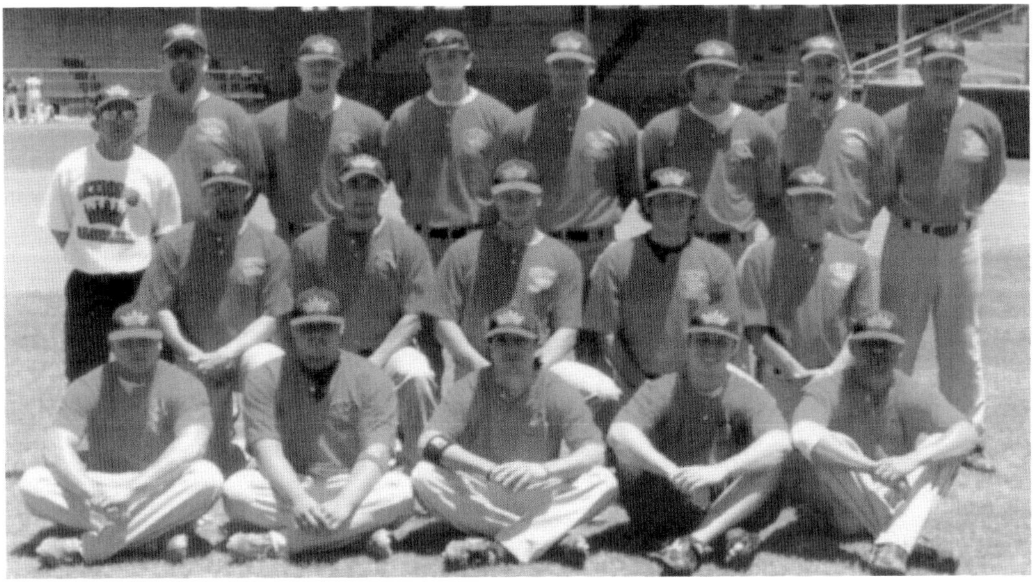

The minor league Copper Kings and the Arizona-Mexico League folded after less than three weeks, leaving local fans angry and resentful. League president Bob Lipp tried again with the semiprofessional Bisbee Kings in 2006. This time, the less ambitious experiment worked. Once again, Butch Hammett was the team's field manager, ending the season with a 15-4 record. (Author's collection.)

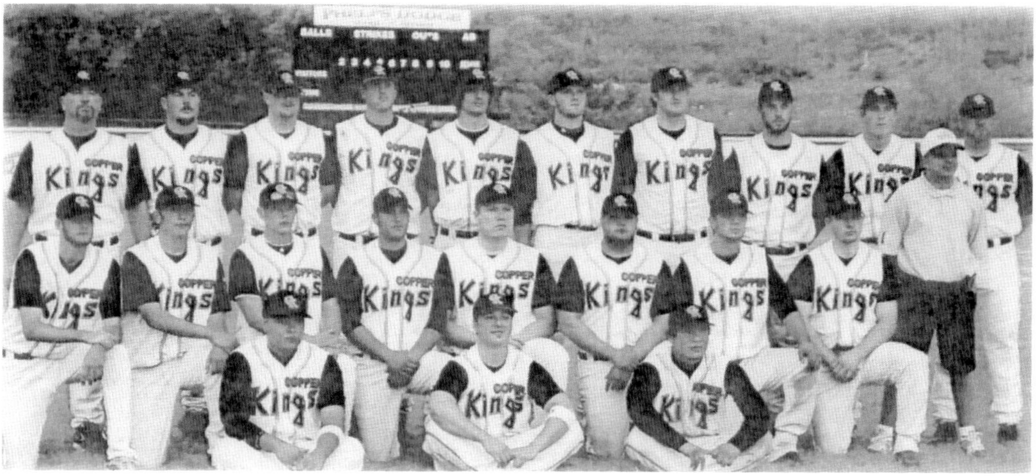

Bisbee businessmen Frank Barco and Tom Mosier took over the semiprofessional team in 2007 and renamed it the Bisbee Copper Kings. Under manager Butch Hammett, the Copper Kings played a winning season (18-12) in the Centennial League against other semiprofessional teams in southeast Arizona and northern Mexico. (Author's collection.)

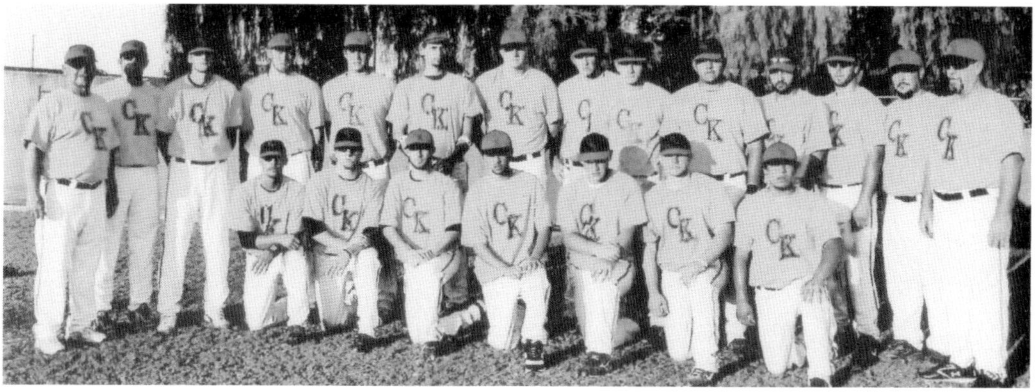

The Copper Kings returned again to play under Hammett in 2008 and remained winners. Hammett recruited extensively among local college players and former high school stars to give the team a strong connection to the Bisbee fans. The Copper Kings finished the summer with 19 wins and 13 losses. (Author's collection.)

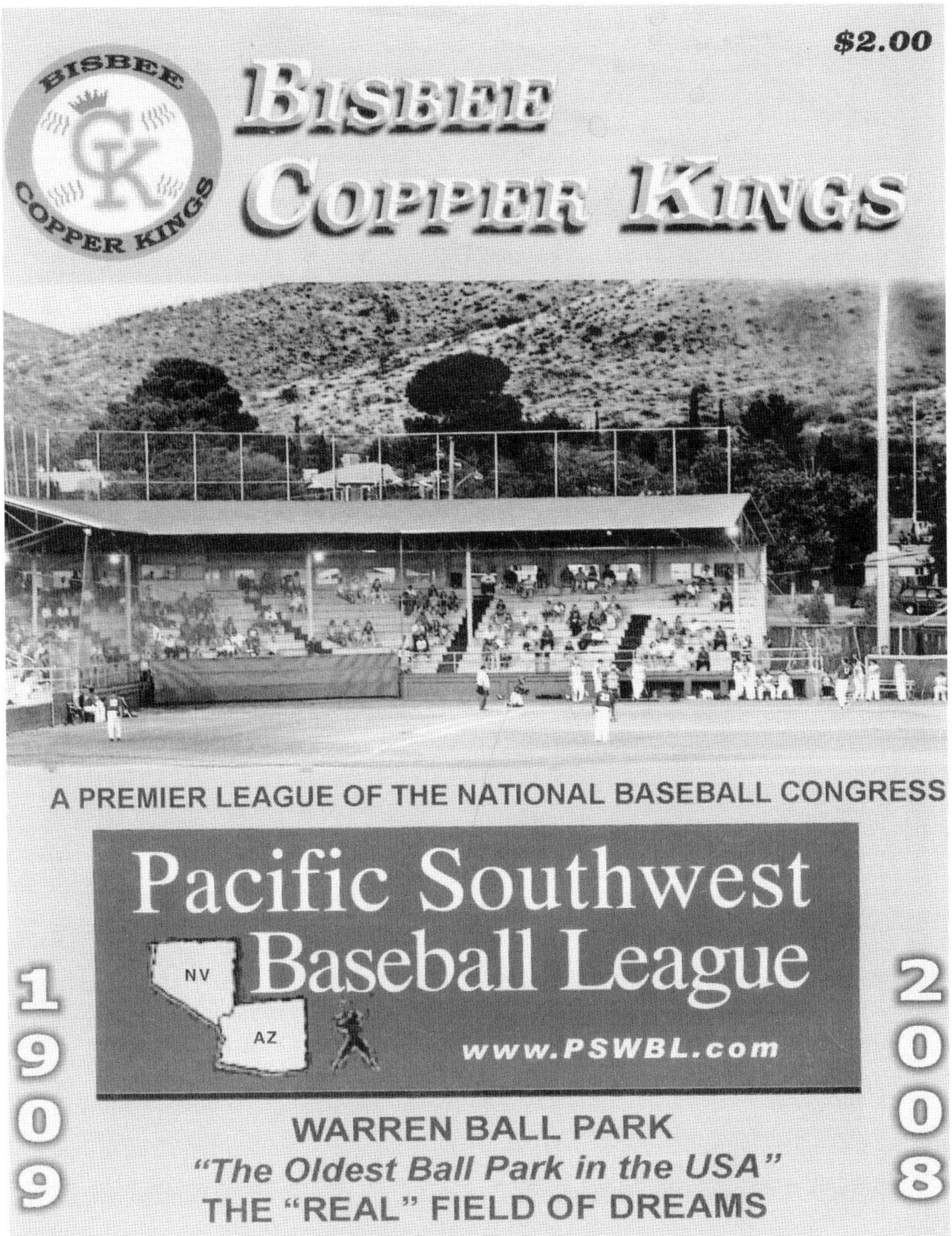

The 2008 Copper Kings played in the Pacific Southwest League, which included semiprofessional teams in Lake Havasu (the Heat), Mesa (the Garden of Gears), Casa Grande (the Cotton Kings), Tucson (the Nationals), and San Luis, Sonora, Mexico (the Banditos). League champions were eligible to play in the National Baseball Congress World Series in Wichita, Kansas. (Author's collection.)

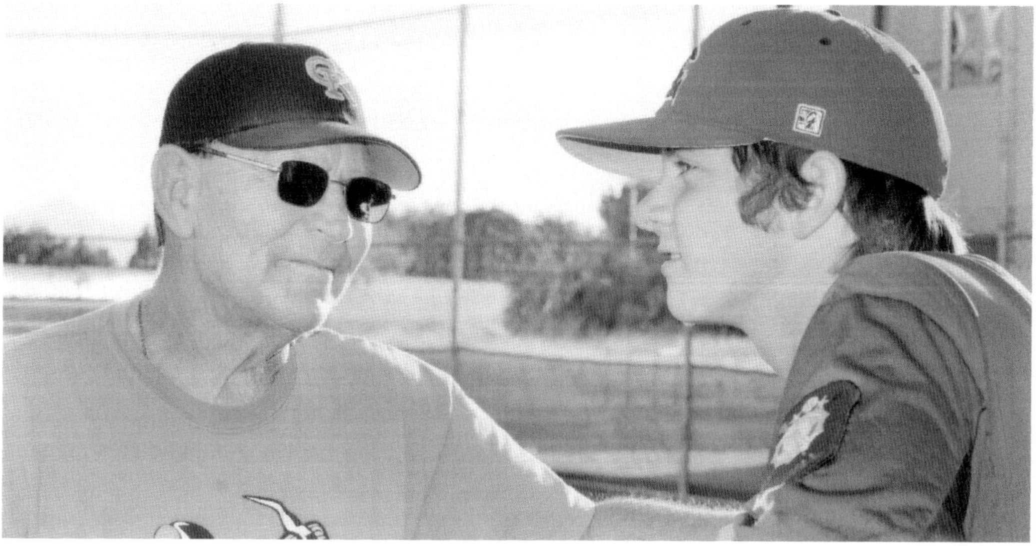

Bill Moore, who has been playing, coaching, and managing baseball for more than 40 years, took over as the manager of the Copper Kings in 2010. The team rebounded from its first losing season in 2009 under Greg Pennington (16-18) to post a winning record in the Pacific Southwest League. In 2012, Moore became the field manager of the Santa Fe Fuego minor league team of the independent Pecos League in 2012. (Courtesy Celina Barco.)

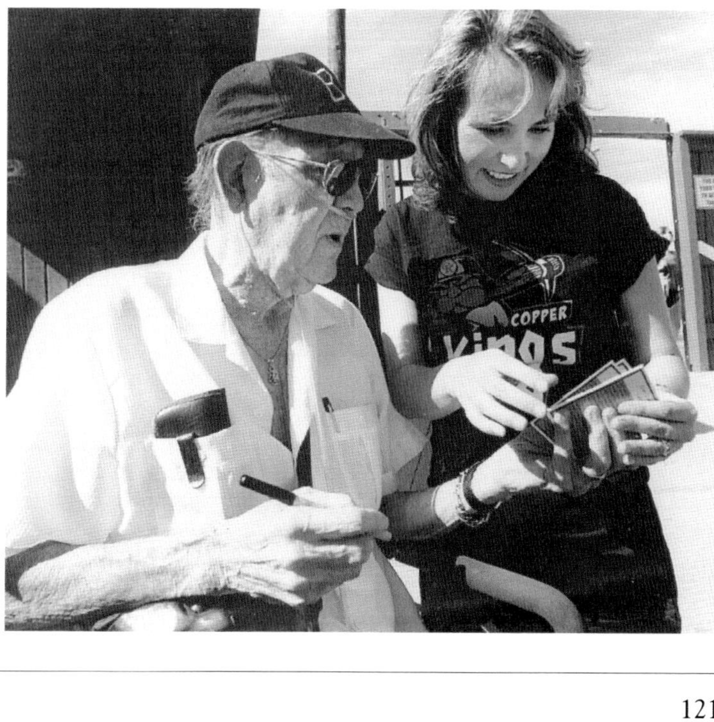

Congresswoman Gabrielle Giffords looks over former Bisbee-Douglas Copper King pitcher Russ Kusmertz's "Bisbee's Boys of Summer" baseball card during a visit to Warren Ballpark in July 2009. Giffords came to the ballpark to present a copy of the statement she read into the congressional record to honor the ballpark's centennial. (Courtesy *Sierra Vista Herald–Bisbee Daily Review.*)

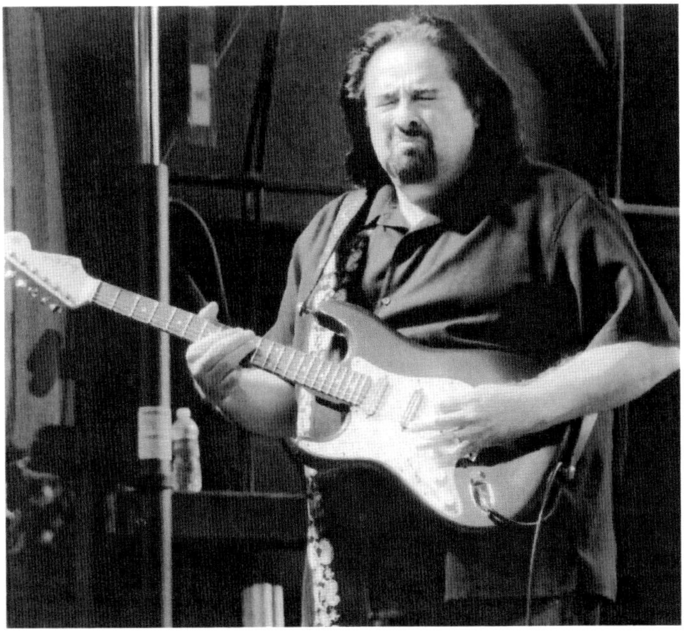

Blues performer Coco Montoya plays some hot licks for an appreciative crowd at the Bisbee Blues Festival, held at Warren Ballpark on September 17, 2011. The annual event, which features some of the best blues performers in the country, was moved to the ballpark from Brewery Gulch in old Bisbee several years ago to accommodate larger crows. (Courtesy *Sierra Vista Herald–Bisbee Daily Review.*)

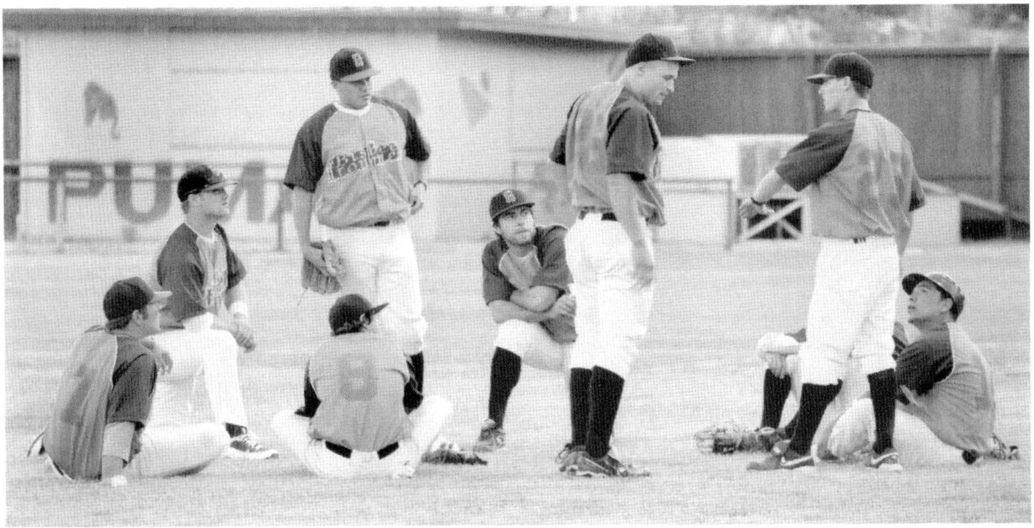

Eric Brown discusses baseball fundamentals with the Ironmen before a game in June 2012. Brown, an assistant baseball coach at Cochise College, led the Ironmen to a very successful inaugural season, fielding a team of college players from several states, as well as a few talented local stars. (Courtesy Celina Barco.)

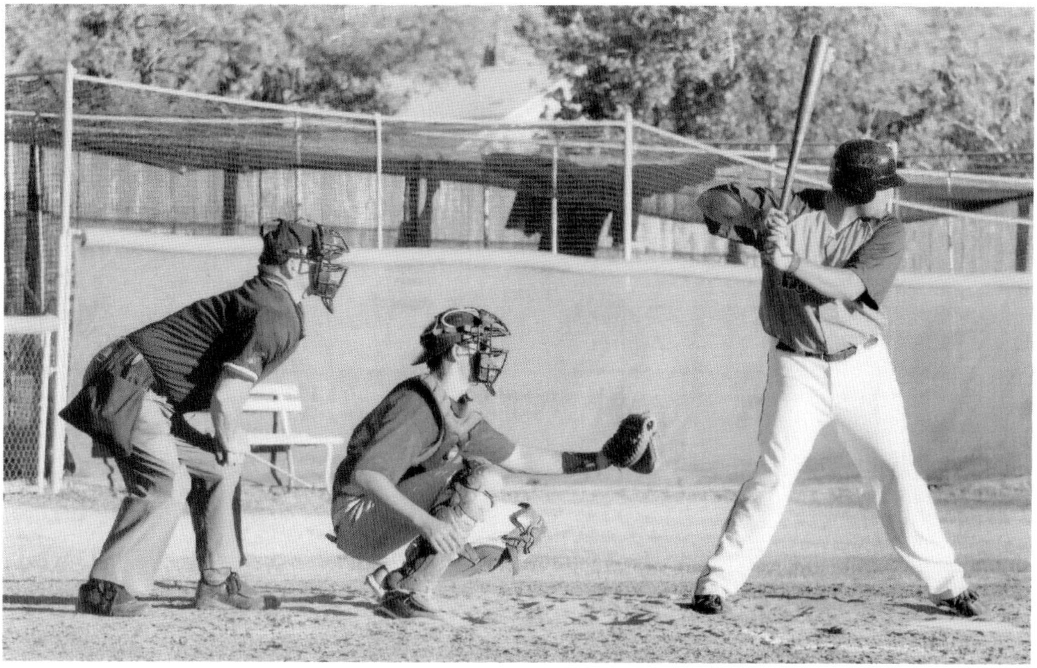

Taylor "Always Smooth" Stone was one of the top hitters for the Bisbee Ironmen in the 2012 summer season at Warren Ballpark. Stone, from nearby Sierra Vista, played first base and was a left-handed pitcher for the Ironmen. The Bisbee Ironmen are owned by Frank and Yolanda Barco. (Courtesy Celina Barco.)

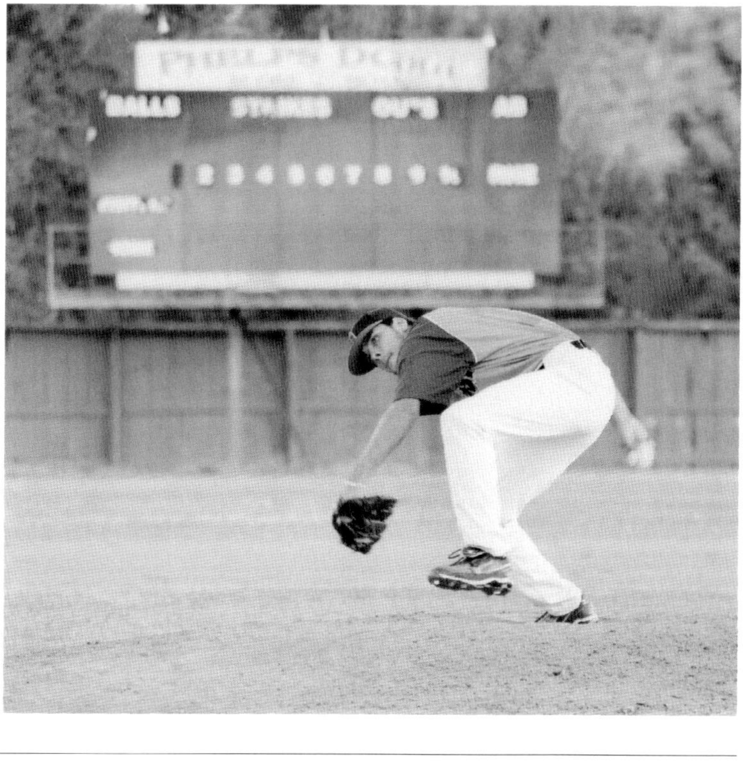

Bisbee Ironmen submarine pitcher Clinton "Red October" Graham confounded the Tucson Yard Dogs during a Kino Sun Belt league semiprofessional game played in June 2012 at Warren Ballpark. Graham, a right-handed pitcher from Alamogordo, New Mexico, was a star reliever for the Ironmen during their successful season. (Courtesy Celina Barco.)

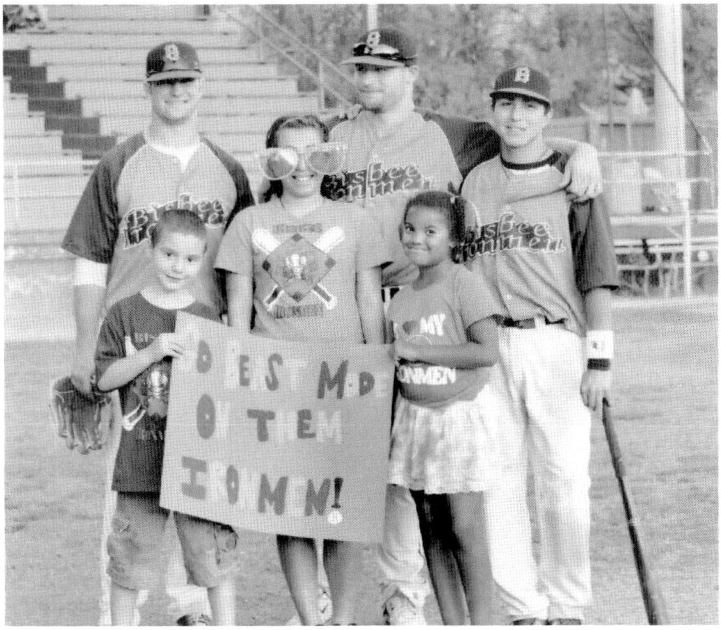

Promotions and special events were a regular occurrence at Ironmen games in the summer of 2012. The team's most ardent fans included a local dance troupe that performed during innings. One of the troupe members and some younger fans posed with Trent "Man Beast" Wilkins, Tyler "Beast Man" Wilkins, and Ray "Ray Ray" Eureste. (Courtesy Celina Barco.)

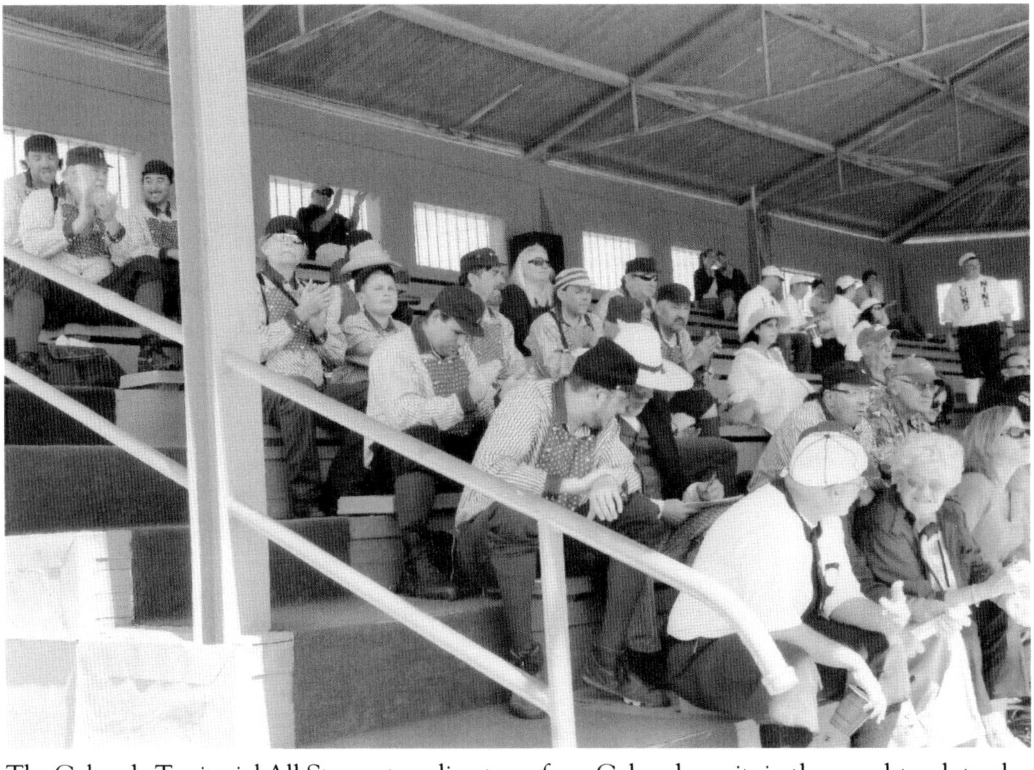

The Colorado Territorial All-Stars, a traveling team from Colorado, waits in the grandstands to play the next game at the third annual Copper City Classic Vintage Base Ball Tournament fundraiser held in March 2012 at Warren Ballpark. The event featured five teams from Arizona, the Colorado traveling team, and the Long Nine from Springfield, Illinois. (Author's collection.)

Jamie Lopata of the Phoenix Senators vintage base ball club belts a long drive into center field at Warren Ballpark during an exhibition game played with the Bisbee Bees in May 2009. Both teams are from the Phoenix metropolitan area and have adopted the names of teams in the old Arizona-Texas League. (Courtesy Larry Elkins.)

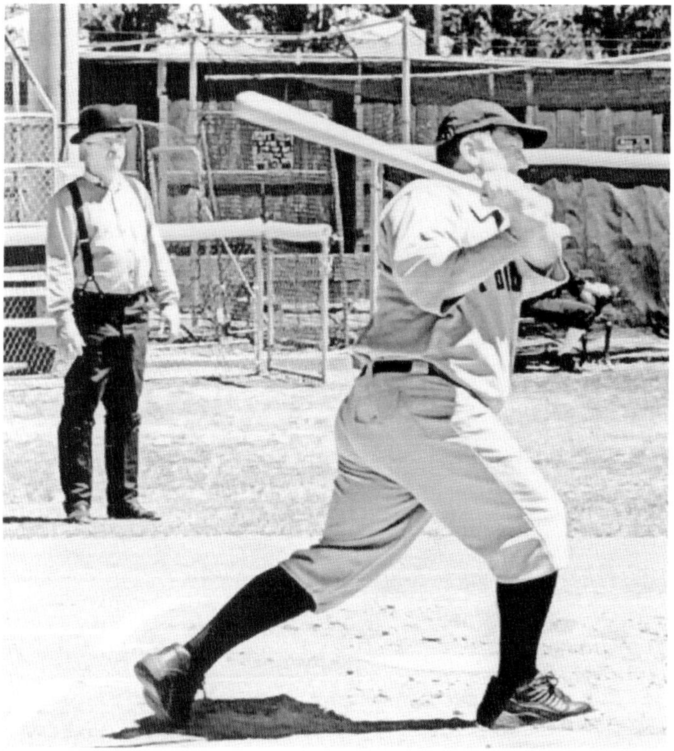

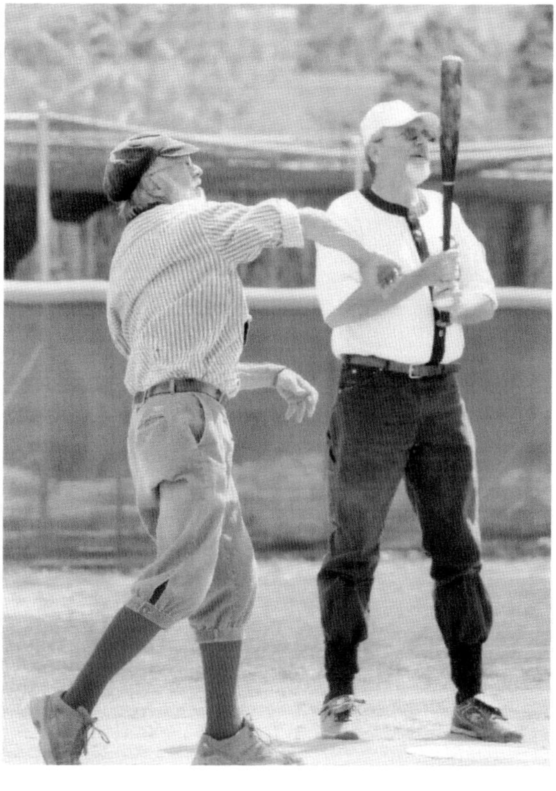

"Hobo" Tom Vaughn, playing behind the plate for Colorado, tosses the ball back to the pitcher as "Piano Legs" Dan Frey, the first baseman for the Bisbee Black Sox, waits for the right pitch. The Black Sox vintage team is named for the outlaw players who appeared at Warren Ballpark after being banished from organized baseball after the Black Sox scandal of 1919. (Author's collection.)

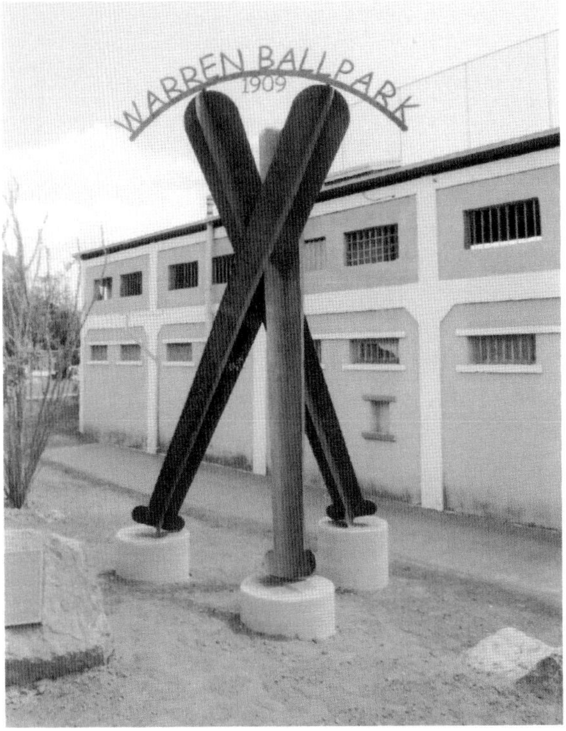

A steel sculpture commissioned by the Friends of Warren Ballpark to identify Warren Ballpark and commemorate its baseball heritage was put in place on July 3, 2012. The sculpture was designed by the Cochise College art department and constructed by the college's welding department. The Bisbee School District, Freeport McMoran Copper and Gold, and the City of Bisbee all assisted in the project. (Courtesy Steve Pauken.)

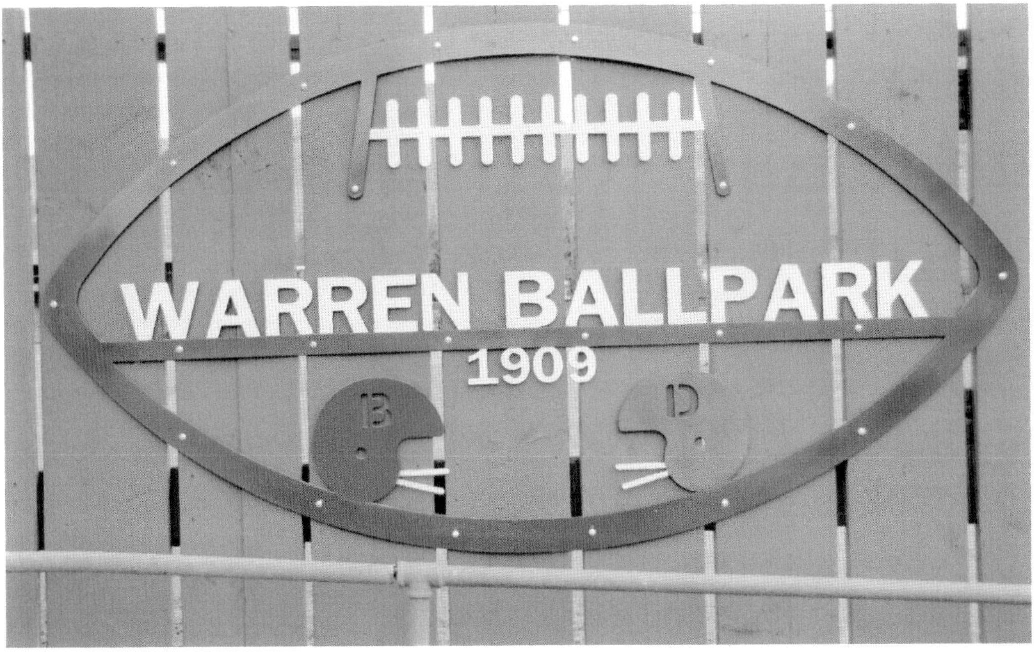

An eight-foot-long steel sign honoring Bisbee High School's football heritage was placed on the perimeter fence of Warren Ballpark shortly before the beginning of the football season in August 2012. The project was funded by the Friends of Warren Ballpark and completed by Cochise College, with assistance from the school district. (Author's collection.)

ABOUT THE ORGANIZATION

This book was produced as a project of the Friends of Warren Ballpark, a tax-exempt 501(c)(3) organization since May 2009, operating under the Bisbee Council for the Arts and Humanities. The mission of the Friends is threefold. Since 2009, we have been involved in a variety of fundraising activities with the purpose of restoring and preserving the historic Warren Ballpark grandstands, clubhouse, and accessory structures. We have completed two projects as of the publication of this book: the replacement of chicken wire in front of the backstop with modern, more durable netting, and the construction of a sculpture and signage to identify and commemorate the ballpark. This book is a product of the second part of our mission, which is to research and share the rich history of the ballpark and of all sports played there. The third part of our mission is to support the continuation of Bisbee's athletic traditions into the future. The Friends actively promote and support high school athletics, semiprofessional sports, and other youth athletic activities that take place within our community of Bisbee. For details, please visit our web site at www.friendsofwarrenballpark.com.